Late Quaternary Environments and Man in Holderness

by

D. D. Gilbertson

with

D. J. Briggs, J. R. Flenley, A. R. Hall,
C. O. Hunt and D. Woodall

and contributions by

Anne Blackham, S. J. Gale, R. D. S. Jenkinson,
H. K. Kenward, P. A. Mellars, N. M. Thew,
V. R. Switsur and Christine Williams

BAR British Series 134
1984

B.A.R.

5, Centremead, Osney Mead, Oxford OX2 0ES, England.

GENERAL EDITORS

A.R. Hands, B.Sc., M.A., D.Phil.
D.R. Walker, M.A.

BAR 134, 1984 :Late Quaternary Environments and Man in Holderness'

Price £ 14.00   post free throughout the world. Payments made in dollars must be calculated at the current rate of exchange and $3.00 added to cover exchange charges. Cheques should be made payable to B.A.R. and sent to the above address.

For details of all B.A.R. publications in print please write to the above address. Information on new titles is sent regularly on request, with no obligation to purchase.

Volumes are distributed from the publisher. All B.A.R. prices are inclusive of postage by surface mail anywhere in the world.

Printed in Great Britain

LATE QUATERNARY ENVIRONMENTS

AND MAN

IN HOLDERNESS

by

D.D. Gilbertson
University of Sheffield

with

D.J.Briggs (University of Sheffield), J.R.Flenley (University of Hull),
A.R. Hall (University of York),
C.O. Hunt and D. Woodall (University of Sheffield),

and contributions by Anne Blackham, S.J. Gale, D.A.Harkness,
R.D.S. Jenkinson, H.K. Kenward, P.A. Mellars, F.B.Pyatt, N.M. Thew,
V.R. Switsur and Christine Williams.

ACKNOWLEDGMENTS

The elucidation of the ecological and human history of Holderness forms an important part of (i) the undergraduate course in Environmental Archaeology and the post-graduate M.A. course in Environmental Archaeology and Palaeoeconomy at the University of Sheffield, and (ii) of courses in Biogeography at the University of Hull. The authors wish to extend their thanks to the numerous undergraduate and post-graduate students who have taken part in these Holderness projects.

The contribution of N.M. Thew is based on a Master's Thesis for the research dissertation component of the M.A. in Environmental Archaeology and Palaeoeconomy at the University of Sheffield which is funded by the Science Based Archaeology Panel of the Science and Engineering Research Council, whose support he acknowledges. The contribution of D. Woodall is based on a Master's Thesis for the research dissertation component of the M.A. in Prehistory and Archaeology. Mr Woodall acknowledges a D.E.S. post-graduate scholarship which financed these studies.

The radiocarbon determinations were generously made available by Dr. V.R. Switsur at the University of Cambridge, under their Mesolithic Radiocarbon Dating Programme, and at the Scottish Universities Research and Reactor Centre at East Kilbride by Dr. D. Harkness with the aid of a grant from the Radiocarbon Panel of the Natural Environment Research Council.

We are most grateful to Dr. M.P. Kerney (Imperial College) and Dr. R.C. Preece (Cambridge) for checking and correcting the identification of the molluscan remains, and their comments and unpublished information on sites in and around Holderness.

Trevor Corns of the Department of Prehistory and Archaeology at the University of Sheffield produced the excellent photographs of plant macrofossils.

Many laboratory and field analyses were carried out by Miss Katherine Groves and Mr. Craig Turner, honours students in Applied Biology at Trent Polytechnic, during the course of industrial placement training in the Environmental Archaeology Laboratories of the University of Sheffield.

Dr. J. Flenley wishes to thank Miss E. Smith for giving permission to publish information from her undergraduate dissertation at Hull, and to thank Miss K. Scurr for drawing the figures in Chapter 7.

The substantial costs incurred visiting the coastal exposures of Holderness have largely been met by dint of the support from the University of Hull and the University of Sheffield.

Finally we wish to thank Valerie Kinsler B.A., for carrying out the onerous task of producing this study on a Compucorp 7 word processor.

The contributors

Anne Blackham B.Sc. Department of Biology, Norfolk College of
Technology, Kings Lynn, Norfolk;
formerly Department of Geography, University of
Hull.

D.J. Briggs Ph.D.   Department of Geography, University of Sheffield.

J.R. Flenley Ph.D.   Department of Geography, University of Hull.

S.J. Gale Ph.D.   Jesus College, Oxford.

D. Gilbertson Ph.D. Department of Prehistory and Archaeology,
University of Sheffield.

A.R. Hall Ph.D.   Environmental Archaeology Unit, University of York.

D.A.Harkness Ph.D.   Scottish Universities Research Reactor Centre, East
Kilbride.

C.O. Hunt Ph.D.   Department   of   Prehistory   and   Archaeology,
University of Sheffield.

R.D.S. Jenkinson Ph.D. Creswell Crags Visitor Centre, Crags Road,
Welbeck, nr. Worksop, Notts, and Department of
Prehistory   and   Archaeology,   University   of
Sheffield.

H.K. Kenward M.Sc.   Environmental Archaeology Unit, University of York.

P.A. Mellars Ph.D.   Department of Archaeology, University of Cambridge.

F.B.Pyatt Ph.D.   Department of Life Sciences, Trent Polytechnic.

V.R. Switsur Ph.D.   Radiocarbon   Laboratory,   Sub-department   of
Quaternary Research, Botany School, University of
Cambridge.

N.M. Thew M.A.   Department   of   Prehistory   and   Archaeology,
University of Sheffield.

Christine Williams   Ph.D. Department of Botany and the Department of
Prehistory and Archaeology, University of
Sheffield.

D. Woodall M.A.   Department of Prehistory and Archaeology,
University of Sheffield.

CONTENTS

RESULTS
    The Till
    The Lacustrine Sequence

THE NORTHERN EXPOSURES
    Plant macrofossils
    Insect assemblages

CENTRAL EXPOSURE
    Plant macrofossils
    Late Devensian clays

SECTION 8
    Biozone SKA
    Biozone SKB
    Biozone SKC
    Biozone SKD
    Biozone SKE
    Biozone SKF
    Biozone SKG
    Biozone SKH
    Biozone SKJ
    Section 3

COMPARISONS WITH OTHER LATE DEVENSIAN DEPOSITS IN
NORTHERN BRITAIN

CONCLUSIONS

by N.M. Thew, D.D.Gilbertson and D. Woodall.

INTRODUCTION

METHODS: PAST AND PRESENT
    Field and laboratory
    Analysis
    Quantification

RESULTS
    Taphonomy
    Juveniles

LOCAL MOLLUSCAN ASSEMBLAGE ZONES

THE MAIN CENTRAL PROFILE
    Local molluscan assemblage zone A_1
    Local molluscan assemblage zone A_2
    Local molluscan assemblage zone A_3
    Local molluscan assemblage zone A_4
    Local molluscan assemblage zone B_1
    Local molluscan assemblage zone B_2
    Local molluscan assemblage zone C
    Local molluscan assemblage zone D

THE NORTHERN PROFILE
    Local molluscan assemblage zone LG
    Local molluscan assemblage zone T
    Local molluscan assemblage zone A_{1-3}
    Local molluscan assemblage zone B
    Local molluscan assemblage zone C
    Local molluscan assemblage zone D_1

THE SOUTHERN PROFILES

MOLLUSCAN BIOSTRATIGRAPHIC CORRELATION BETWEEEN THE
SKIPSEA PROFILES

PREVIOUS STUDIES AT SKIPSEA WITHOW
    Phillips (1826)
    The **Ancylus** faunas

LATE QUATERNARY MOLLUSCAN FAUNAS OF HOLDERNESS
    Late Devensian
    Early Flandrian
    Land Species

THE EFFECTS OF BIOLOGICAL SUCCESSION AND DISPERSAL
AMONG MOLLUSCAN FAUNAS
    Successional developments in the Skipsea Withow
      molluscan faunas

DISTINGUISHING CLIMATIC INFLUENCES ON MOLLUSCAN
ASSEMBLAGES
    Climatic influences and the Skipsea Withow
      Molluscan Assemblages
    The Climatic Significance of other Holderness
      Molluscan Assemblages
    The Wider Climatic Significance of the Skipsea
      Withow Molluscan Sequence
    Nazeing, Essex
    White Bog, Co. Down
    Sturton, Lincolnshire
    Berkshire valleys
    Staines, West London
    Seamer Carrs
    Early and Mid-Devensian molluscan faunas

    FUTURE PROSPECTS

    INTRODUCTION

    A POLLEN ANALYTICAL STUDY OF FLANDRIAN VEGETATIONAL
    HISTORY AT SKIPSEA WITHOW MERE
    by Anne Blackham and John Flenley

    TECHNIQUES

RESULTS

DISCUSSION
    Zonation of the pollen diagram
    Correlation with the pollen diagram of
      Godwin and Godwin (1933)
    The development of Skipsea Withow mere
    History of the regional vegetation

FLANDRIAN PLANT MACROFOSSILS FROM SKIPSEA WITHOW MERE
by A.R. Hall

    Timber orientation studies (DDG)

TOWARDS A VEGETATIONAL HISTORY OF THE MERES OF
HOLDERNESS
by J.R. Flenley

POLLEN DIAGRAMS FROM HOLDERNESS MERES: THE DATA

DISCUSSION
    Stratigraphy
    Pollen assemblages

CONCLUSIONS

INTRODUCTION

PALAEOLITHIC AND MESOLITHIC FINDS FROM THE SKIPSEA
WITHOW MERE DEPOSITS
by Paul Mellars

    The Skipsea Withow Blade
    The Skipsea Withow Harpoon
    Artefacts excavated by Armstrong (1923)

CONCLUSIONS

NEOLITHIC WOODWORKING AND WOODLAND MANAGEMENT

EARLY NEOLITHIC ROD

IN SITU ROD AND PEG
    Unprovenanced timbers

river to the meres to the west. The "lake dwelling" site reported by Smith (1911) is located near Skipsea Low mere.

CHAPTER 1

INTRODUCTION

<u>HOLDERNESS</u>

The name Holderness is a compound of the Old Norse **holder** - "a higher yeoman, an owner of alloidal land" or the Old English **hold** "an officer of higher rank", and the Old Norse **nes** "a cape or headland". The principal early reference to **Heldernes** is in the Domesday Book of 1086 (Smith 1937).

The low lying triangle of Holderness is bounded by the North Sea to the east, to the south by the Humber and to the west and north by the Chalk hills of the Yorkshire Wolds (Figure 1.1).

A simplified view of the geological context of the region is shown in Figure 1.2. Holderness lies on the gently undulating surface of a till sheet which laps onto the Yorkshire Wolds to the west (Figure 1.2). The redrawn map of the Drift Geology of the Skipsea area of Holderness shown in Figure 1.3 indicates that the surface of the till sheet comprises a mosaic of sands and gravels, clay and silt rich soils and natural hollows. These have given rise to one of the most characteristic features of Holderness - its abundance of wetlands and mires. Today only Hornsea Mere survives as open water lake surrounded by reedswamp (Plate 1.1) and Alder/Oak carr (Plate 1.2). The remainder of the very large number of lakes and mires known or suspected in medieval times (Figure 1.4) has been lost by coastal erosion, natural and accelerated siltation, and drainage. A general impression of the earlier wetland landscapes of Holderness can be gained by an examination of Plates 1.1 and 1.2. The richness of environment and resources represented by these habitats is obvious.

In general, Holderness is a neglected and by-passed region of Britain. Its low terrain and contemporary, open, bleakness are not to many peoples' taste. In all probability, it is best known for its problems of coastal erosion, with erosion relentlessly occurring at a rate of 1-3m of cliff retreat each year. These problems of coastal erosion have proved a blessing for archaeologists and geologists because they have provided a continuing series of important exposures in mire and lake deposits. Many of these have yielded artefacts or fossils which have attracted both attention and controversy. As Thomas Sheppard (1909:500) noted:

> "Possibly no district in the British Isles offers such a variety of lessons as does the coastline between Bridlington and Spurn Point and the Humber Estuary. On the one hand enormous tracts of land have disappeared within historic times; whilst on the other, large areas have been formed, embanked and cultivated.
>
> The district is also especially worthy of attention from the fact that data of a most reliable character relating to these changes are available."

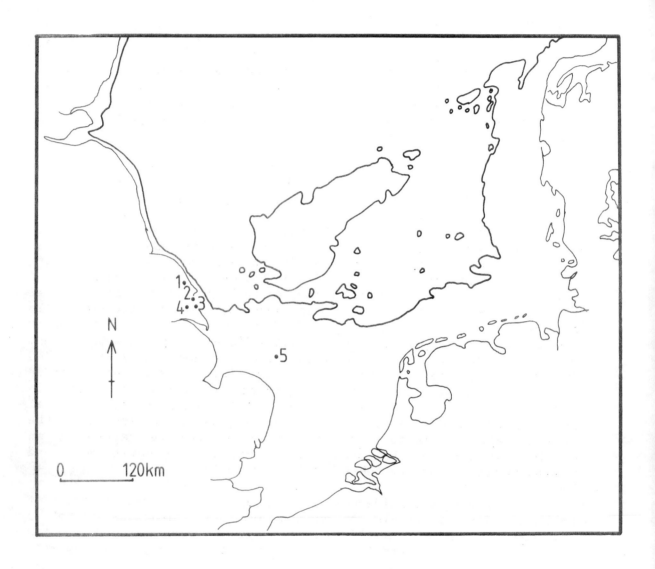

Figure 1.1   The location of Holderness, Yorkshire. Holderness is the
triangle between Flamborough Head immediately north of
Skipsea Withow mere (point 2), the Humber estuary to the
south and the North Sea. The Late Devensian and Flandrian
marine transgression has effected notable changes in the
geography of the present North Sea basin. For comparison
the thicker line indicates the approximate position of the
North Sea shoreline c. 9-10,000 yrs b.p. Important
Mesolithic sites located are (1) Star Carr, north of the
Yorkshire Wolds; (2) Skipsea Withow mere; (3) Hornsea; (4)
Brandesburton; (5) "moorlogs".

by kind permission Leicester University Press; after Clark
1972, and Evans 1979.

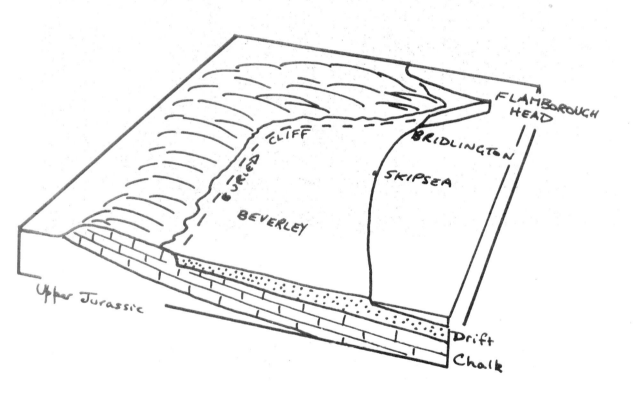

Figure 1.2 Block diagram showing the general geological setting of
Holderness: the "Drifts" are mainly Till of Late Devensian
age, which bury the underlying Chalk and Pleistocene beach
deposits and their associated cliff and shoreline platform.
These are exposed at Sewerby Cliff, immediately north of
Bridlington.

Plate 1.1 Reedswamp dominated by **Typha, Phragmites** and **Carex** spp.
fringing open water at the present Hornsea mere, Holderness:
taken at the east end of the lake (Figure 1.4).

Plate 1.2   Semi-natural alder and oak carr adjacent to the till surface
at the western end of the present Hornsea mere, Holderness
(see Figure 1.4).

The great potential for archaeological and palaeoecological research in Holderness has been only partially realised since Sheppard's notes (see Catt, 1977). Unfortunately any analysis of the literature concerning the series of interesting sites exposed by coastal erosion tends to produce a characteristic sequence of responses in the reader - interest and excitement, followed by suspicion and then frustration. Typical are the "Maglemose harpoons" (Figure 1.5) reported from the depositional remnants of the margins of the former Skipsea Withow mere (Figure 1.6). These were found by a Mr. B. Morfitt (Junior) in 1903. A carved bone harpoon was found:

> "lying in silt at a depth of 5 feet, beneath a lacustrine peat and immediately under the skeletal remains of an elk (**Cervus giganteus**), which he was excavating. Other fauna associated was Reindeer, red-deer, and ancient ox."

(Armstrong, 1923b:60).

Armstrong's initial excitement is evident in his accounts in which he related these finds to those in the recently investigated Maglemose bog sites in Denmark (Armstrong 1922, 1923a). He was especially excited by the faunal and depositional context of a harpoon which indicated very ancient hunting. His subsequent frustrations are evident in his rebuttals of the public and private allegations that the Morfitts had manufactured and planted these harpoons (Figure 1.5; Sheppard 1923, 1929; Armstrong 1923b).

Modern sympathies probably lie with Armstrong. Nevertheless it is undoubtedly the case that consultation of his stratigraphic descriptions does not remove lingering uncertainties concerning the provenance, age, stratigraphic relationships, environmental and palaeoeconomic significance of the finds.

These problems recur when one considers the other remarkable vertebrate faunas recovered from this site that were reported by Phillips (1829) (Figure 1.7) and Armstrong (1923b). These derive from lake silts beneath lake and carr peats (Figure 1.7). The literature suggests giant elk and similar taxa associated with cold, open landscapes were inhabiting temperate Flandrian woodlands.

There are also numerous records of later prehistoric stakes, piles, and 'crannogs' also associated with the remains of former meres or lakes which characterise Holderness. Their archaeological and palaeoecological richness is in contrast to the uniformity of the present landscape. Its monotonous topography reflects the very gentle slopes of the undulating surface of late Quaternary till sheets (Figures 1.3 and 1.4). The meres occupy the broad basins underneath the slightly higher mounds of till or gravel ridges which rarely exceed 30m O.D.

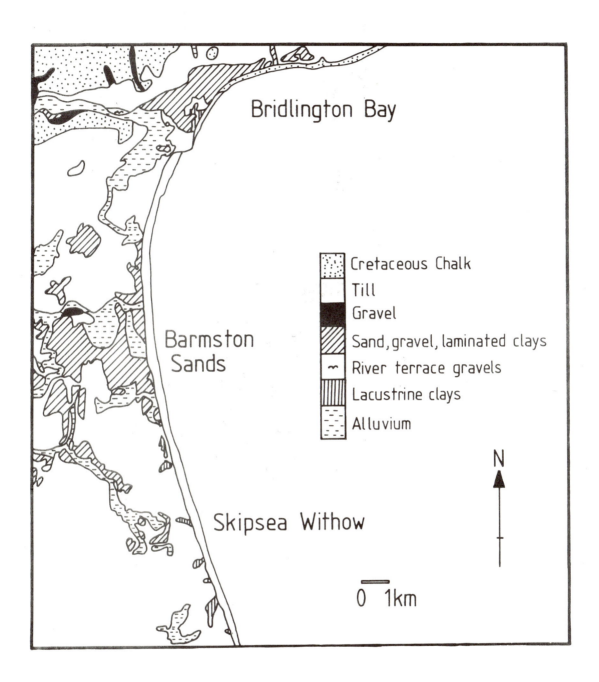

Figure 1.3 The drift geology of the northern part of Holderness near Skipsea emphasising the pedological lithological complexity of the Late Devensian till sheet's surface deposits.

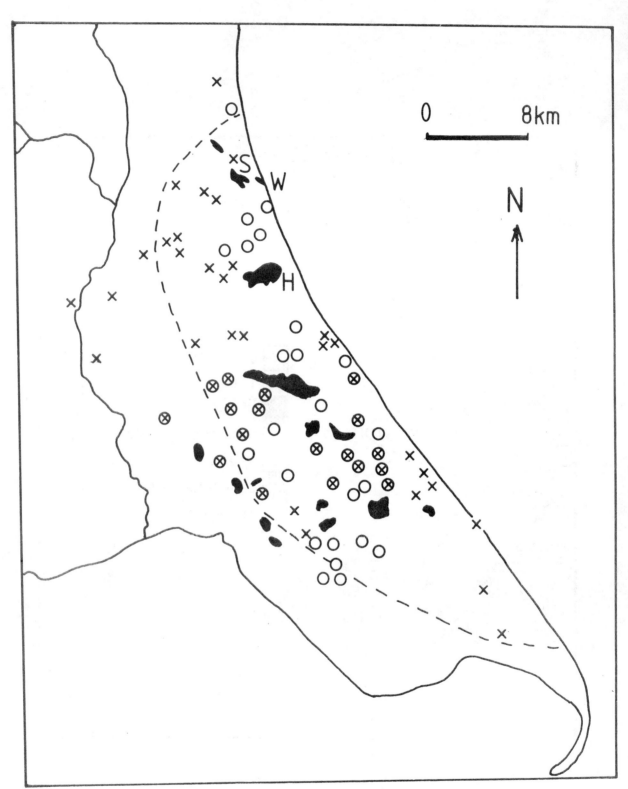

Figure 1.4   The locations of known and suspected lakes and mires in
Holderness in the medieval period.   The dotted line
indicates the westward and southern limits of the Late
Devensian ice and the resultant till sheet.   The symbols
indicate the strength of the evidence used to make this
reconstruction: see Chapter 2:   the outlines of the
principal meres/lakes are shown:-
closed areas - definite geological and historical evidence
of a former mere; open shapes - geological evidence of a
former mere; cross - historical evidence suggests a small
mere; open circle - evidence of the 1946-7 floods suggests
a former small mere; open circle enclosing cross
- historical evidence and 1946-7 floods suggest a small
mere. (After June Sheppard 1957).

LAKES AND MERES

The lakes and meres have formed in original depressions in the till sheet, kettle holes, perhaps in decayed pingos, and occasionally solutional hollows in the Chalk-enriched tills. These features developed in the late-Devensian and Flandrian to produce a landscape mosaic of lake, marsh, wet woodland, and higher, better drained ground with denser woodland. Subsequent forest clearance, soil erosion, land drainage and rapid coastal erosion have all combined to cause the loss of nearly all these meres (Figure 1.4; Chapter 2).

Nowadays, the only survivor of the very large number of lakes which existed into medieval times is Hornsea Mere (Figure 1.4). This lake, with its fringing marsh and carr, offers contemporary analogues to aid our reconstruction of lake habitats and environmental change over the past 13-14,000 years in the region. But for the construction and maintenance of the Hornsea seawall in the late nineteenth/early twentieth century, Hornsea Mere would have been breached and drained by coastal erosion - the fate which befell its former eastward counterpart (Hornsea Old Mere) and numerous other former large meres and indeed towns and ports of Holderness.

In this account, attention focuses on the remains of Skipsea Withow mere (Figure 1.6), the source of the Morfitt's finds. The lacustrine deposits which collected at the western margins of this mere have been the focus of geological, archaeological and palaeoecological research for over 150 years. It appears to have been a sizeable lake, perhaps over 1km in length, in the medieval period (Chapter 2). Coastal erosion proceeding at a rate of 1 to 2m each year since then has resulted in only the furthest west marginal deposits surviving today in the low cliffs of the Skipsea Withow gap (Figure 1.6, Plate 2.2). The cliffs continue to retreat at approximately this rate today, under the combined attack of wave and sub-aerial erosion. In a decade, little of what is left of the former mere will remain. Three or four decades into the future, erosion will start to expose the deposits of the next, smaller, silted mere further inland. Similar fates await the other exposures of former meres which can be studied at Sand le Mar, Ulrome, and Barmston.

THE RESEARCH AND TEACHING POTENTIAL OF HOLDERNESS MERES

The longer term future of the Withow mere section is unfortunate. Nevertheless the excellence of both the exposures and the conditions of preservation offer the prospect of realising some of the immense palaeoecological potential of this coast. In particular, research could develop the Withow mere story as an illustration of the archaeological, ecological and geomorphic evolution of Holderness wetlands and lakes.

The site has great significance for improving our understanding of a variety of inter-related problems - some of local or regional significance, others concerning questions of fact; yet others of broader methodological or educational significance:-

Figure 1.5 "Maglemose harpoon" reported by Armstrong (1923b:60).

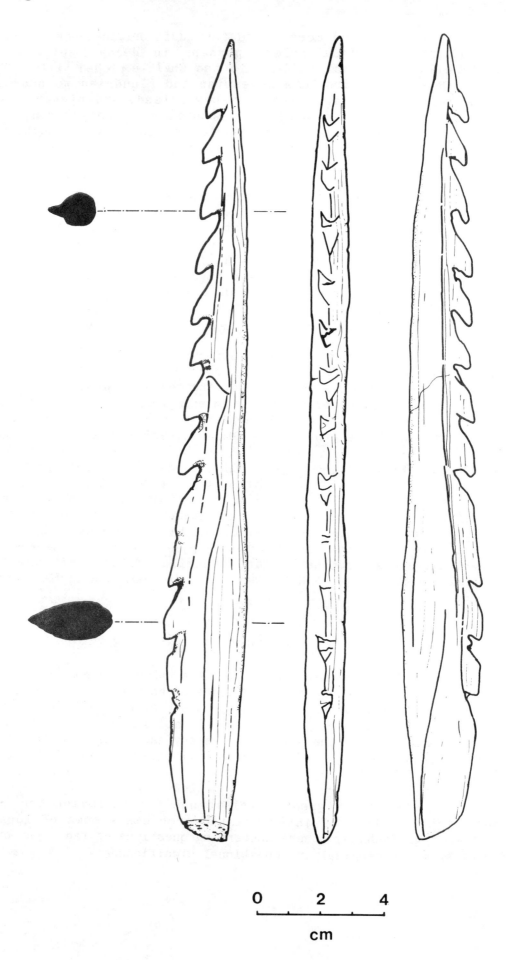

0   2   4
cm

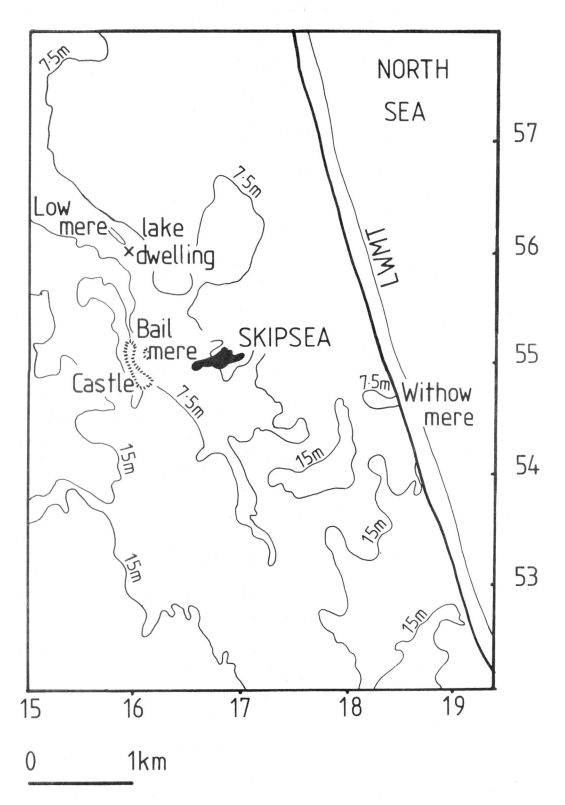

Figure 1.6   The location of the coastal exposures of the former Skipsea
Withow mere, Skipsea Bail mere and Low mere around the
village of Skipsea, Holderness. The contours confirm field
observation that the western margin of the Withow mere is
not linked by steram or river to the meres to the west.
The "lake dwelling" site reported by Smith (1911) is
located near Skipsea Low mere.

(1) Skipsea Withow mere, and Holderness in general, are important because of their location close to one of the last migration and colonisation routes into the British Isles across the North Sea floor from continental Europe. Figure 1.1 shows the approximate location of the coastline at the position of the present 20 fathom isobath as occurred in the Late Devensian, early Flandrian. The present sea level was attained approximately 3-4,000 years ago (Gaunt and Tooley, 1974). Palaeoecological analyses of the Withow mere sediments will provide important information on the pattern of species arrival from their glacial refuges in mainland Europe and the subsequent vegetational and faunal development of Holderness.

(2) The topographic situation of the Withow mere as an enclosed basin resulted in the sediments and stratigraphy of the site reflecting past lake levels, primarily controlled by climate in this region. Similarly, the deposits also reflect palaeoecological changes in the surrounding catchment, as well as the impact of past human activity on the soils and vegetation of the area.

(3) The exposures also offer valuable insights into the ecological and geomorphic processes and environments which have occurred at the important, but infrequently studied, habitat and depositional environment of the lake margin. The quite remarkable degree of complications found in this marginal lacustrine facies exposed at the Withow Gap are of archaeological and palaeoecological importance. Such complexity is, typically, **not** observed in many palaeoecological studies of lakes and meres. Most stratigraphic data tend to derive from coring with a Russian or boat-launched corer, and the palaeontological study invariably tends to be in the more central zones of lake basins, normally associated with 'continuous' deposition. The latter policy aids understanding of 'regional' vegetational change from pollen analytical data. However, archaeologically and geologically important evidence is often to be found at the margins of the lake and is liable to be missed in such conventional sampling strategies. Only the absence of a small incurrent stream causes it to fall short of Coope's (1977:326) ideal location for Quaternary environmental analyses which are based on macrofossil studies. Very little is known of the geomorphic/sedimentological properties and development of such marginal locations.

(4) It is clear that many of the Holderness meres contain deposits of Late Devensian age. This is a most fascinating and complex period of time. Its problems have stimulated considerable research and controversy in the past two decades (Mitchell and West 1977). Inspection of the distribution maps of the Late Devensian sites studied reveal a marked concentration in the "highlands" of western Britain. In many ways the pattern of Late Devensian climatic change identified differs from that originally postulated on the basis of palynological research in the countries of north west Europe from northern France to Denmark (e.g. Hammen, Maarleveld, Vogel and Zagwijn 1967).

In general there is little dispute that the Loch Lomond stadial (the Younger Dryas of continental workers) was associated with an extremely cold climate across northern Europe in the period c. 11,000 - 10,000 years b.p. In highland Britain corrie glaciers developed. However the characteristic vegetation of the time is

SKIPSEA - SKELETON OF MEGACEROS

Further on the pebbly clay sinks below the level of high water, and forms a wide hollow, in which is as

an extensive and interesting lacustrine deposit.

General appearance of the Peat-deposit at Skipsea. Shelly clays underlie the peat; but near the north end,

at * the peat touches the boulder clay for a space.

The series of depositions from freshwater is as follows:-

Peat, with roots, branches, and hazel nuts: its utmost thickness is 7 feet; where this happens the lower
4 feet 6 inches are solid, and break like clay; the upper part is then fibous. Yellowish clay, full of
Bithynia tentaculata, Cyclas cornea, C. Lacustris, and a few specimens of Lymnaea stagnalis: this is seen
only on the southern side of the hollow. Blue clay, full of Cyclades; here is some phosphate of iron; this
rests upon gravel, under which is blue or brown boulder clay.

    In this deposit an old man, who was employed collecting gravel, accidentally discovered the head and

antlers of Cervus megaceros,... . Subsequently the lower jaw was discovered by the researches of Mr. Arthur

Strickland. The antlers .... measuring 11 feet 4 inches by the circuit, and 6 feet 8 inches between

the tips. ....   . This is the second and largest specimen of the gigantic elk which has been found in

Yorkshire.

After Phillips, 1829, 80 - 81.

Figure 1.7   Phillips' (1829) records of the stratigraphy at Skipsea
             Withow mere in 1826 and the provenance of the remains of a
             "gigantic elk". Taken from Phillips (1829:80-81).

imperfectly known, especially from the eastern side of the country.
Starkel's (1977) reconstruction (based on Grichuk 1973) of the
vegetation of Europe at that time indicates that Holderness lay in a
zone of "tundra" immediately north of a zone of "forest tundra with
birch" which covered most of south and south east Britain. There are
suggestions that tree birch actually survived within Holderness near
Hornsea mere (Beckett 1981), and even as far north as the Leven Valley,
Cleveland (Keen, Jones and Robinson 1984).

Nowadays the Pennines act as a major topographic and
climatic divide in Britain, and further research in Holderness has the
interesting prospect of testing these biogeographic reconstructions and
assessing the extent to which the vegetation of the "highland zone" at
that time differed from that of the more continental, eastern parts of
Britain.

The preceding period from 11,000 to 11,800 years b.p., has
long been claimed to be an interstadial period - the Allerød
interstadial. It was believed to be the warmest episode in the Late
Devensian. The climatic inference derived from the evidence that this
period saw the arrival and growth, and then the sudden decline of tree
birch and some pine in Britain. This period was thought to be
separated by a cold phase - the Older Dryas - from the preceding
milder episode which was called the Bølling interstadial (c. 12,000
-13,000 years b.p.) The latter was inferred from palynological
evidence which suggested the presence of a shrub tundra. Before this
period the climate was thought to have been warming, but still
essentially cold, as the Devensian (Weichselian) icesheets melted and
retreated from the maximum extent c. 18,000 - 20,000 years b.p.

Recent studies from the west of Britain have suggested a
different model of the course of climatic change (Coope and Pennington
1977). In this model Coope (1977) suggests that a single warm
interstadial - the Lake Windermere interstadial - commenced about
15,000 years b.p., and terminated suddenly about 11,000 years b.p.,
with a brief cold snap at c. 12,000 - 12,200 years b.p. The highest
temperatures were thought to have been achieved at about 13,400 years
b.p. Pennington (1977) generally concurs, but places the start of the
interstadial at about 13,000 years b.p.

There are several reasons why suggest discrepancies might
have occurred. First they might stem from differences in technique. The
older ideas derived from the pollen analytical studies which depended
heavily upon the relative abundance of pollen types, whereas the more
recent ideas stem from absolute counts of pollen per sample, and the
analysis of beetle remains which are thought to respond to climatic
amelioration more rapidly than tree taxa. Studies of beetle remains
have not been carried out in detail on the Skipsea Withow deposits
described in the text; however, there has been a detailed investigation
of another animal group which can be transported very rapidly across a
landscape -freshwater molluscs. The palaeoenvironmental and
biostratigraphic importance of land molluscs is now well known as a
result of the important studies of Kerney (1964, 1977) and Evans
(1972). However, the freshwater molluscs have received relatively
little attention.

Alternatively, the differences might reflect genuinely different environmental histories. Holderness and Denmark would both have been parts of the extended North European Plain with a continental climate; a situation somewhat different to the highland zone of Britain adjacent to the Atlantic Ocean.

(5) The Withow mere site is also very important in its own right. The lacustrine deposits have been the subject of many archaeological or palaeoecological studies; several of which were either unique in their day or were associated with considerable discord and controversy. The authenticity of the 'Maglemosian' harpoons not only caused acrimonious discussion (Figure 1.5, Armstrong 1923b), it also prompted Professor Sir Harry and Lady Godwin to carry out the first attempt in the British Isles to date archaeological remains (the disputed harpoons) by pollen analysis (Godwin and Godwin 1933). This biostratigraphic approach represented a major innovation in archaeological research and was to have profound consequences in later decades for understanding chronology and environmental change in prehistory.

(6) Finally, good exposures appropriate for teaching environmental archaeology and palaeoecology, are relatively few and far between in lowland Britain. The unfortunate realities of the Withow mere sequence results in a little over-enthusiastic over-trowelling being of little consequence. It is very helpful to students if they can compare detailed descriptions of former exposures, found in the literature, with their own field observations. The three dimensional geometric properties of sedimentary bodies become apparent. Similarly it is much easier to appreciate in this situation both changing research paradigms and the development of particular arguments which deal with a specific location.

This volume represents a first step along the path of realising these research and educational objectives. One part of its contents derives from post-graduate and undergraduate projects carried out at the site by students of the University of Sheffield and the University of Hull. On three occasions in the text we have provided particle size distribution data and molluscan data with little interpretation. The reason is that at present there are insufficient theoretical understanding or empirical observations with which data to interpret the significance of the present data from Skipsea Withow. However we are aware of current research programmes that will help resolve these problems. In order to facilitate future research and teaching in Holderness, we have also included full details of the original stratigraphic, archaeological and palaeontological descriptions, together with key sentences from the more important of the earlier studies.

CHAPTER 2

PREVIOUS RESEARCH

The remains of Skipsea Withow mere are situated in a cliff exposure on the Holderness coast at 53°58'N; 0°12'W; National Grid Reference TA 184547 (Figures 1.4 and 1.6; O.S. Sheet 107, Kingston upon Hull), 1.6km south east of the small village of Skipsea.

Stratigraphic nomenclature used here (Table 2.1) follows Mitchell, Penny, Shotton and West (1973), although this scheme may need modification at a future date (Briggs and Gilbertson, 1980; Briggs, Coope and Gilbertson, 1984). The Godwin (1975) pollen zonation scheme inevitably figures largely in this study. Its relationship to West's (1970) proposed chronozones is given in Table 2.1.

QUATERNARY RESEARCH

The mere deposits are now exposed over a length of less than 100m located in Figure 2.1. They occupy a shallow depression in the surface of till sheets which constitute the dominant deposit exposed along the Holderness coast. The general field relationships between the underlying Chalk, the till sheets, and the mere deposits are summarised in Figures 1.2 and 1.3.

The Tills

The origins and stratigraphic relationships of the tills exposed on the coasts of Holderness have been the subject of research for many years. Consequently the descriptive nomenclature and interpretations have undergone many changes which are summarised in Table 2.2.

The till exposed beneath the lacustrine deposits at Skipsea Withow is now termed the Skipsea Till, after this its type location (Madgett and Catt 1978). At present there are two different interpretations of the till stratigraphy of Holderness. The first envisages the till sheet as the result of deposition by a complex layered ice mass which penetrated along the Holderness coast inland to the Yorkshire and Lincolnshire Wolds, extending as far south as the Norfolk coast (Figure 2.2). At Dimlington (Figure 2.3) it overrode moss-filled hollows which yielded radiocarbon dates of 18,240+250 b.p. (BIRM 108) and 18,500+400 b.p. (I-3372) (Penny, Coope and Catt 1969).

When first published, these dates produced considerable surprise, since they indicated that the Devensian glacial maximum in eastern Britain (Figure 2.2) was much younger in that cold stage than previously suspected. The tills subsequently were bracketed in time by being shown to be overlain by lake deposits which yielded a radiocarbon date of 13,045+270 (BIRM 317). The last glaciation in Holderness was thus shown to be attributable to the period 18,250 to 13,000 years b.p.

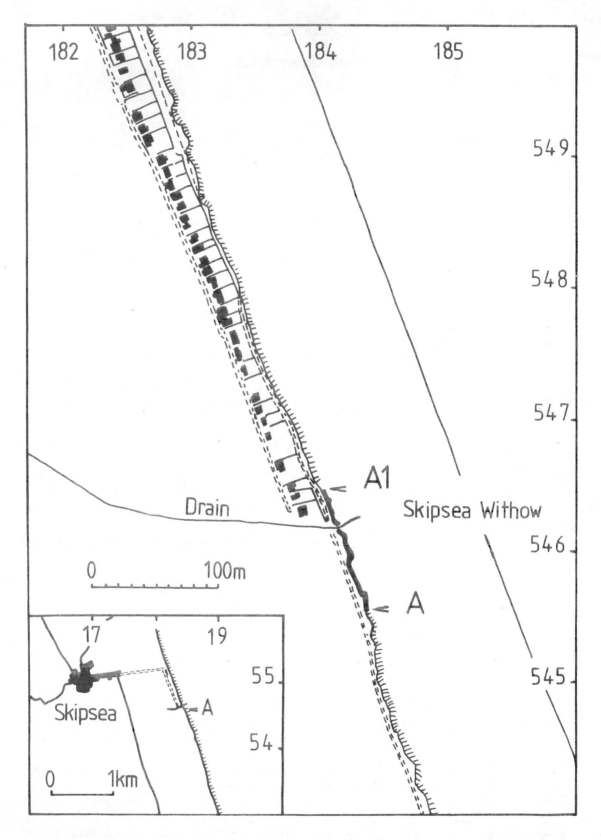

Figure 2.1 The location of the exposures (A to A1) of deposits collecting at the western margin of the former Skipsea Withow mere at the 'Withow Gap'.

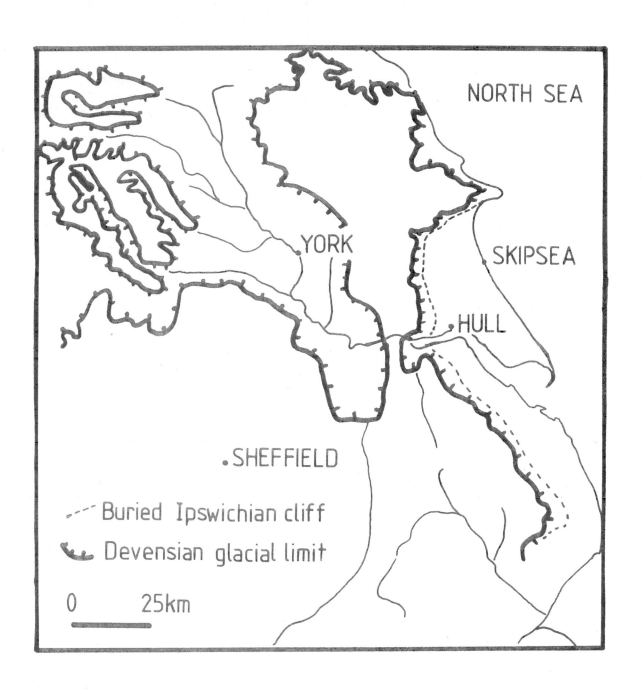

Figure 2.2 The Late Devensian glacial limit c. 18,000-14,000 b.p. and Ipswichian shoreline in and around Holderness (largely after Catt 1977).

This ice advance may be the result of a 'glacial surge' as described by Boulton, Jones, Clayton and Kenning (1977), and 'slightly' younger than the maximum Devensian ice extension in the Midlands and west of Britain, where the Devensian tills currently can be shown only to post-date c. 30,000 years b.p. (see Shotton 1977,1981).

The complexity of the ice mass in Holderness has been demonstrated in a series of major studies by Catt and Penny (1966), Catt and Madgett (1981), Madgett and Catt (1978), Penny and Catt (1967). This work follows on from the pioneering studies of Reid (1885), Bisat (1939) and Bisat and Dell (1941).

The general picture as currently understood in this first model (Catt 1977, Catt and Madgett 1981) is that between c. 18,250 and c. 14,000 years ago, ice masses crossed the Pennines via the Stainmore Gap and Tees valley, carrying rocktypes from the Lake District. East of the Pennines these ice masses formed two ice sheets which passed on either side of the North York Moors. The western branch then penetrated into the Vale of York, extending south across the line of the present Humber estuary. The eastern branch, in the vicinity of the present Tees estuary, over-rode another ice mass which was moving southwards along the coast. This lower ice sheet had crossed the dry North Sea floor from a source region in Scandinavia.

A complex two-tiered ice sheet was produced. It carried quite distinct assemblages of rock types in each layer. The ice pressed into the bays and against the former cliffline of the Ipswichian embayment of Holderness (Figure 2.2) over-riding at Dimlington the sub-arctic mosses and lacustrine silts in the hollows of an older till sheet.

On melting, the lower layer of the compound ice sheet yielded the Skipsea Till, which was termed the 'Drab Till' (Chocolate brown matrix 10 YR 3/2) by Bisat. The upper ice melted to yield the Withernsea Till - the 'Purple Till' (7.5 YR 3/2) of Bisat. This latter till does not occur in the Skipsea area, but thick exposures (c. 15-20m) occur at Dimlington (Catt 1977).

The second model seeks to explain the complex till stratigraphy in terms of multiple glacial re-advances in the Devensian (Straw in Straw and Clayton 1979:24). Straw indicated that, contrary to the predictions of the "ice-sheet sandwich" model, there was evidence that notable erosion between the till layers could be detected (Bisat 1939). Second, there are distinct variations in the extent to which different areas of the present till surface had been eroded. This suggested major differences in the periods of time which these various parts of the till surface had been exposed to the atmosphere.

Bisat (1939) beleived further sub-divisions of the tills could be made as set out in Table 2.2. One further division was the recognition of the Hessle Till. This was believed to overlie both Drab and Purple (Skipsea and Withernsea) Tills. This Hessle Till has now been shown to be a weathering product developed upon and across the Skipsea and Withernsea Tills. It is not therefore a distinct sedimentary unit.

Stage	Approximate age – southern England ^{14}C Time	West Chronozones		Godwin Zones	Characteristic pollen	Land Mollusc Zones
FLANDRIAN	1000	Fl III	Sub-Atlantic	VIII	Alnus-Quercus-Betula	f
	AD / BC		Sub-Boreal			
	1000					
	2000			VIIb	Alnus-Quercus-Tilia	e
	3000				Arboreal Pollen decline	
	4000	Fl II	Atlantic	VIIa	Alnus-Quercus-Ulmus-Tilia	d2
	5000				c Quercus-Ulmus-Tilia	d1
	6000	Fl I	Boreal	VI	Pinus b Quercus-Corylus Ulmus	c
					a Ulmus-Corylus	
	7000		Pre-Boreal	V	Corylus-Betula-Pinus	b
	8000			IV	Betula-Pinus	a
LATE DEVENSIAN		III	III	III	Herbs	
	9000	L-De	II	II	Betula-herbs	z
	10,000		I	I	Herbs	y

Table 2.1   SCHEMES OF CHANGE, DIVISION AND CORRELATION IN THE LATE DEVENSIAN AND FLANDRIAN OF ENGLAND AND WALES: AMENDED FROM JONES AND CUNDILL (1978), GODWIN (1975) AND KERNEY (1977).

Bisat (1939, 1940)	Catt and Penny (1966)	Madgett and Catt (1978)	British Quaternary Stages Mitchell et al (1973)
Upper Purple Clays (2 beds)	Hessle Till	Withernsea Till	Late Devensian
Gravels			(18,000-13,000 B.P approximately)
Lower Purple Clays (3 beds)	Purple Till	Skipsea Till	
Upper Drab Clay Middle Drab Clay Chalk rafts	Drab Till		
Lower Drab Clay Sub Drab Clay Basement Drab Clay	Dimlington Interstadial Beds	Dimlington Silts	Late Devensian (18,240±250 B.P.)
Basement Clay	Basement series	Basement Till	Wolstonian
Sub-Basement Clay			

Table 2.2. Subdivision of the Holderness glacial sequence recognised by W.S. Bisat, and their relation to those of later workers. (after Catt and Madgett, 1982).

In places, the complex ice mass, or ice re-advances, which eventually deposited the Skipsea Till also dragged up, and partially incorporated, much older previously deposited tills of Wolstonian or Anglian age (Table 2.2). This older till is termed the Basement Till and is to be found in tight folds within the Skipsea Till. Elsewhere "erratic rafts" of derived masses of cold, shallow estuarine marine deposits, of presumed Pastonian age also occur in the Till. These marine deposits are known as the Bridlington "Crag".

The Kelsey Hill gravels

Rather different fossiliferous, but very coarse, glacio-genic gravels, known as the Kelsey Hill Gravels, also occur on Holderness (Catt 1977). These contain a rich, but derived ?Ipswichian interglacial fauna (Penny 1963, 1974; Prestwich 1861). In archaeological terms these are important because of their slightly higher elevation and gravelly texture, which have led to better drainage and lighter soils than occur over much of Holderness. These areas may have been preferred for occupation in early Flandrian times. For example, presumed Mesolithic barbed harpoon points have recently been recovered from Hoveringham's Gravel Pit (TA 12544654) near Brandesburton (Davis-King 1980). Such finds need to be regarded with caution. Their relationship with the Quaternary stratigraphy is frequently unknown. Knowledge of their distribution is obviously biased towards areas where gravel is quarried.

The origins and stratigraphic position of the Kelsey Hill Gravels is not fully clear. They often appear to lie stratigraphically between two Devensian tills - the Skipsea and Withernsea Tills. Consequently they may date to the period 18,250-14,000 years b.p., or a period between major ice readvances; a complete knowledge of the palaeogeography at deposition is not yet available. The derived fauna contained within them is surprising. There are frequent remains of large, 'resilient' Ipswichian vertebrate and molluscan fossils. The further re-working of these fossils into Flandrian sequences ought to be detectable by consideration of the taxa concerned: e.g. **Palaeoloxodon antiquus**, **Dicerorhinus hemitoechus**, **Corbicula fluminalis**; and marine molluscan taxa such as **Cardium** and **Littorina** (see Penny 1963).

The Sewerby Raised Beach

At Sewerby, immediately north of Bridlington (Figure 1.2) exposures in the sea cliff reveal Skipsea Till overlying chalky hillwash, dune sands and beach deposits of presumed Ipswichian interglacial age. These rest against a fossil sea cliff and associated shoreline platform eroded into the Chalk and across pre-Devensian tills. The platform and cliff may be ultimately of greater antiquity than the Ipswichian, possibly having only been exhumed and further eroded in that interglacial stage (Boylan 1967; Catt, Weir and Madgett 1974; Catt 1977).

THE MERES AND WETLANDS OF HOLDERNESS

Location and abundance: cartographic, documentary and place name evidence.

The original distribution of lakes, meres and wetlands on Holderness is not easy to reconstruct. Land drainage, reclamation, agricultural improvements, siltation and coastal erosion have all produced major changes in the landscape.

The best palaeogeographic reconstruction published is that of June Sheppard (1957). Five techniques were employed (Figure 1.4). First, the topography of the area was examined and likely locations of former large meres determined (e.g. Plate 2.1). Shallow meres on flat ground are clearly likely to be missed using this approach. On the other hand, the surface relief of other areas has been altered by peat cutting and peat shrinkage - possibly allowing some areas to flood and hence generate meres. Sheppard suspected Burton Agnes mere might have been enlarged by these processes.

Second, examination of drift geological maps provided clues, but small meres or shallow accumulations of lake silts/peats will not necessarily be noted on the published 1:63,360 sheets or even on the unpublished 1:12,500 field mapping sheets held by the Institute of Geological Sciences, recently renamed the "British Geological Survey". Very small meres are therefore likely to be missed with this approach.

Third, examination of aerial photographs taken during flooding in the extremely bad winter of 1946-47 was useful since it is quite probable Holderness must have resembled its earlier undrained conditions (Sheppard 1957). The larger areas of flooding clearly correlate with large former meres, but the significance of the smaller flooded areas was not always clear.

The importance of place names for palaeogeographic reconstructions has been stressed by numerous writers including Sheppard (1957). For example, Ekwall (1936) explained the name Skipsea as Old English or Anglo-Saxon for "Lake for Ships", providing a clear indication that the former lake was of substantial dimensions.

Place names including 'mere', 'mar(r)', 'marsh', and 'sea' indicate the former presence or proximity of lakes, meres or wetlands in the fifth to ninth century, when the names were given by Anglo Saxon and Danish occupants. This list of names is long but not complete.

> Marton and Sallymarr, near Burton Constable; Sand-le-Marr, near Withernsea; Marfleet near Hull; Longmarhill, near Welwick; Bowmerehill in Owstwick; Pilmar Lane in Roos; Hornsea mere; Withernsea mere; Pidsea; Rowmere and Giltsmere in Tunstall; Redmere in Preston; Braemere in Flinton; 'The Marrs' in Swine; Crossmerehill in Aldborough; Braemarr Drain in Beeforth; Gunnymarsh Drain in Ottringham; Slightmarsh and Ryehill marsh in Ryehill; Ottringham marsh; Atwick marsk; 'The Marsk' in Nunkeeling; and Soumers, Whitmarr, Bassmarr, Lowmere, Bailmere and Skipsea Withow mere

Plate 2.1 The silted up and drained remains of the former westward extension of the main Skipsea Withow mere, photographed from the Withow Gap (Figure 1.6).

Figure 2.3 The location of towns and meres of Holderness lost as a
result of coastal erosion (after Sheppard 1912): Dots
correspond to villages; open symbols correspond to meres.
1 - Wilsthorpe; 2 - Auburn; 3 - Hartburn; 4 - Hyde; 5 -
Withow; 6 - Cleton; 7 - Northorpe; 8 - Hornsea Burton; 9 -
Hornsea Beck and Southorpe; 10 - Great Colden; 11 - Colden
Parva; 12 - Old Aldborough; 13 - Ringborough; 14 -
Monkwell; 15 - Monkwike; 16 - Sand-le-mere; 17 - Waxholme;
18 - Owthorne or Sisterkirke; 19 - Newsham; 20 - Old
Withernsea; 21 - Out Newton; 22 - Dimlington; 23 - Turmarr;
24 - Northorp; 25 - Hoton; 26 - Site of Angell's Light; 27
- Sunthorp; 28 - Orwithfleet; 29 - Ravenspurn; 30 -
Ravenser Odd.

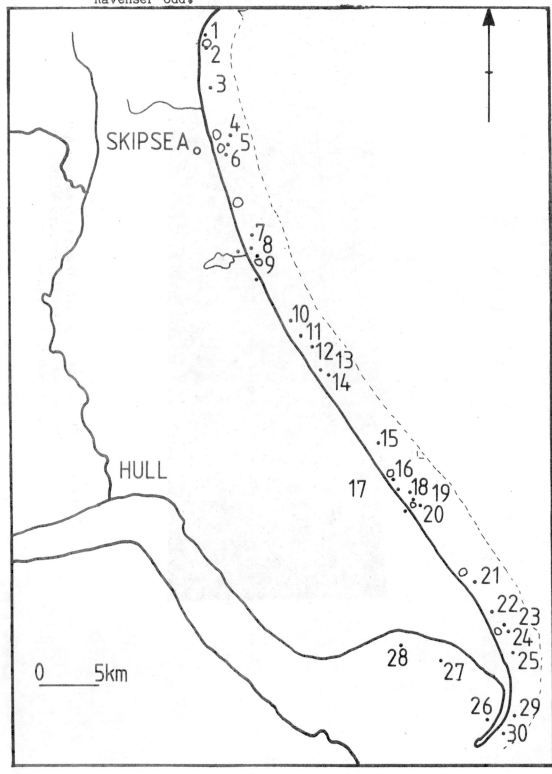

at Skipsea (Figure 1.6). Goose island near Ulrome is a hillock surrounded by fields, the site is no longer an island. According to Sheppard (1909:503-504) in medieval times this vast area of wetlands constituting the 'Isle of Holderness' could itself be circum-navigated by vessels entering from the North Sea near Barmston and then sailing west and then south down the River Hull to the Humber estuary.

The modern maps of the region are relatively poor guides to this wealth of names. Much better are the Ordnance Survey First Edition Six Inch Maps (1854-1855), and the Tithe Surveys which give the names of most of the fields in the areas surveyed.

The results of these combined surveys are reproduced in Figure 1.4 which indicates the former presence of over 70 meres in Holderness. The figure is probably too low since all of these survey methods inevitably tend to under-estimate the numbers of small, economically unimportant meres.

The disappearance of the Holderness meres.

Sheppard (1957) also documented in detail the disappearance of many meres known to exist from medieval records. She suspected that many of the smaller meres and one larger mere (Lambwith - Figure 7.5) had completely silted up (Plate 2.1) by the fourteenth century. The reasons for the developments are not fully clear. Many possibilities spring to mind. It may have been the consequence of deliberate draining, or failure to clear weeds and hence maintain open water as economic interest in freshwater (subsistence?) fishing declined.

The Reformation led to further declines in interest in maintaining open water, as sea fishing continued its rise in importance at the expense of freshwater fishing. Documentary records of the seventeenth century show that by this time penalties had been established for failure to properly maintain drains in the area. These records, 'The Pains' of the Court of Sewers for the East Parts of the East Riding which are now held in Records Offices, suggest that only the meres at Hornsea, Skipsea (Bailmere and Lowmere) (Figure 1.6) and Pidsea still survived; Withernsea and Skipsea Withow meres had disappeared as a result of coastal erosion. In the late seventeenth and early eighteenth centuries further meres/wetlands were drained as local land owners 'improved' their properties. Now only Hornsea mere survives.

Documentary evidence of coastal erosion.

"Hornsea as an old market town probably little dreamed of becoming a seaside resort. But coast erosion brought the possibility nearer, and the building of a concrete foreshore at once serves the purpose of keeping back the sea and provides the essentials of a seaside resort."

(S.E.J. Best 1930:146-147)

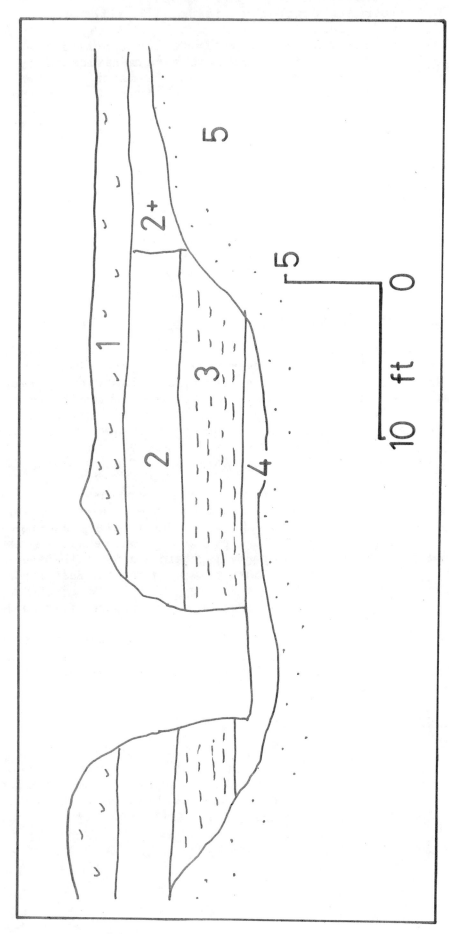

Figure 2.4 Peat stratigraphy at Ulrome, West Furze: 1 - peaty marl; 2 - peat; 3 - brushwood and logs with piles; 4 - peat with logs (After Smith 1911).

Several historical documents compiled in Sheppard (1909, 1912) provide clues on the loss of meres and coastline by coastal erosion, and more specifically upon the loss of revenue previously generated by them.

"From an inquisition held at Wagen about 1288, it seems Robert de Chester enjoyed the tythe of fish in Skipsea Marr. Possibly this mere was in existence and well stocked with fish at that time. It would certainly be some distance from the cliff edge in the thirteenth century."

"Inquisition at Hedon 1400: £46:13/4 from Ulrome, Cleton, Skipsea and Villam de Hythe (£30) to Convent of Meaux 'chiefly in the tythe of fish - all destroyed'."

"1396: 'the place (Hythe) is now totally destroyed'. Hythe: east of Skipsea, included with Skipsea in Cleton in the reign of Edward II.
Edward III was petitioned for a reduction of tythes because of 'devastations of the sea' in Skipsea parish. Withow: Waghen Inquisition: tithed like Skipsea to Robert to Chester. Only the name is now left. It was in the township of Skipsea."

(Sheppard 1912:192-193).

Further estimates of land loss were made by Sheppard (1909) by comparing his estimates of the arable acreage of coastal towns in Holderness derived from data in the Domesday Book with the results of a survey conducted in 1800. Whilst the reliability of the estimates is open to question, their general import is clear.

Township	1086	1800
Easington	2400 acres	1300 acres
Holmpton	1280 acres	900 acres
Tunstall	1280 acres	800 acres
Colden	1920 acres	1100 acres

If these figures are attributed and averaged according to the relevant sections of the Holderness coastline, an average rate of retreat of 2.2m each year is suggested for the Holderness coast as a whole. This estimate is slightly higher than that derived by Valentin who initially calculated the average rate of retreat of the Holderness cliffline to be 1.2m each year (Valentin 1952) and subsequently modified this figure to 1.4m each year (Valentin 1972). These estimates were obtained by comparing modern Ordnance Survey maps with those of the Ordnance Survey's First Edition Six Inch map which was published in 1852, and based on surveys conducted immediately before this date.

Several other early maps and hydrographic charts are also relevant in this context. The sixteenth century map entitled **"Plotte made for the description of the River Humber and of the Sea and Seacoast from Hull to Skarburgh"** held in the British Museum shows a predecessor of modern Hornsea. It was located east of the present

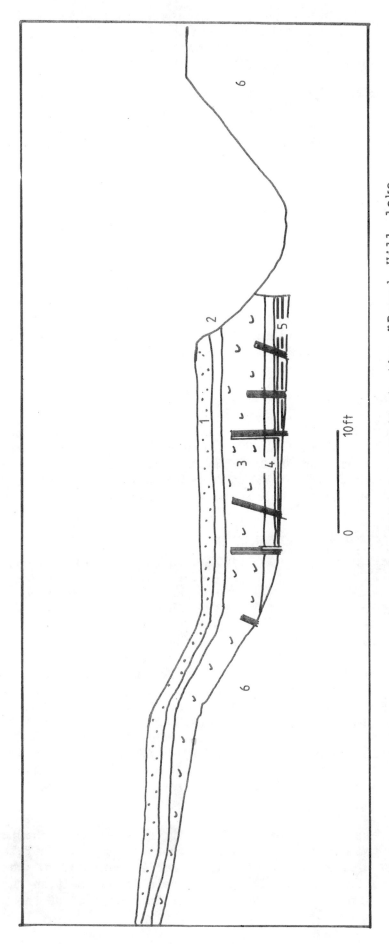

Figure 2.5 Lake stratigraphy recorded at the "Round Hill lake dwelling", Skipsea by Smith (1911): 1 – "Warp"; 2 – Peat; 3 – Freshwater marl; 4 – peat; 5 – gravel; 6 – Till.

settlement and is shown to be connected to the sea by a long straight river or creek. This town was later abandoned and the newer settlement located further inland. The construction of seawalls necessary to protect it from coastal erosion began at the end of the nineteenth century.

From the end of the eighteenth century numerous maps were made of the coast. These are especially interesting since they utilised measurements obtained from fixed points. The documentation is particularly good for Spurn Head at the entrance to the Humber. This spit is the subject of a classic study using such documents by De Boer (1964, 1982).

The above data are summarised in Figure 2.3 which shows the lost towns and coastal erosion on Holderness.

ARCHAEOLOGY AND STRATIGRAPHY OF HOLDERNESS MERES

The earliest finds of worked timbers from Holderness meres are recorded in Smith (1911) who noted that in 1880, oak piles and bones were found at West Furze and Round Hill, Ulrome (TA 161566) during the clearing of the Skipsea branch of the Barmston Drain (Figure 1.6). Shortly after 1880, Thomas Boynton, a Drainage Commissioner, began a small scale, but pioneering, programme of excavations of waterlogged sites around Skipsea. The work was recorded by Smith (1911) whose paper became the major source for later workers.

Ulrome

The stratigraphy of the Ulrome – West Furze 'lake dwelling' is shown in Figure 2.4. The undifferentiated peats – presumably peaty detritus muds – are shown to be divided by a carr peat upon which the structures were built.

The stratigraphy of the Round Hill 'lake dwelling' is more interesting (Figure 2.5). Freshwater 'marl' – a calcareous deposit with freshwater mussel shells and a human skull (Smith 1911:605) – is shown forming the centre of a sandwich between the peat layers. During the period of occupation, broadly attributed to the Bronze Age, the lake appears to have contained highly calcareous water.

Hornsea Old Mere

The 'Old Mere' is nowadays a dry, landscaped depression to the east of the present Hornsea Mere. It is protected by the modern seawall. The general stratigraphy and archaeology of these lake deposits are imperfectly known. Whilst Phillips' (1829) early sketches are rather general, his later interpretations which were reproduced after his death (Etheridge 1875) are more informative. These diagrams suggest that at least part of the lake sequence is faulted. The later observations of Clement Reid (1885) and Sheppard (1912), made after severe storms had eroded the foreshore, suggests an alternation of layers of lacustrine peats and shelly calcareous marls, reproduced as Figure 2.6. . This feature is essentially similar to that observed at Ulrome - Round Hill by Smith (1911; Figure 2.5 in this text).

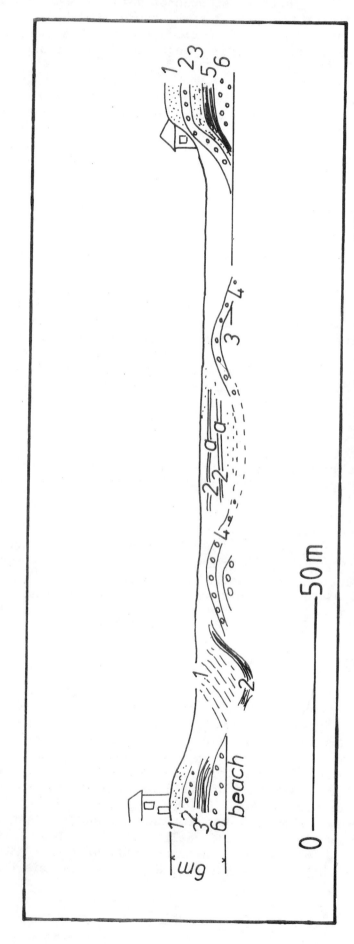

Figure 2.6 Stratigraphic sections of the former exposures of Hornsea
Old Mere at Hornsea beach, recorded by Sheppard (1912).

Bisat's sketches in Catt and Madgett (1981) provide little further information. However, detailed stratigraphic and palynological data are available from a core by Beckett (1977, 1981) from the remains of Hornsea Old Mere at NGR TA 1947. The lake sequence encompasses the Late Devensian and Flandrian. The Late Devensian sequence exhibits the classic lithological sequence of (oldest) minerogenic gravel clay - organic detritus mud - pinkish grey silty clay (youngest) typical of many Late Devensian sequences in northern Britain. The middle detritus mud contains a pollen flora indicating the presence of **Betula** woodland and is correlated with the Allerød interstadial period.

The enclosing mineral-rich layers are characterised by pollen and spores indicative of the 'open' vegetation of Late-Devensian zones I and III.

The overlying brown, homogeneous detritus muds reveal an early Flandrian landscape dominated by **Betula** and **Pinus**. This was followed by a mixed deciduous woodland with **Ulmus**, **Quercus**, **Tilia**, **Corylus** and **Alnus** - which is fairly typical of sites in northern England. **Alnus** is recorded very early in the Flandrian.

The 'elm decline' was accompanied by parallel declines in the abundance of **Tilia**. Minor forest regeneration then took place, with further forest clearance taking place in the Bronze Age. Beckett (1977) felt the extent of the clearances were of smaller scale or intensity than are reported on upland sites in Britain.

The sequence is terminated by slopewash sediments being deposited in the lake as it silted/dried up. This may have occurred c. 2000 B.P. when Beckett (1977:38) suspected the lake may have been breached and drained by the sea.

The lithological fluctuations noted by Sheppard (1906) in the sea wall exposure were not reported.

Armstrong (1922, 1923a, 1923b) reported the find in 1905 of a 'Maglemose harpoon' from a depth of 15 feet (4.5m) from these deposits during the excavation of a gas holder. The harpoon is similar to several others found since in the area; however Armstrong's view of its provenance must remain doubtful. An extensive coring programme by Godwin failed to locate the deposit from which the harpoon was reported to have been found (Clark and Godwin 1956:11). A later harpoon find found on Hornsea beach in 1932 is also unprovenanced and was presumed to have derived from the Old Mere lacustrine deposits by Clark and Godwin (1956:11).

Grimston

Late Devensian lacustrine clays and peats radiocarbon dated to 11,250+170 b.p. (BIRM 301) and 11,230+120 b.p. (BIRM 298) were obtained from a former kettle peaty infill exposed in a landslip at Grimston (TA 289352) further south on the Holderness coast (Catt 1977:39, 40).

Barmston

The Ulrome and Barmston sites described by Smith (1911) were surveyed by Varley in 1960 and the results of his re-examination of the Barmston site published in 1968 (Varley 1968). The stratigraphy established at Barmston is shown in Figure 2.7. The wooden piles of buildings were found lying upon, or driven into, the 'Shell Bed' which overlies gravels, themselves resting unconformably upon 'late-glacial' varved silts. The wooden stakes and piles were associated with Bronze Age implements. Varley (1968) reported radiocarbon dates of 2960+150 and 2890+150 for these. The molluscan palaeoenvironmental studies of Boylan (1966) at the site are discussed in Chapter 6 here. They led him to infer the former presence of a seasonally flooded lake or fen surrounded by carr at the site. Pollen analysis of the overlying peats suggested clearance of the mixed deciduous forest cover and agricultural activity after the Bronze Age occupation of the site (Varley 1968).

These data indicate both stratigraphic parallels and notable differences with the sequence at the Skipsea Withow mere site. Of particular interest is the major stratigraphic break below the 'Shell Bed', and the demonstration of Bronze Age occupation of the wetlands. Varley (1968) preferred to regard the structures, not as crannogs -i.e. piled lake dwellings - but as the remains of Bronze Age buildings initially built in a damp hollow. He believed these had to be abandoned due to environmental changes which eventually led to the site being buried and preserved beneath peat.

Varley's section (Figure 2.7) reveals substantial exposures of varved clays which he associates with lake-freezing/unfreezing in a deglacial phase. The contact with the overlying lacustrine deposits is clearly erosional. The molluscan palaeontology (Chapter 6), pollen biostratigraphy and archaeological finds in the overlying shell bed and peats suggest this part of the sequence is attributable to Bronze Age and post-Bronze Age times.

The colluvium (Units 4 and 5) is also interesting. Two pieces of green-glazed medieval pottery referred to the thirteenth century "rested upon" the sandy clays of Unit 4; whilst Unit 5 - of similar texture - was overlain by the upcast from the Barmston Drain which was excavated about 1800 A.D. (Varley 1968:16).

Skipsea Withow Mere

"Skipsea" - Old English - "a lake for ships".

The cliff exposure at the Withow Gap of the former deposits of the Skipsea Withow or Witthow mere are notable for two reasons. They possess the most complete and complex sequence of Late-Devensian and Flandrian deposits known in Holderness. They are also unrivalled for possessing the most confused literature describing any Holderness lacustrine sequence.

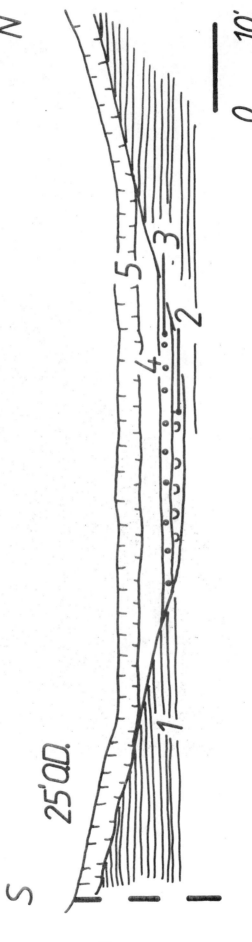

Figure 2.7 Lake stratigraphy at Barmston, near Skipsea (after Varley 1968).
1) Skipsea Till; 2) Gravel; 3) Varved clays; 4) Peat;
5) Hillwash.

Plate 2.2 The present Withow Gap; the exposures studied by Armstrong
(1923b) and Godwin and Godwin (1933) lay seawards of the
collapsed pillboxes, bottom right.

Plate 2.2 shows the present Withow Gap and the buildings mapped on Figure 2.1 as photographed pointing north from location A. The rate of coastal erosion may be appreciated by recognising that the location of the exposures noted by Godwin and Godwin (1933) lay well seawards of the fallen remains of concrete pill boxes seen collapsed on the beach in the bottom right hand corner of the photograph.

'The Withow Gap or Withow Hole'

The oldest references to the former Skipsea Withow mere are recorded in the Yorkshire Archaeological Society's Record Series. Skipsea Withow mere is identified in them by the name Fwitthouker (Sheppard 1957), who records:

> "In 1260, one William de Fortibus, Earle of Albemarle is described as owning 'four meres and a half, to wit Lambwad, Skipsea, Fwitthouker and Wythornse meres and a moiety of Pidsea mere, with a fishery throughout the whole. The other moiety is the Lord William de Ros with fishery through the whole'." (pp. 80-81).

A second document quoted by Sheppard (1957:82) provides further details of economic and social interest, indicating that in Skipsea the arable land and meadow were valued at 4d and 8d an acre respectively; whereas the eels from Skipsea and Withow meres were valued at 10 shillings. The Withow mere had disappeared from the documentary record by 1660, presumably having been lost by coastal erosion. The Skipsea meres - Bailmere and Low mere can both be traced on the ground today and have been cored and investigated (Figure 1.6; Flenley and Maloney 1975, 1976).

SEDIMENTS AND STRATIGRAPHY

The nineteenth century

The progress of argument and the development of our understanding of the sediments, stratigraphy, chronology, palaeontology and archaeology at the Skipsea Withow mere site are subjects which merit considerable interest. The general principle appears to be that the stratigraphic problems which became clear in the late 1970's derive from a lack of detailed information on the stratigraphy of the lower part of the sequence. It is especially instructive to establish exactly what the various research workers actually wrote, and compare their views with the information found in secondary sources.

The exposures at Skipsea Withow mere were first described by Phillips in 1829. His fullest sections and descriptions are given in Figure 1.7. His belief, that the tills (boulder clays) were the result of deposition in glacial seas, was in keeping with the wisdom of the times, and did not colour or distort his description of the exposures.

Several points, clearly illustrated in Phillips, are relevant to a fuller understanding of the archaeological and palaeontological remains later found at the site.

1.   The length and thickness of the exposure in the 1820's. It
was recorded as over 400m long, compared with less than 100m exposed
nowadays. A broad, dish shaped basin is implied, the coast having
retreated c. 225m in the intervening period.

2.   The shape of the contact between peat and clay in Phillips'
(1829) section is illustrated in Figure 1.7, together with his notes.
The contact indicates the underlying lake silts must have been eroded
prior to the deposition of the infilling peats. This important
observation was also made by Bisat, whose carefully drawn sections also
reveal the major unconformity between the peat and underlying
lacustrine silts/clays (in Catt and Madgett 1981).

3.   An important gravel member is described (although not
illustrated) within the 'clay' stratum by Phillips (1829a). This
gravel member was largely overlooked in later studies. This is
unfortunate since one possible interpretation of Phillips' text is that
the head and antlers of the **Cervus megaceros** were obtained from this
member by the 'gravel collector' who found them. It is exceedingly
unlikely such a combination of finds would be obtained from the many
nearby gravel lenses found in the adjacent Skipsea Till.

          Phillips (1829) and several other later workers (e.g. Reid
1885, Sheppard 1906, Bisat in Catt and Madgett 1981, and Varley 1968)
indicate basically similar late- and/or post-glacial sequences
infilling hollows on the till surface elsewhere along the Holderness
coast. The most recent detailed descriptions derive from Hornsea
(Beckett 1981) and Barmston (Varley 1968).

The Maglemosian harpoon controversy

          Whilst the palaeontology and 'lake dwellings' of this and
similar sites on Holderness were becoming well known, little further of
scientific significance was found at the Withow mere site until 1903.
At this time, a 'Mr. B. Morfitt Junior' found a carved bone harpoon
(Figure 1.5)

          "lying in silt at a depth of 5 feet, beneath lacustrine peat
          and immediately above the skeletal remains of an elk (**Cervus
          giganteus**) which he was excavating. Other fauna associated
          was reindeer, red-deer and ancient-ox.

          The Skipsea harpoon --- is 4.9 inches long, exceedingly
          well finished, barbed on one edge only ---"
          (Armstrong 1922:60).

          These finds were written up by A. Leslie Armstrong in a
series of papers (1922, 1923a, b). They represented the first finds of
such artefacts in the British Isles. He noted that irregular holes
infilled with peat or twigs had been observed at the contact between
the peat and underlying clays. These were also detected by Armstrong
in his own excavations. They were thought to be too narrow and
irregular to represent the remains of timber piles, and were regarded
as more likely to be the result of using poles to propel boats across
the former lake by 'Maglemosian' rather than the Bronze Age people
associated with the nearby crannogs (Smith 1911).

MUSEUM OF NATURAL HISTORY,
ANTIQUITIES & APPLIED ART
ROYAL INSTITUTION, ALBION STREET.
TEL. CENT. 8136.

MUSEUM OF FISHERIES
AND SHIPPING:
PICKERING PARK.
TEL. CENT. 37234.

HULL HISTORICAL MUSEUM:
WILBERFORCE HOUSE,
HIGH STREET.
TEL. CENT. 2328.

MUSEUM OF COMMERCE AND TRANSPORT:
OLD CORN EXCHANGE,
HIGH STREET.
TEL. CENT. 2328.

MORTIMER MUSEUM
OF PREHISTORIC ARCHAEOLOGY.
CARR LANE.
TEL. CENT. 31012.

T. SHEPPARD, M. SC., F.G.S., F.S.A. SCOT.
M.B.O.U., F.R.A.I.,
DIRECTOR.

THE MUNICIPAL MUSEUMS,
HULL.

17th September 1929.

Dear Mr Hazzledine Warren,

Thanks for yours. The Maglemose harpoons were made by Mr B.Morfitt in the presence of his sister who was spending a weekend with Mrs Sheppard and I and told us how it was done. (see enclosed pamphlet).

Since then a special committee appointed by the British Association has examined the site at Hornsea and made excavations and no peat exists anywhere near the Gasworks and the men say nothing of the sort was found there during excavations.

The Skipsea site still has to be examined by the Committee but I am sure will be equally unproductive. Don't forget that Sir Hercules Reid stated that both harpoons has been made by the same individual.

Yours sincerely,

T Sheppard

S.Hazzledine Warren, Esqre.,
Sherwood,
Loughton,
Essex.

Are the Morfitts now dead!

Figure 2.8 Sheppard's (1929) correspondence on the authenticity of the harpoon remains recorded by Armstrong (1923b).

Unfortunately for Armstrong, the harpoons became the subject of unpleasant controversy. Sheppard, who was Director of the Municipal Museum, Hull, and Editor of the influential northern journal 'The Naturalist', always doubted the authenticity of the harpoons. His attack was three pronged.

Armstrong was clearly regarded as not playing the scientific game in the approved manner:

> "One of the most extraordinary newspaper 'stunts' in recent years has been the method adopted by Mr. Leslie Armstrong, of Sheffield, in endeavouring to convince the world that the two bone harpoons which he exhibited at Hull are genuine, and that the opinion expressed by the present writer to the effect that the harpoons are forgeries, has been proved to be wrong. Mr. Armstrong alleges that two committees have proved conclusively that the harpoons are twelve thousand years old, whereas the committees have proved nothing of the sort, and in fact could not do so."
> (Sheppard 1923:169).

In the longer run, much more interesting are the many criticisms Sheppard records on the circumstances and reports of the initial finds. Several important discrepancies can be identified in Armstrong's accounts in the fencing match represented by their literature (Armstrong 1922, 1923a, b, Sheppard 1923, newspaper articles therein, and 1929 reproduced as Figure 2.8 here).

Armstrong's (1922) report gives a different account of the faunal context of the harpoon, especially as it relates to the giant elk (**Cervus giganteus** = **Megaceros giganteus** Blumenbach).

> "The harpoon --- was resting in silt, under five feet of overlying peat. Above it and enclosed in the peat was the complete specimen of a female elk (**Cervus giganteus**). At the same level as the harpoon, remains of reindeer, red deer, and pike were discovered ---"
> (Armstrong 1922:131).

The harpoon remains were <u>in</u>, <u>not on</u> the silt, although other references to peat staining indicate close proximity to the peat. The reindeer, red deer and pike similarly are regarded as found in the silt. The giant elk has, however, been transferred to the peat.

Current knowledge of vertebrate palaeoecology summarised in Stuart (1982) records that reindeer and giant elk were both creatures of the 'cold' open tundra or birch/pine/poplar-aspen parklands of British cold stage climates (it is not possible to distinguish between the pollen of poplar and aspen). Stuart (1982) indicates <u>c</u>. 11,000 years b.p. as the youngest reliable antiquity yet attributed to this giant elk. Reindeer is known from Late Devensian zone L-De III. Even in Phillips' (1829) days, the Withow mere peats were recognised as essentially the products of temperate landscapes. Hazel nuts, in particular, are abundant and give unequivocal indications of temperate forest trees/shrub occurring in the area.

In 1923 Armstrong (1923a:136) states that these same silts which yielded the harpoon, and certainly the reindeer, also "contain plant remains, nuts and freshwater shells". These nuts can only be hazel nuts.

These data indicate curious overlaps between essentially cold stage faunas of open environments and temperate forested early-mid Flandrian landscapes. Whilst the quantity of better authenticated harpoons subsequently deriving from the area, described in Clark and Godwin (1956), Bartlett (1969), Radley (1969) and Davis-King (1980) suggests Armstrong's harpoons may have been genuine, the basic stratigraphy of the site and consequently palaeoecological context still remains confused in this literature.

Committees of Enquiry

Two committees of archaeologists and geologists were convened in 1922 to discuss the authenticity of the harpoons. Their views are given in Armstrong (1922). The first panel, comprising Haddon, Burkitt and J.E. Marr, expressed their view that "on the evidence placed before us, we are satisfied as to their provenance." (p. 65). The second group of Read, Smith-Woodward and Kendall, made the telling point that at the time of their discovery, no other harpoons were available to be seen from Denmark, from which they were alleged to have been copied. Sheppard's "strong grounds for doubting the authenticity of the harpoons" was found to be non-verifiable.

These answers were clearly favourable to Armstrong, but insufficient to vindicate fully his position. Sheppard's view was not dismissed, it remained non-proven; these opinions did nothing to sort out the basic stratigraphic problem.

The reports of the committees stimulated further research by Armstrong, and a decade later by the Godwins (1933) which was to clarify some points, but also to introduce further uncertainties into the understanding of the palaeontology and age of the lower lake silts.

In 1922, Leslie Armstrong carried out further excavations. These yielded further collections of flint implements of Mesolithic type from the upper layers of the clay/silts, from the silt/peat boundary, and the lower layers of the peats. The implements were adjudicated by the committees, and one of Armstrong's flint implements (Armstrong 1922:figure 4) was stated to be early Neolithic, rather than Mesolithic, but still regarded as contemporary with the harpoons.

The advent of pollen biostratigraphy

The harpoons and their chronological problems clearly fascinated the Godwins. In the summer of 1932, they visited the section with Armstrong and brought to bear the new science of Palynology. This represented their first attempt to date archaeological remains by pollen biostratigraphy in the British Isles, and established principles and standards of great significance. The original harpoon site had by this time been lost by three decades of coastal erosion.

At the sampling site the section was as follows:

(0.76m) 2 feet 6 inches, fine brown clay - now cracking into columnar
    form. A fresh water deposit.

(2.13m) 7 feet, solid black or brown amorphous peat with large
    numbers of horizontal tree branches or trunks, including much
    oak (**Quercus**) especially in the upper two feet, which is
    almost solid with them. Hazel nuts found at 4 feet 4 inches, 5
    feet 6 inches and 6 feet 4 inches, from the top of the bed, and
    at its very base.

(0.15m) 6 inches, brown sandy silt - with fragments of **Pinus** bark,
    fins of pike (**Esox lucius**) and flint artifacts. Stone fruit
    of (?) **Prunus**. Buttery Blue Clay.

During the sampling further artifacts were found in the sandy silt just
underlying the peat: these are in the possession of Mr. Armstrong and
clearly are of the same type as those described by him in 1923.

Table 2.3   DESCRIPTION OF THE SKIPSEA WITHOW MERE SEQUENCE BY GODWIN AND
            GODWIN (1933).

"Submerged forests on the Northumberland coast give only
indefinite evidence of a small transgression later than zone
VI, and the same may be said of the site at Skipsea Withow on
the Yorkshire coast, where erosion has now exposed on the
beach the lowest layers of a freshwater lake. In these
layers, which belong to zone VIc, there probably occurred not
only remains of elk, reindeer, and a freshwater **Ancylus**
fauna, but in all probability another Maglemosian fish spear
of the type mentioned as found between the Leman and Ower
banks. Marine deposits do not, however, enter the deep
profile of the deposits succeeding these basal layers."

(Godwin 1943:236).

Table 2.4. Godwin's (1943) re-interpretation of the antiquity of the
lake silts at Skipsea Withow mere.

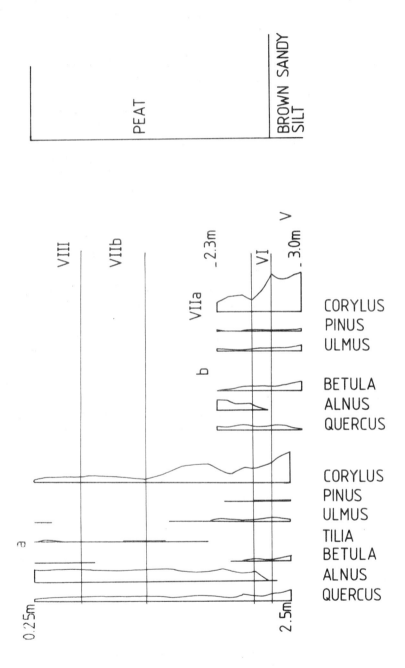

Figure 2.9 Summary of the pollen diagram from Skipsea Withow mere published by Godwin and Godwin (1933).

43

The section described by Godwin and Godwin (1933) is set out in Table 2.3. The results of their palynological studies are re-drawn in Figure 2.9.

A new stratigraphic member was noted. Table 2.3 describes a brown sandy silt immediately below the peat from which artefacts were obtained. At the time of this description, this may or may not have been mistaken for the silts described by Armstrong (1923). It certainly appears to have been mistakenly equated with them later in the 1940's.

The dominance of pine, birch, hazel and subsequent rise in Alder suggested that the brown sandy silt should be referred to the late Boreal (zone VI - Table 2.1) of the definitive Godwin (1975) scheme. In the 1940's, stratigraphic complications were introduced in the review section of Godwin (1943), specifically in his seminal paper on coastal peat beds and sea level change. The critical sentence is set out in Table 2.4. The lowest layers of the freshwater lake at Skipsea Withow mere (not just the brown sandy silt below the peat) were thus all attributed to zone VI: an early mid-Flandrian date.

Molluscan biostratigraphy

A combination of the application of molluscan biostratigraphy and (apparently) lithostratigraphic correlation combined with Godwin's review (1943) prompted Boylan (1966) to confirm the early mid-Flandrian view from his molluscan studies (see Chapter 6 here and Table 2.5).

The excellently exposed fossil molluscan faunas found in lake silts at Skipsea Withow mere and other former meres in Holderness are described in Bisat (1932), Drake and Sheppard (1910), Ellis (1951), Petch (1904), Spalding (1962) and, most recently, by Boylan (1966) who reviewed all previous work. Boylan (1966) also described the unpublished notes of A.S. Kennard, which are held in the British Museum (Natural History), Department of Palaeontology. The faunal list, and its associated habitat/climatic interpretation scheme, is set out here as Table 6.5 in Chapter 6.

This study by Boylan played a crucial role in attributing the 'harpoons' and, by implication, the vertebrate remains previously described to the early mid-Flandrian. The critical sentences are:

> "There is little evidence of climate, since the land shells are so few, and freshwater molluscs are very poor indicators, but the scarcity of warm-loving species, such as **Discus rotundatus**, that are so common in the Sub-Boreal faunas of North Lincolnshire (Kennard and Musham 1937) is noteworthy. The author therefore agrees with Kennard's (manuscript) opinion that both Skipsea and Barmston molluscs are Late-Boreal in age." (Boylan 1966:117).

Barmston is located immediately north of Skipsea. Close examination of Table 6.5 reveals that the woodland, and indeed warmth indicators, such as **Clausilia bidentata** or **Discus rotundatus** are present at Barmston, but are totally absent in the lake silts at Skipsea Withow. There are other suggestions of warmth at Barmston -

Number of specimens of mollusca in the samples from Skipsea (1929, 1936 and 1937) and Barmston (1945A and B, 1946, 1947).

Number of specimens in:

	Species	Skipsea			Barmston				New fossil record for:-
		1929	1936	1937	1945 A	1945 B	1946	1947	
4	**Theodoxus fluviatilis** (Linne)	0	0	0	1	5	7	0	E.Y.
3	**Valvata cristata** (Müller)	C	13	+	258	496	269	222	
4	**V. piscinalis** (Müller)	C	153	+	74	120	70	71	
4	**Bithynia tentaculata** (Linne)	C	32	+	53	118	81	38	
4	**B. leachii** (Sheppard)	0	0	+	1	20	18	11	
M	**Carychium minimum** (Müller)	0	0	0	0	0	11	7	
W	**C. tridentatum** (Risso)	0	0	0	1	3	0	0	
1	**Lymnaea truncatula** (Müller)	0	0	0	0	1	0	0	
2	**L. palustris** (Müller)	0	0	0	0	1	0	0	
4	**L. stagnalis** (Linne)	0	1	0	1	0	20	1	
2	**L. pereger** (Müller)	C	36	+	239	270	226	165	
3	**Myxas glutinosa** (Müller)	C	0	0	0	0	0	0	
4	**Physa fontinalis** (Linne)	C	0	0	0	1	2	2	Skipsea; E.Y.
3	**Planorbis planorbis** (Linne)	0	2	0	0	0	4	0	Skipsea; E.Y.
1	**P. leucostoma** (Millet)	0	0	0	1	5	7	5	
-	**P. laevis** (Alder)	12	5	0	0	0	0	0	Skipsea; E.Y.
2	**P. albus** (Müller)	0	0	0	5	21	14	6	
2	**P. crista** (Linne)	C	132	+	5	17	13	11	
2	**P. contortus** (Linne)	C	23	+	24	75	116	57	
2	**Segmentina complanata** (Linne)	C	19	+	0	0	0	0	
3	**Acroloxus lacustris** (Linne)	0	0	0	19	48	20	20	E.Y.
4	**Ancylus fluviatilis** (Müller)	0	0	0	45	220	83	82	E.Y.
OM	**Succinea pfeifferi** (Rossmassler)	0	0	0	0	1	0	0	E.Y.
MW	**Lauria anglica** (Wood)	0	0	0	0	0	0	1	
OD	**Vallonia excentrica** (Sterki)	0	0	0	0	1	0	0	E.Y.
W	**Clausilia bidentata** (Strom)	0	0	0	1	0	0	1	
-	**Cepaea nemoralis** (Linne)	0	0	0	0	2	1	4	
OD	**Helicella itala** (Linne)	0	0	0	0	0	2	0	E.Y.
W	**Discus rotundatus** (Müller)	0	0	0	1	0	0	1	
-	**Arion sp.**	0	0	0	3	5	2	1	E.Y.
M	**Retinella radiatula** (Alder)	0	0	0	0	0	0	1	
W	**R. pura** (Alder)	0	0	0	0	0	0	1	
M	**Zonitoides nitidus** (Müller)	0	0	0	0	0	1	0	
W	**Limax sp.**	0	0	0	0	4	0	0	
4	**?Anodonta cygnaea** (Linne)	2	0	0	0	0	0	0	
2	**Sphaerium corneum** (Linne)	C	0	+	0	0	0	0	
4	**Pisidium amnicum** (Müller)	0	-	0	16	71	41	29	E.Y.
1	**P. casertanum** (Poli)	1	-	+	50	835	360	5	
1	**P. personatum** (Malm)	1	-	0	35	137	212	176	
2	**P. milium** (Held)	0	-	+	15	0	0	8	
2	**P. subtruncatum** (Held)	C	-	+	0	0	0	0	Skipsea; E.Y.
4	**P. henslowanum** (Sheppard)	0	-	+	0	0	0	0	Skipsea; E.Y.
2	**P. nitidum** (Jenyns)	C	-	+	0	0	0	0	
-	**Pisidium spp.**	-	42	-	-	-	-	-	

| | Total number of specimens in sample:- | Not known | 458 | Not known | 849 | 2477 | 1580 | 925 | |

E.Y. = East Yorkshire.   C = recorded as common, but no details available.
       + = recorded as present, but no details available.

LAND MOLLUSCA

M: Marsh and associated species
W: Woodland species
O: 'Open' species (i.e. unwooded conditions)
D: Dry ground species.

FRESHWATER MOLLUSCA

1: 'Slum' species (i.e. showing a preference for, or tolerance of, poor water conditions, such as small bodies of water subject to drying, stagnation or considerable temperature variation).
2: 'Catholic' species (i.e. tolerant of a wide range of habitats, other than the worst slums).
3: Ditch species (such as are found in ditches with clean, slowly-moving water and abundant aquatic plants).
4: Moving water species (such as are more commonly found in slightly larger bodies of water, for example moving streams and ponds, where the water is moved by currents and the wind).

Table 2.5. HOLOCENE MOLLUSCAN FAUNAS FROM SKIPSEA WITHOW MERE AND BARMSTON DESCRIBED BY BOYLAN (1966): FOR MODERN NOMENCLATURE SEE WALDEN (1976) AND KERNEY (1976).

Theodoxus fluviatilis, Cepea nemoralis - which are also absent from the Skipsea Withow silts. The shell bed at Barmston was later to be associated with the Flandrian by Varley (1968) in his description of the Barmston 'crannogs'.

The weaknesses in the argument are now clear. The association of the Skipsea Withow lake silts and the harpoons and vertebrate remains with each other and the early-mid-Flandrian certainly does not automatically follow from the molluscan faunas reported, as the first line quoted from Boylan (1966) (Table 6.5 here) indicates. The Skipsea Withow silts are completely lacking diagnostic obligate thermophiles or specific indicators of temperate woodland. The understanding of molluscan biostratigraphy at this time was relatively limited. The impact of the seminal papers of Kerney and Evans (Kerney 1963, Kerney, Brown and Chandler 1964, Evans 1966, 1967, and see also Kerney 1977, Kerney, Preece and Turner 1981, Evans 1972) was only just starting to be felt. In any case, the published work largely concerned land faunas from the hillwashes on the Chalk of southern England.

The environmental significance of the molluscan fauna from the lake silts at Skipsea Withow mere was consequently much clearer. The freshwater faunas indicated the former presence of a large, open body of clear water. The absence of terrestrial taxa pointed to either a lack of streams or rivers nearby which might have introduced such shells, or a lack of trees and shrubs, or both features in combination.

A recent model of the stratigraphy of the former Withow mere at the Withow Gap

The stratigraphic conclusions derived from the early stages of the present research programme were published in Gilbertson (1983). The results are summarised in Figure 3.1. The lowest non-glacial units recognised were the lacustrine silts, sands and gravels of Units 2a and 2b of that figure. These were seen to be separated by an erosional episode from the base of lacustrine organic muds (Unit 3) radiocarbon dated to 9880+60 radiocarbon years b.p. (SRR 1944). The complexities of the Late Devensian sequence were not resolved. The Flandrian organic lake muds of Unit 3 gave way to wood-rich carr peats (Unit 4) and overlying detrital and in situ carr/marsh peats which were strongly laminated, and contained abundant evidence of minor episodes of erosion and re-working. These contained a re-worked carved stake of Alder (**Alnus**) radiocarbon dated to 4770+70 b.p. (HAR 3378). Peat formation was shown to end shortly after 4,500+50 years b.p. (SRR 1942) - this date being obtained from a 5cm thick slice of peat at the top of this deposit. The sandy silts burying this layer were regarded as colluvium resulting from soil erosion of the adjacent till ridges, rather than reflecting any possible later marine or freshwater influences (see Catt 1977).

The source of the confusion in this review of the literature concerning the Skipsea Withow site derives from the lack of reliable information on the stratigraphy, palaeoenvironments and development of the Withow mere and its neighbours in Holderness. The research programme described here was initially directed towards resolving these fundamental problems.

CHAPTER 3

THE LATE QUATERNARY SEQUENCE AT THE SKIPSEA WITHOW GAP

D.D.Gilbertson, D.J. Briggs, D.A.Harkness, C.O. Hunt, F.B.Pyatt,
V.R. Switsur, N.M. Thew and D. Woodall

The deposits noted at the Withow Gap between 1978 and 1984 are shown in Figures 3.1 to 3.4, 3.7 to 3.10, and are summarised below. The details of litho-biofacies variations, erosional events and post-depositional movements are set out in the later sections.

Unit No.	Maximum Thickness in m.	Description
11	0.15	Made ground - concrete, narrow gauge bullhead rail, hardcore, pill boxes, deposited 1939-45.
10	0.10	Clay silts; grey [2.5Y 7/4]; blocky/prismatic structure. Soil 'B' horizon, clay enriched (10b) beneath a thin, compacted turf line (10c). ?Colluvium: ploughwash? Unconformably resting on:-
9	0.20	Sandy silts; grey [2.5Y 5/2]; occasional peaty inclusions. Colluvium - hillwash? Unconformably resting on:-
8d	2.50	Detrital and in situ marsh and carr peats; moderately humified, includes sandy partings in strongly laminated, quasi-horizontally bedded layers. Cut-and-fill stratification present near stream. Dense packing of brushwood, with larger flat-laying trunks of **Alnus, Fraxinus, Quercus** and **Corylus**; abundant hazel nuts.
8e	0.10	Well-sorted sand lens, thins into lake deposit: ?beach sand derived by erosion and sorting of till or Unit 4.
8b	0.05	Silt, blue, pebbly in parts: ?reworked from Unit 3.
8a	0.05	Poorly sorted pebbles, silts: ?slump or inwash from Unit 4? Erosional surface below 8a with flint and chalk fragments; acorns and hazel nuts.

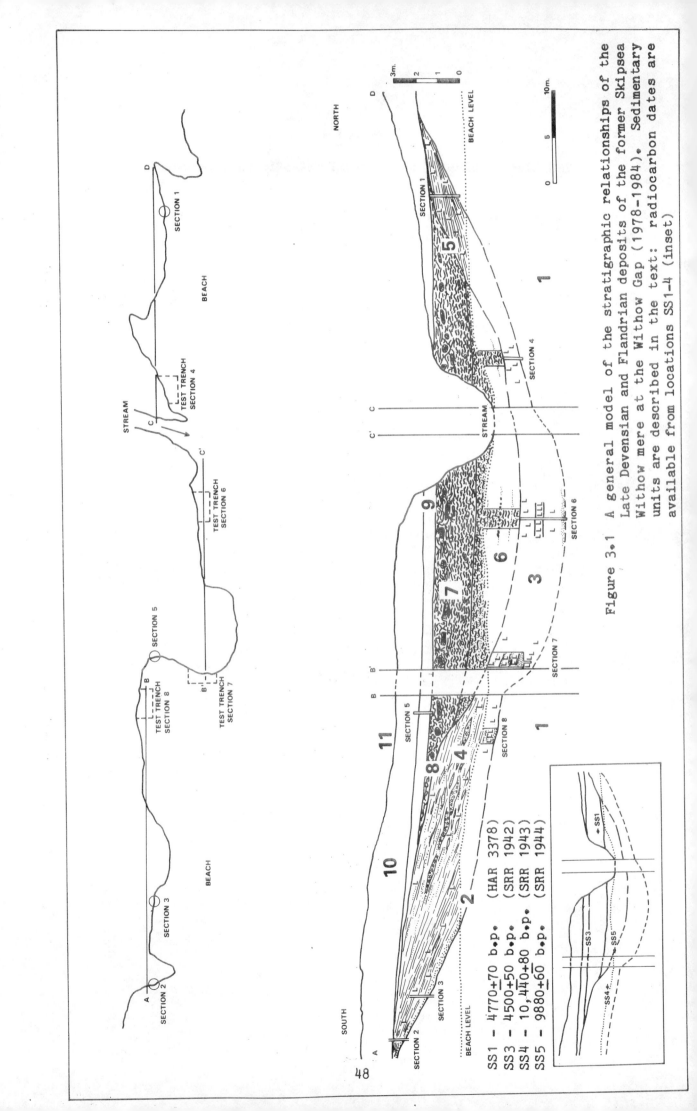

Figure 3.1 A general model of the stratigraphic relationships of the former Skipsea Late Devensian and Flandrian deposits of the Withow Gap (1978–1984). Sedimentary units are described in the text: radiocarbon dates are available from locations SS1–4 (inset)

SS1 – 4770+70 b.p.   (HAR 3378)
SS3 – 4500+50 b.p.   (SRR 1942)
SS4 – 10,440+80 b.p. (SRR 1943)
SS5 – 9880+60 b.p.   (SRR 1944)

48

The *in situ* and reworked Alder carr is also associated with early neolithic wooden rods and pegs (Plates 8.1-5). One carved wooden stake (Plate 8.1) at this level yielded a radiocarbon date of 4770+70 b.p. (HAR 3378 - sample SS1). The uppermost 0.05m of Unit 8 at section 4 yielded a radiocarbon date of 4500+50 years b.p. (SRR 1942 - sample SS3). This unit continues below without apparent break into:-

7	1.70	Silty peat; brown (black on exposure to the atmosphere), strongly laminated, with abundant flat-bedded brushwood and numerous substantial horizontal branches and tree trunks up to 0.3m diameter of **Quercus, Pinus, Alnus, ?Fraxinus** and **?Corylus.** Lacustrine shallow water deposits. Apparently conformable transition below to:-
6	1.25	Silty peat; dark brown (black on exposure to the atmosphere); occasionally horizontally bedded trunks and branches up to 0.2m diameter of **Alnus** and **Betula.** The basal 0.05m of this deposit at section 7 yielded a radiocarbon date of 9880+60 years b.p. (SRR 1944 - sample SS5).
6b	0.05	Occasionally separated from the deposits below by a 'lag' deposit of angular to rounded flints. Unit 6 rests unconformably upon:-
5a (north exposure)	0.10	Sandy silt, often strongly weathered, orange-brown;
5b (south exposure)	0.16	As 5a - [5Y 5/3 at top, changing to 2.5Y 4/2 at base],thinly downslope bedded; moderately sorted,occasional small rounded pebbles <0.015m diameter; apparently cross-laminated, but may be infill of root holes. At 5b (Figure 3.5) in the central exposure, the layer is distorted by slumps, minor folds and erosional hiatuses, predating the peats of Unit 6.
4vii	0.02	Reworked detrital peat pellets on clear erosional surface developed upon Unit 4vi. It is uncertain whether this surface extends above or below Unit 5b.
4vi	0.15	Sandy gravel; poorly sorted, often structureless; ?slump or reworked gravel? Underlain by

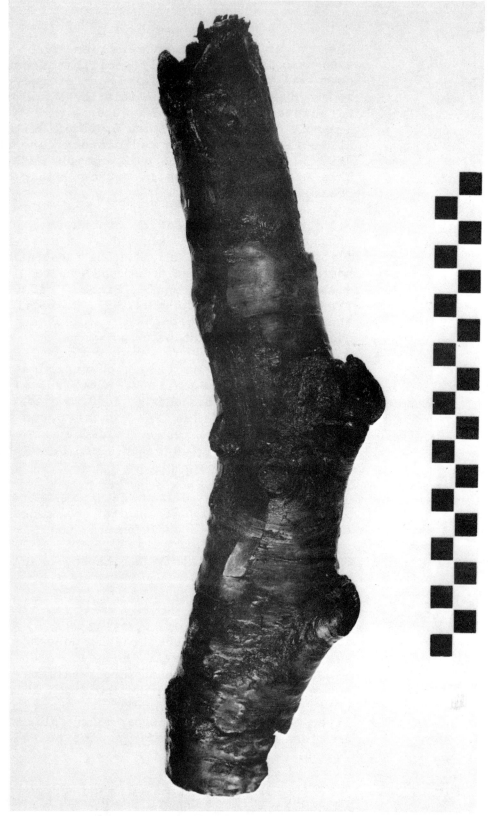

Plate 3.1 A branch of a tree birch (**Betula** sp.) incorporated into
Unit 4ii, section 5 (Figure 3.5). The wood was identified
as tree birch by Dr. Allan Hall: the scale is in
millimetres. The branch gave a radiocarbon date of
10,440±80 yrs b.p. [SRR-1943 - (Skipsea code SS4 - inset
Fig. 3.1)].

4v		Erosional surface, developed across Unit 4d; it is uncertain whether this surface extends above or below Unit 5b.
4d	1.4	Coarse gravels and pebbles; poorly sorted; in layers 0.05m to 0.2m thick; gravel comprises rounded to angular pebbles up to 0.03m diameter. Interfingers with alternating layers (0.2m to 0.02m thick) of silts/clays, often pebbly and dipping north east: frequent graded bedding fining upwards in and between layers. Unit coarsens to the southwest and former lake margin where clasts 0.05 to 0.15m occur. Lobes due to slumping bring both deposits and macrofossils into this layer. Sample SS4 may have been incorporated in such a lobe. Colour of gravels and matrix variable – brown/grey/orange [2.5Y 5/6 to 2.5Y 4/2]: ?slump reworked in lake at lake margin? Apparently conformable relationships below with:-
4iii	0.15	Sandy silt; poorly sorted; occasional small rounded gravel; twigs of **Betula** at base; thickens to the east to form a depression 0.30m thick – possibly a slump into a slump scour hollow. Colour variable [5Y 4/3 top to 5Y 5/4 base]. The layer rests unconformably upon:-
4ii	0.06	Detrital **Carex** peaty silt with plant and molluscan remains; occasionally disturbed by folds/slumps; yielded a tree birch log (Plate 3.1; Figure 3.7) which yielded a radiocarbon date of 10,440±80 years b.p. (SRR 1943 – sample SS4). Downward penetrating lobes of sediment caused by slumping and load casting, bring both superjacent deposits and macrofossils down into this layer. The tree birch sample SS4 may have been introduced in this manner. Colour 5Y 3/1 to 5Y 2.5/1. In situ and reworked marsh/lake margin soil/ sediment surface. This layer rests unconformably upon an erosional surface truncating:-
4c	0.45	Coarse gravel, poorly sorted, in layers 0.05m to 0.16m thick downslope bedded, [5Y 4/2] alternating with, and fining upwards into, intrusive layers of laminated dark blue/grey silts of Unit 3; often weathered – colours blue to orange/brown [2.5Y 3/0 to 5Y 4/2].

4b	0.5	Gravels and pebbles as 4c; with clasts up to 0.08m diameter. This layer is divided from 4c by the plane of a major lateral slide (4Fi) which appears to have an eastward component of 1-2m lateral displacement.

4a   1.6

Gravels and pebbles: poorly sorted, alternating layers, 0.4m to 0.1m thick, forming four couplets, with clasts up to 0.08m in diameter; thins rapidly to the east/north east. Colour grey/brown/orange [often 2.5Y 4/2 to 2.5Y 4/4]: lateral transition to sorted sand 0.22m thick at P83.

Throughout sections 7 and 8, the deposits of Unit 4 are affected by slumps and a complex sequence of faults (4F$_2$ - 4F$_3$) etc., which are often further displaced by a later lateral slide 4Fi, and

3   2m+
[B/C/D]

Silts and clays; thinly laminated; occasional discontinuous, thin 1mm detrital peat/(soil?) layers (Unit 3:- section 2; Figure 3.7) and pebble bands, both at former lake margin: plastic-sticky-texture; colour grey/blue [2.5Y 4/1]; occasional blue crystals of vivianite: the unit interdigitates with the gravels of Unit 4.

Fragmented plant debris and molluscan remains common in some locations, especially the decomposing/rotten shells of large freshwater bivalves ?**Anodonta** sp. A compressed log of tree birch in 'blue' clay stratigraphically equivalent to or slightly below the gravels of Unit 4, was found in situ exposed on the beach 100m south east of the Withow gap. This log yielded a radiocarbon date of 10,710+70 years b.p. (Q 3035). It is uncertain whether or not the blue clays of Units 3 B/C/D are separated by an erosional surface from the underlying clays/silts of:-

3A   1m+

Pale grey/white/brown clays and silts. Lowest 0.4m contains textural varves at northern exposure [Units 3(1/1) to 3(1/4) - Figure 3.3]. These are overlain by 0.4m of silts with thin layers of white precipitated carbonates in layers 2-3mm diameter, alternating with grey silts [Units 3(1/6) to 3(1/7) - Section 1 - Figure 3.3]. Mottles and brown discolouration suggest minor episodes of weathering and the former development of 'gley' soils. Occasional very thin, discontinuous, 1-2mm thick layers of compacted in situ and detrital peats.

Flint blade (Figure 8.1) found in Unit 3, section 2 (Figure 3.2) associated with a thin detritus, silty peat. Sporadic fragmented plant macrofossils; rich in molluscan remains, especially **Valvata piscinalis.**

In the northern and central exposures -sections 1, 7 and 8, these (Unit 3) deposits are affected by a complex sequence of normal faults and a lateral slide (4Fi).

2b	0.1+	Sands, well sorted: downslope bedded; occasional rounded or angular pebbles - apparently barren - ?lag deposit?
2a	0.2+	Sandy clay; poorly sorted; quasi-bedded downslope, elsewhere showing slump structures, folds. Includes striated clasts of cobbles from tills below. Weathered on upper surface - brown/orange/grey mottles - [5Y 4/1 to 4/2 to 3/2]. Mudflow, slumps and downslope hillwash weathered and ?affected by later development of gley soils?
1	>1.5m	Till. The Skipsea Till [5Y 4/1 - 3/2]. Surface is weathered, often sandy with brown sandy weathered zone around 0.2m deep, 0.002m wide fissures - ?tension cracks?

THE LATE-DEVENSIAN LACUSTRINE SEQUENCE AT THE WITHOW GAP

Lithofacies variation

The details of the evolution of the Late Devensian lacustrine deposits may be examined by describing three sequences (Figure 3.1): those from the southern exposures (section 3); the northern exposures (section 7) and the very complex central exposures (sections 5, 7, 8).

THE SOUTHERN MARGINS OF THE LATE DEVENSIAN LAKE
(sections 2 and 3, Figures 3.1 and 3.2)

Slumps or mudflows

The earliest lacustrine deposits in this area are the diamicton of Unit 2a. This has not previously been recognised in the sequence. Its properties of downslope, quasi-stratification, poor sorting, and the downslope orientation of its contained clasts all suggest that it formed as a slump or mudflow from the subjacent till from which it is derived. In contrast to the Till it lacks a blocky or prismatic structure. The upper levels of the unit are slightly redder/browner and sandier, suggesting both slight weathering and subsequent elutriation of the fine fraction.

Figure 3.2 The sequence at the southern exposure of the deposits of
            Skipsea Withow mere (Figure 3.2, sections 2 and 3).
            20cm dia tape is scale; Units are described in text;

            + is find spot of Mesolithic blade; see Figs. 5.11, 8.1
            and Table 6.14.

Lag deposits

The upper surface (Unit 2b) is notably richer in rounded pebbles and coarse sands. This appears to be a lag deposit in which lake waves or currents have removed the fine fraction and concentrated coarser materials. No fossils or dateable material has been recovered from this layer.

The lacustrine silts

These pale grey silts are often strongly laminated or varved and dip steeply downslope, parallel to the lake bottom topography. They are largely free of coarser sand or gravel components for a thickness of 1.1m. Their very fine grade and laminations suggest very quiet water deposition, possibly under ice for a significant part of the year. The occasional interbedded, thin (0.5cm) band of detrital plant debris reflects the development of organic detritus/soils from lake margin vegetation. The worked flint blade (Figure 8.1) was found 5cm above one such band. The silts are overlain conformably by 5 to 10cm layers of well sorted sands and gravels (Unit 4) and colluvium/plough soils. The pollen, molluscs and archaeological evidence from this face are discussed later.

Conclusions

The import of the sequence lies in the presence of evidence of mass movement, re-working and very quiet water-deposition (possibly in a seasonally frozen lake) (?shortly?) after deglaciation, during a period of human activity at the lake, prior to the period represented by the major influxes of gravels into the lake.

THE NORTHERN MARGINS OF THE LATE DEVENSIAN LAKE

with D. Woodall

Full details of the sequence are given below (Plates 3.2 and Figures 3.3 and 3.4): pollen and molluscan studies are given in Chapters 5 and 6.

Stratigraphy

Section 1. (Figures 3.1 and 3.3/3.4, Plate 3.2)

Unit	Thickness	Sample	Stratum
6	5cms	47	Detritus peat (10YR 3/2) overlain by carr peat of Unit 6. Rests unconformably on:
5a	6cms	46	Brown/orange/grey (2.5Y 4/2) sandy silt; laminated with thin layers of $CaCO_3$ precipitate: an ?in situ or reworked weathering product.

Figure 3.3 Stratigraphy at the northern exposures of the deposits of
the former Skipsea Withow mere at section 1: Figure 3.1.

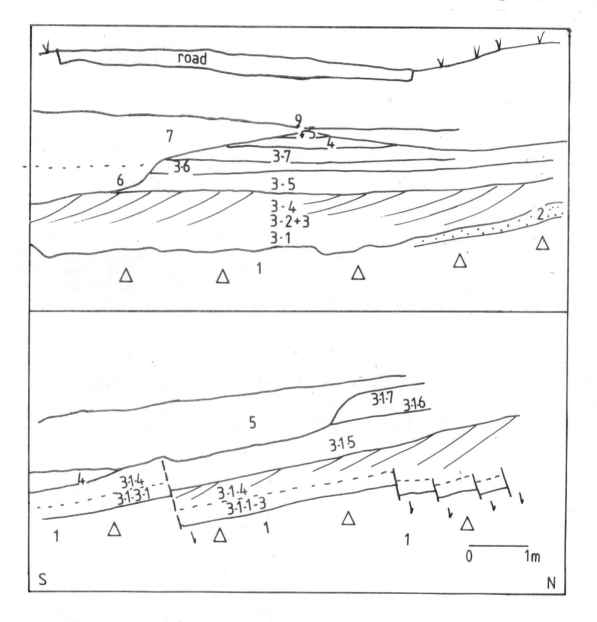

Figure 3.4 Faulting of Late Devensian deposits at the northern margin
of the deposits of the former Skipsea Withow mere.

Plate 3.2 The exposure of the deposits of the former Skipsea Withow mere at the northern margins of the late-section 1: Figure 3.1 and Figure 3.3. Peats rest on an erosional surface and cliff, presumably by lakewater, although faulting is undoubtedly also responsible for the small scarp (left, above trowel). The upper peats rest upon a brown, sandy silt - possibly that noted by Godwin and Godwin (1933) which then yielded Mesolithic implements. The present brown, sandy silt is a weathering deposit developed upon silts with many thin laminae of carbonate precipitates - here attributed to pollen zone III. The point of the trowel rests upon an erosional surface developed upon texturally varved lake sediments. These are sterile in their lowest levels and attributed to pollen zone I. The original lake bed/till surface is denoted by the surface of the till - black line: bottom right. The till is readily distinguished by its colour, clast content and blocky structure.

3(1/7)	24cms	45	Clay, marl (2.5Y 7/2); strongly laminated with downslope-dipping, alternate layers of dark grey and white clays; layers 20-50mm thickness: overall a white colour. Noticeable sub-unit of dark brown loam, 5mm thick, 5cms from top of layer. Gastropods common, no bivalves noticed.
3(1/6)	23cms	43/42	Clay marl (5Y 4/2); strongly laminated with alternate layers of dark grey and white clays 20-50mm thick, however predominantly dark in colour. Many bivalves present.
3(1/5)	28cms	41/40	Clay, soft, 'sticky' (5Y 3/1): shelly. Gleyed in lower 10cms: poorly developed laminations; grey: faulted
			- MARKED NON-SEQUENCE-
3(1/4)	34cms	7/6	Clay: laminated downslope (5Y 3/1); occasional whiter laminae: brown; very shelly: faulted.
3(1/3)	4cms	4	Clay, laminated; shelly; brown (10YR 4/2); faulted.
3(1/2)	5cms	3	Clay (7.5YR 4/2 dark grey); strongly laminated with alternate layers represented by slight differences in grain size, not colour. Sandy at base, fines upward. Plant debris in upper part: faulted; occasional shells. Dark brown.
3(1/1)	35cms	5/2	Clay: strongly laminated with individual layers identified by differences in texture; occasional shells; dark grey (10YR 3/1); faulted. Sandy at base where it overlies Till unconformably.
1			Till

Sediments

The sedimentological properties of the sediments are shown in Figures 3.5 and 3.6. Several important trends are illustrated. Analytical methods are summarised in the Appendix.

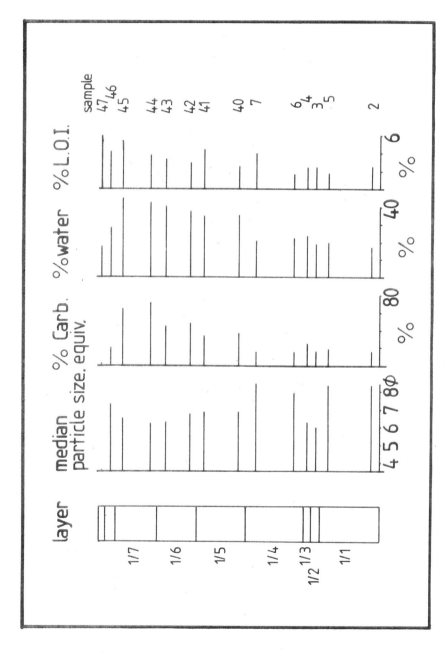

Figure 3.5 Sedimentary properties of the Late Devensian and Flandrian deposits at the northern margin of the former Skipsea Withow mere – section 1: Figure 3.1; for description of site see text.

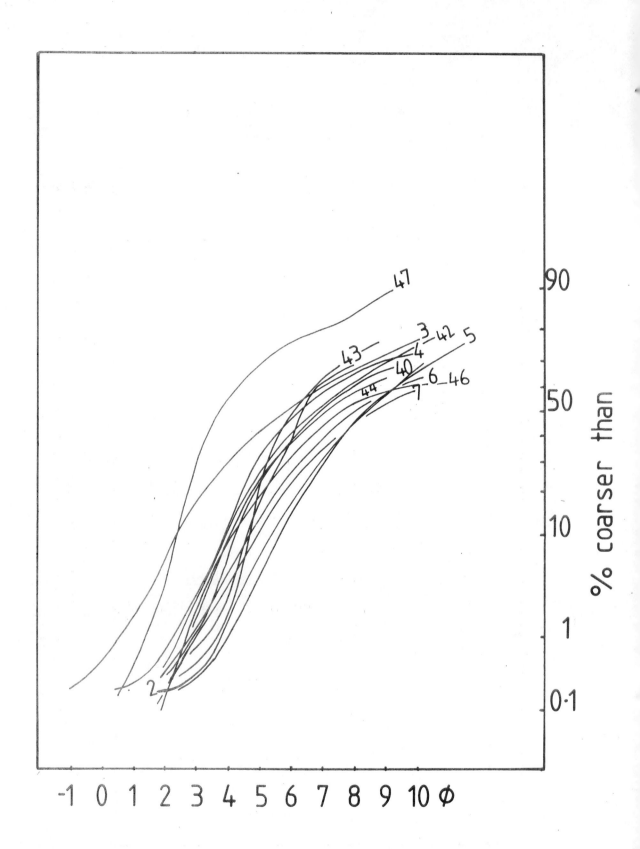

Figure 3.6   Textural properties of the Late Devensian and Flandrian
deposits at the northern margin of the former Skipsea
Withow mere - Section 1; Figure 3.1.

The data given on the median grain size indicates the predominantly very fine-grade characteristics of the silt and clay sediments collecting in the lake: quiet water conditions are indicated. There was a brief influx of coarser sands in Units 3/1/2 - 3/1/3 when slightly more energetic conditions prevailed. A slight change in depositional conditions are indicated at the junction between Units 3/1/4 and 3/1/5: more energetic conditions prevailing, until the weathering episode and erosional hiatus between 3/1/7 and Unit 5a. Not surprisingly, water content reflects the available pore space suggested by the median particle size curve. The carbonate equivalent data indicate that the lower sediments of Units 3/1/1 to 3/1/4 are essentially similar with notable levels of carbonates. This is also true for the loss-on-ignition data. The overlying sediments of Units 3/1/5 to 3/1/7 all display sympathetic trends in median particle size, carbonate equivalent and loss-on-ignition. Grain size decreases slowly, whereas carbonate equivalent and loss-on-ignition show gradual increases.

Episodes of freezing and non-freezing of the lake surface

A possible interpretation of these sequences is as follows and incorporates the field observation of textural varves frequently occurring in Units 3/1/1 to 3/1/4, and layers of precipitated carbonate occurring above these levels. All these phenomena would be obtained if the deposits of Units 3/1/1 to 3/1/4 were associated with frequent, probably seasonal, freezing of the lake. This would permit the deposition of the finest grade of deposits in winter and encourage the formation of varves.

The molluscan studies described in Chapter 6 indicate only limited biological activity within the lake and at the lake sediment surface at this time. The result was little disruption of sedimentary strutures by bioturbation.

In such a periodically frozen landscape, at the earliest time available for its colonisation, the rates of input of organic detritus and carbonates (in solution or as particulates) are likely to have been lower than at later stages when biological and fluvial processes would have been more active. The upper deposits are therefore seen as those of a more frost and ice-free landscape, with increasing biological activity, soil maturation, nutrient cycling, and disturbance of lake sediments by wind and waves throughout much greater parts of the year. It is impossible to identify the time gap represented by the junction between Units 3/1/4 and 3/1/5.

The properties of the sediments of Unit 5a suggest weathering, loss of carbonates, colour and pedogenic mottling developing upon lake sediments. These 'browner' sediments may be the equivalent of those identified in the earlier studies of Godwin and Godwin (1933) which were associated with Mesolithic implements.

Erosional episodes

The stratigraphic relationships of these deposits are shown in Figure 3.3 These data show the presence of a notable episode of erosion within the clay-silt sequence (between 3/1/4 and 3/1/5) and

61

that its upper limit is marked also by a notable unconformity (between Units 5 and 6). These erosional episodes might correspond to either increased storm activity generating erosive lake side waves, and/or falls in lake level exposing the uncohesive sediment surface to erosion by overland flow, rain splash, and wave action during the regression and transgression of the lake margin waves. The weathering associated with the upper unconformity (to yield Unit 5a) indicates at least proximity to the atmosphere if not actual exposure as a soil surface.

Faulting

Two episodes of normal faulting are detectable (Figure 3.4). One set of faults affecting Units 3/1/1 and 3/1/4 and the till are let down in an en echelon series of normal faults with throws of 5 to 18cms. These faults do not affect the unconformable boundary between Units 3/1/4 and 3/1/5. Consequently, they appear to be associated with the period of time thought to relate to frequent freezing of the lake.

However, both these layers are affected by a further set of normal faults (F_2) with a throw of between 30 - 60cms. The woody peat of Unit 6 is inflexed over a small, eroded scarp left by this second phase of faulting. The inherent erodibility of the lake deposits suggests this minute 'fault scarp' would not greatly pre-date the deposition of the peats of Unit 6; shown elsewhere to be Flandrian. The faulting episodes are therefore thought to be Late Devensian - (during the very early history of the lake) and pre-dating Unit 3/1/5 and much later in the Late Devensian, affecting Units 3/1/5 and 3/1/6. The mechanisms responsible for this faulting are unclear. Fluctuations in permafrost state might be associated with both the first and second phases; and additionally dewatering or compaction in the second. The limited spatial extent of these faults is indicated by their being detectable in the 1982 exposures, but not the 1981, 1983, 1984 exposures.

THE SOUTH WEST AND CENTRAL MARGINS OF THE LATE DEVENSIAN LAKE

with N. Thew and C.O. Hunt

Stratigraphy and Interpretation

The stratigraphic relationships of the Late Devensian deposits in the central areas of the exposure (sections 8, 5, 7: Figure 3.1) are shown in Figures 3.7, 3.8 and Plate 3.3. The locations and details of the sampling points for the pollen, molluscan and palaeomagnetic samples are shown in Figures 3.7 and Table 3.1.

(i)   Buried and foreshore exposures

The trial pit and coring study in the central area of the exposure indicated the presence of a shallow clay/silt filled trough beneath the beach linking the former Withow mere with the enclosed basin immediately inland of the exposures. No sand or gravel dominated lithofacies were identified in this region. Deposits similar to the blue/grey vivianite-rich silts in this area are exposed on the foreshore at very low tides after winter storms in the area 100 - 250m

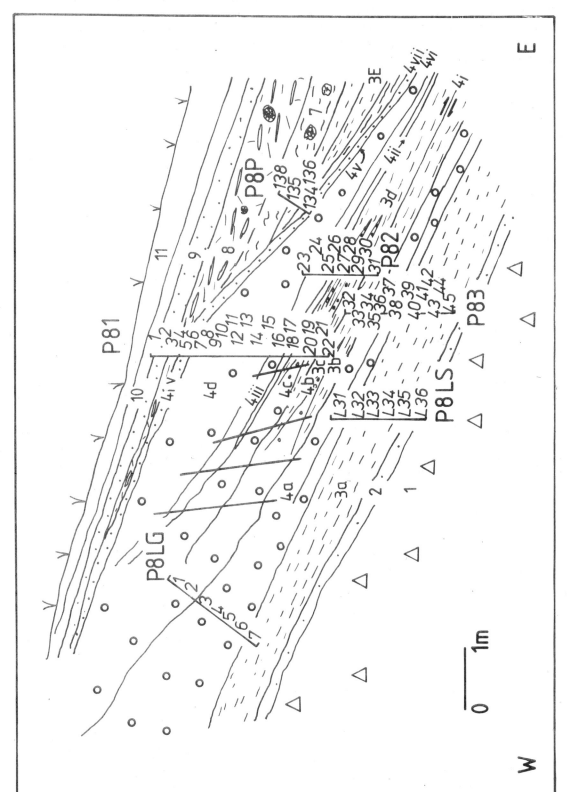

Figure 3.7 Stratigraphy, faulting and sample provenance in the central
exposures of the deposits of the former Skipsea Withow mere
– sections 8, 5 and 7: Figure 3.1.

S.E. of the stream exit. These rarely yield fossils, although one substantial piece of compacted tree birch branch was excavated and yielded a radiocarbon date of 10,710$\pm$70 years b.p. (Q-3035). Unfortunately, the continued re-discovery of even more complexities in the sequence makes it impossible to relate these foreshore and buried deposits reliably with each other, or Units in the main exposure of Sections 7, 5, 8 (Figure 3.1), even though they are similar lithologically.

(ii)   Cliff-exposures - sections 7, 5, 8: Figure 3.1

The details of this sequence are shown in Figures 3.7 and 3.8 and described previously.

Several important points emerge from these data. The blue-grey silts containing the flint blade exposed at section 3 pass under the gravel unit 4. The gravel (Unit 4) interdigitates with the fine grain lake silts of Unit 3B, C, D, for three reasons. In several cases the gravels and silts are genuinely interbedded, demonstrating synchroneity. In other cases the contact may be due to the presence of faults or a low angle slide (4Fi) with a lateral displacement of 1-2m. At other locations, the contacts indicate the presence of major unconformities (4vii), and in some cases a period of time sufficient for the development of a peaty lake margin soil or detrital sediment formed (4ii).

Throughout this period the gravel lithofacies north and west of section 6 obviously collected within the lake. This is indicated by the presence of prominent graded bedding and well sorted sediments. Further upslope south and west of section 6, stratification becomes less clear, there are no clear sorting or fabric in the gravel sequence. In this area, these gravel-rich sediments have the properties of those generated by slump, slide or other mass movements. The general interpretation of the sequence therefore consists of:

(a)   an open clear water lake;

(b)   localised instability of the adjacent hillslope leading to episodic mass-movement, slumping, mudflow, and slides into the lake which led to:

(c)   interbedding with fine grained sediments of the lake; graded bedding, sorting and re-working of the gravels occurring in water at the lake margin by wave action. This might relate to daily or seasonal fluctuations.

(d)   major slides, slumps, folds and normal faulting developed (Plate 3.3) at several times. At least three episodes of faulting are noted (Figure 3.8). Normal faults XX are disrupted by the lateral slide (YY), which appears to have occurred along a line of peaty detritus; finally YY is affected by a series of normal faults ZZ with very small downthrows. Since the XX and ZZ series die away in Gravel member 4d, they presumably date from this period, placing them relatively late in the Late-Devensian sequence.

64

Plate 3.3 Normal faults (throw **c.** 0.5m) which developed before the
final stages of the deposition of the gravel body (Unit 4):
section 5: Figure 3.1. Scale total length 50cms: see also
Figure 3.8; Oct. 1983.

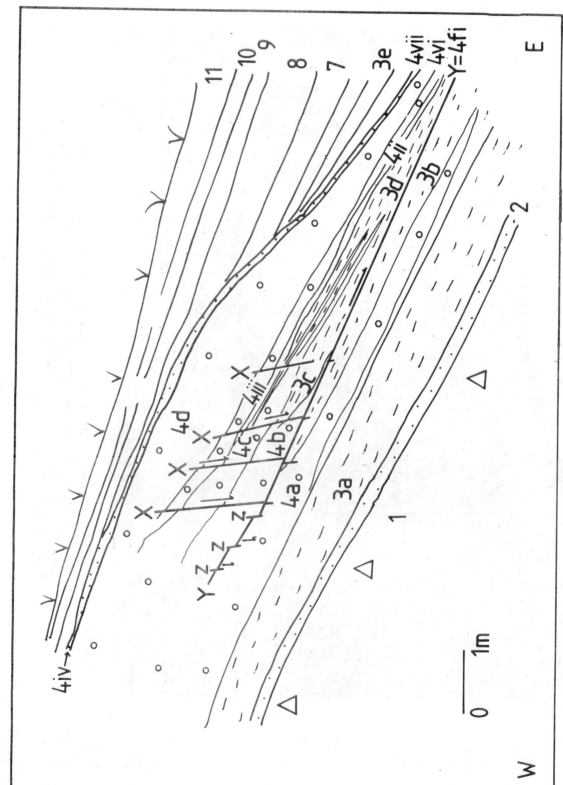

Figure 3.8 Faults and lateral slides in the central exposures of the deposits of the former Skipsea Withow mere – sections 8, 5, 7: Figure 3.1.

(e) on three occasions (4ii, 4v and 4vii) the lake margin sediments
     were eroded, either by increased wave action, and/or as a result
     of a lowering of lake level. The erosional surface 4ii is very
     clear. Each erosional episode was followed by the accumulation of
     peaty detrital sediments including the remains of tree and dwarf
     birch (Chapter 5). Branches of tree birch from 4ii yielded a
     radiocarbon date of 10,440+80 b.p. (SRR 1943). The stratigraphic
     evidence suggests that at least some of these macrofossils
     (including sample SRR 1943) have been incorporated into lower
     deposits by slumps or in load structures. These events must post
     date the formation of Unit 4, but the period of time involved is
     unknown.

(f) A cessation of slope instability followed the latter phase of
     erosion (4vii) with the return to the deposition of essentially
     sand and gravel free blue silts (Unit 3E). There is no evidence
     to indicate slumping and folding continued into this period.

(g) A final phase of erosion affecting all these deposits occurred to
     produce a low-angle unconformity between 3E and the Flandrian
     lacustrine peats of Unit 6. The base of these overlying deposits
     (Unit 7) yielded a radiocarbon date of 9880+60 b.p. (SRR 1944).
     Accelerated wave erosion and/or lake lowering are probably again
     responsible. A thin long deposit is also present at this
     stratigraphic level (Unit 5a).

(h) finally, weathered, brown water-washed lake silts (Unit 5) are
     also present at the top of the Devensian sequence. The layer is
     affected by small scale mass-movement. It is overlain by peats
     relatively late in the Flandrian peat sequence: it may be the
     brown sandy silt yielding Mesolithic remains noted by earlier
     workers (e.g. Godwin and Godwin 1933). The date of the weathering
     may range from final Late-Devensian to early-mid Flandrian.

        The actual cause(s) of the mass-movement are not fully clear.
Their fossil content (Chapters 5 and 6) indicate cool/cold climates
with tundra and milder oscillations. A likely cause is the localised,
repeated thawing of frozen ground on the local hillside, possibly
brought about by milder climatic fluctuations as well as the thermal,
mechanical, erosional effects of the lake itself. These agents would
also give rise to the recurrent faulting, sliding and slumping noted in
the section.

        Biostratigraphic evidence for the more precise correlation,
dating and interpretation of these deposits are presented in Chapters 5
and 6.

Textural properties

        Particle size distribution data for the samples located in
Figure 3.7 are given in Table 3.2. The analyses concentrated on the
coarse fraction. Simple inspection of the Table indicates clasts size
in the gravel member varies significantly, and sorting varies from poor
to very good; thus confirming field observations. Further detailed
numerical manipulations of these data await clearer understanding of
the mathematical methods, their appropriateness and objectives with
these categories of deposit.

Sample Number	Profile	Layer	Weight (wet-grammes)	Colour (Munsell)
1	P8 1	10	501.6	2.5Y 7/4
2	P8 1	9	425.0	2.5Y 5/2
138b	P8 P	3E	595.8	5Y 3/1
135	P8 P	3E	604.8	5Y 4/1
136	P8 P	3E	607.3	5Y 5/1
137	P8 P	4vii	564.9	5Y 25/1
5	P8 1	4iv	966.0	5Y 5/3
6	P8 1	4iv	473.9	2.5Y 4/2
7	P8 1	4d	326.9	2.5Y 5/4
8	P8 1	4d	828.7	2.5Y 5/6
9	P8 1	4d	336.9	5Y 5/4
10	P8 1	4d	692.3	2.5Y 4/4
11	P8 1	4d	333.6	2.5Y 4/4
12	P8 1	4d	741.9	2.5Y 5/6
13	P8 1	4d	540.1	5Y 4/3
14	P8 1	4d	538.9	2.5Y 4/4
15	P8 1	4d	499.4	5Y 4/2
16	P8 1	4iii	878.5	5Y 4/3
23	P8 2	4iii	774.0	2.5Y 4/2
17	P8 1	4iii	978.9	5Y 5/4
24	P8 2	4iii	909.3	5Y 4/2
25	P8 2	4iii	611.2	5Y 3/1
18	P8 1	4ii	523.2	5Y 3/1
19	P8 1	4c	674.6	5Y 4/2
20	P8 1	4c	855.9	5Y 4/3
21	P8 1	4c	567.7	2.5Y 4/0
30	P8 2	4c	584.3	2.5Y 3/0
22	P8 1	4c	500.0	5Y 4/2
32	P8 3	4b	586.5	2.5Y 3/0
33	P8 3	3b	577.6	2.5Y 3/0
34	P8 3	3b	593.8	2.5Y 3/0
35	P8 3	4a	579.4	5Y 4/1
LS7	P8 LS	4a	508.9	2.5Y 4/4
36	P8 3	4a	753.8	2.5Y 3/0
37	P8 3	4a	602.6	2.5Y 3.5/0
38	P9 3	$3a_3$	595.6	2.5Y 3/0
39	P8 3	$3a_3$	606.5	2.5Y 3/0
40	P8 3	$3a_3$	481.7	2.5Y 3/0
41	P8 3	$3a_2$	581.5	2.5Y 3/0
42	P8 3	$3a_2$	346.4	2.5Y 3/0
43	P8 3	$3a_1$	582.9	2.5Y 3/0
44	P8 3	$3a_1$	599.9	5Y 4/1
45	P8 3	$3a_1$	597.4	5Y 4/1
LS4	P8 LS	$3a_1$	582.1	2.5Y 4/0
LS5	P8 LS	$3a_1$	582.2	2.5Y 3/0

TOTAL 27,194.3; Average 604.3

Table 3.1: SAMPLE PROVENANCE, WEIGHTS AND MUNSELL COLOURS FOR THE CENTRAL EXPOSURES AT SKIPSEA WITHOW (Section 8: Figure 3.7, see also Figure 3.1)

TABLE 3.2 — Block 1

Layer	10	9	3e	3e	3e	4vii	4iv	4iv	4d	4d	4d	4d	4d	4d	4d	4d	4d	4ii	4ii	4ii	4ii	4ii	4ii
Sample	1	2	138b	135	136	137	5	6	7	8	9	10	11	12	13	14	15	16	17	23	24	25	18
* Gravel 2mm	3.8	0	1.5	3.8	4.8	9.6	18.8	55.9	69.8	172.7	88.2	261.0	151.1	157.4	94.4	320.5	38.2	28.1	8.8	4.9	23	1.5	41.3
Sand 1.4mm	1.2	0.7	0.2	0.5	1.5	1.9	2.5	12.7	9.2	23.7	20.5	19.6	21.3	25.1	17.0	31.2	5.2	4.4	0.9	1.2	12	1.0	7.1
Sand 1.0mm	1.8	1.2	0.3	0.7	2.1	2.5	2.9	14.1	11.3	17.6	18.4	16.0	18.9	20.2	18.5	34.1	5.0	5.9	2.9	2.2	18	1.5	7.3
Sand 0.71mm	2.6	3.5	0.3	1.0	2.6	3.2	4.1	14.3	12.5	11.1	12.8	11.7	14.1	15.8	15.9	27.6	5.2	6.9	4.1	3.0	30	1.8	6.9
Sand 0.5mm	6.2	9.9	0.7	1.7	5.4	6.5	11.0	22.2	18.4	13.0	15.7	15.4	18.0	19.0	20.4	37.1	9.4	15.0	9.9	6.3	60	4.1	10.9
Sand 0.355mm	11.0	20.9	1.3	3.0	11.9	9.7	27.9	24.5	21.1	15.7	21.7	15.9	19.5	19.5	20.7	33.6	15.0	23.2	20.4	11.2	110	8.7	11.3
Sand 0.25mm	21.7	63.8	4.0	10.4	52.5	26.2	83.5	42.8	43.5	29.0	42.4	26.6	37.8	36.8	32.2	40.5	40.2	51.2	54.2	27.5	320	35.5	15.1
Total Sand	54.5	100.0	6.8	17.3	76.0	50.0	131.9	130.6	116.0	110.0	131.5	105.2	129.6	136.4	124.7	204.1	80.0	106.6	92.4	51.4	550	52.6	58.6
* Sand 0.355mm	22.8	36.2	2.8	6.9	23.5	23.8	48.4	87.8	72.5	81.0	89.1	78.6	90.8	99.6	92.5	163.6	39.8	55.4	38.2	23.9	230	17.1	43.5

TABLE 3.2 — Block 2

Layer	4c	4c	4c	4c	4c	4b	3b	3b	4a	4a	4a	4a	3a3	3a3	3a3	3a2	3a2	3a1	3a1	3a1	3a1	3a1
Sample	19	20	21	30	22	32	33	34	35	LS7	36	37	38	39	40	41	42	43	44	45	LS4	LS5
* Gravel 2mm	173.3	73.1	35.1	33.0	199.2	65.6	0.5	0.3	17.6	389.7	34.1	88.6	3.4	2.3	2.1	15.8	25.7	1.4	0.2	0.3	0.7	1.2
Sand 1.4mm	29.2	13.3	10.2	8.7	34.6	10.4	0.3	0.2	9.1	56.4	8.8	11.6	1.0	0.7	0.4	3.6	5.8	0.5	0.2	0.2	0.2	0.2
Sand 1.0mm	24.3	14.4	12.0	8.4	26.8	9.4	0.5	0.7	13.3	57.2	9.2	10.1	1.3	1.2	0.6	3.1	5.2	0.5	0.2	0.3	0.3	0.5
Sand 0.71mm	20.8	13.9	12.3	8.0	17.2	7.5	0.7	1.5	12.8	49.9	8.9	9.0	2.0	1.3	1.5	2.6	4.3	0.7	0.2	0.5	0.3	0.5
Sand 0.5mm	25.5	20.4	19.4	13.3	18.8	11.6	1.9	3.2	15.4	66.6	16.1	13.6	4.5	2.6	2.5	3.1	4.9	1.0	0.7	1.5	0.7	0.7
Sand 0.355mm	24.2	21.1	21.1	11.5	13.8	10.1	2.6	4.0	15.4	71.3	24.9	17.1	6.4	3.1	3.7	2.9	4.3	1.4	1.0	2.7	1.2	0.9
Sand 0.25mm	28.8	35.9	34.3	15.9	18.4	23.2	14.4	12.8	35.0	83.9	57.2	39.7	15.4	7.3	7.5	4.6	6.1	3.1	4.0	7.5	3.3	1.5
Total Sand	152.8	119.0	109.3	65.8	129.6	72.2	20.4	22.4	100.6	385.3	125.1	101.1	30.6	16.2	16.3	19.9	30.6	7.2	6.3	12.7	6.0	4.3
* Sand 0.355mm	124.0	83.1	75.0	49.9	111.2	49.0	6.0	9.6	65.6	301.4	67.9	61.4	15.2	8.9	8.7	15.3	24.5	4.1	2.3	5.2	2.7	2.8

TABLE 3.2: PARTICLE DISTRIBUTION SIZE DATA (PER 1000g) OF SEDIMENTS FROM SECTION 8, SKIPSEA WITHOW MERE. SAMPLE PROVENANCE IS GIVEN IN FIGURE 3.7.

THE FLANDRIAN SEQUENCE

Examination of the stratigraphic record at the start of this chapter and detailed stratigraphic sections indicates that the Flandrian peats overlie the Late Devensian silts and gravels with a marked angular unconformity (Figures 3.1-3.4, 3.7) which is also evident in the sedimentological and palaeontological properties of the deposits.

The sedimentological characteristics of the peat indicates that at about 9880+60 b.p., the Skipsea Withow mere continued to be a largely open-water lake, but was now characterised by the deposition of organic, nekron muds (Unit 6) reflecting the natural mineral enrichment and associated aquatic algal growth in the lake. Initially, few woody remains were incorporated into the accumulating organic muds; however after c. 1m of such deposits had accumulated, isolated branches and trunks were deposited. Presumably these fell into the lake with bank collapse and eventually sank. There are occasional thin (1cm) thick layers of reworked brushwood, suggesting a brief phase of lake lowering and reworking by overland flow or lake margin waves.

At approximately 7000 b.p. (Chapter 7) there is a transition (Unit 7) to _in situ_ and reworked carr peats. There is abundant flat-bedded, reworked brushwood, with many sandy partings (Unit 8) and cut-and-fill stratification. Widespread reworking and erosion of hillside soils by overland flow is indicated. The extent of humification varies suggesting a series of brief and longer exposure times to the atmosphere.

This sequence demonstrates the spread of Alder dominated carr woodland by successional processes into the lake. Plant macrofossils indicate the abundance of Alder, Ash, Oak and Hazel. However the presence of early neolithic carved stakes, coppiced timber and wooden pegs and 'fixings' (Plates 8.1-8.5, Chapter 8) indicates both use and management of the local woodland. In this context, the presence of sandy lens and partings might suggest soil erosion caused by forest clearance. There is no evidence to suggest fluvial or lacustrine erosive agents were responsible for the initial erosion, although the latter no doubt reworked sediment inputs in the lake beach zone.

The formation of carr peats at the site terminated at about 4500+50 b.p. (SRR 1942) when the entire sequence became buried in a clay-silt-gravel lithofacies (Units 9 and 10), whose field relationships indicate it is largely a slope wash deposit. Field examination indicates this is a complex deposit, affected by subsequent pedogenic processes. It has not been examined in any detail. The available field evidence suggests it may also have formed as a result of accelerated soil erosion consequent upon forest clearance and early farming.

CORRELATIONS WITH PREVIOUS STUDIES

Establishing the nature of the lithostratigraphic and biostratigraphic correlation between the previous studies of the exposures at the Withow Gap by Phillips (1826), Armstrong (1923) and

SOUTH SIDE		NORTH SIDE	
Phillips logged 1826* published 1829	Sheppard T., logged 1894*	Armstrong logged 1922* published 1923	Godwin and Godwin logged 1932* published 1933
Section ¼ mile long, 3.6m OD S. end 1.2 - 1.5m OD in middle, 235.5m from 1983 exposure	Peat 2.1m at thickest point 133.5m from 1983 exposure	Peat over 1.85m thick in centre, 91.5m from 1983 exposure	Peat c. 90m long, 2.7m thick in centre, 76.5m from 1983 exposure
NO DATA	c. 0.1m surface earth	0.31 humus 0.61m clay	0.76m fine brown clay, columnar cracking
"PEATS" 0.75m fibrous	0.96m trees, branches, etc.		0.6m fibrous, solid peat with branches etc.
2.1m peat with roots, branches and hazelnuts.	2.1m peat	1.75m peat with large trees, branches, etc. plus elk and auroch bones.	2.13m peat with horizontal branches, trunks, etc. especially oak (Quercus). Hazelnuts at 1.25m, 1.70m, 1.92m and base
1.35m solid peat; breaks like clay	1.20m black peaty clay		1.53m solid, black or brown, amorphous.
"CLAYS" 0.30m yellowish clay = nekron mud		Silt with Ancylus, interpreted here as Acroloxus lacustris, red deer, reindeer, pike and flint artifacts.	0.15m brown sandy silt with fragments of pine bark, pike, Ancylus, interpreted here as Acroloxus lacustris, cherry(?) stones, and flint artifacts.
NOT PRESENT		0.23m blue silt with freshwater shells, and plant remains	buttery blue clay
0.90m blue clay	0.60m marl		
0.30m gravel	0.90m gravel	NOT PRESENT	NOT PRESENT
		BOULDER CLAY	

* assuming 1.5m cliff retreat per annum

Table 3.3: SUMMARY OF PREVIOUS STRATIGRAPHIC RECORDS OF THE DEPOSITS OF SKIPSEA WITHOW MERE (after Thew 1983)

Godwin and Godwin (1933) is very difficult. It is salutory to note that the exposure seen by Professor and Lady Godwin would have been at least c. 50m seaward of the line of collapsed pillboxes now found on the beach and shown in Plate 2. The present study of lithofacies variation only serves to emphasise the extent to which such variation also occurred in the seaward direction from the present exposure.

The sequences are summarised in Table 3.3. There is a clear parallelism in the basic sequence of:-

YOUNGEST

colluvium

'woody'

peat

'muddy'

brown

silts/clays

blue 'buttery'

gravel   -

boulder clay

OLDEST

The lithostratigraphic parallels suggest it is probably broadly correct to provisionally correlate these units as shown in Table 3.3, and make the obvious correlates with Figure 3.1.

Five further points merit stating. First, as today, the gravel member (Unit 4) was restricted in 1826 to southern exposures at the Withow Gap. Second, the present studies have located fossiliferous clay/silt members (Unit 3a) occurring beneath the gravels of Unit 4. It is not clear whether Phillips and Sheppard were in error, or whether the gravels of Unit 4 completely cut out the underlying fossiliferous silts except at the **very** margins of the former lake, as represented today. Third, the present study has detected notable unconformities/ erosional episodes within the clays/silts of Unit 3 and the gravels of Unit 4. Textural and palaeontological studies (Chapters 5 and 6) emphasise the regional climatic, biogeographic and local significance of these erosional episodes. Fourth, weathering and slumping episodes are noted, pre-dating the earliest lake deposits, and affecting the Till surface. Finally, although it cannot in any sense be demonstrated the brown sandy silts with Mesolithic artefacts which interested Armstrong (1923a,b) have the general textural, palaeontological (Chapters 5 and 6) and field relationships of Unit 5 in the present study. This is interpreted as a (very late) Late Devensian - early Flandrian reworked weathering product developed upon an exposed surface of Late Devensian lake deposits. It would therefore suggest one episode of lower lake levels during a period of mesolithic occupation. It follows from this interpretation that the artifacts, floral and faunal remains noted in earlier studies in association with this stratum, are likely to represent an assemblage deriving from a number of periods of the Late-Devensian, and possibly very early Flandrian.

CHAPTER 4

PALAEOMAGNETIC STUDIES OF LATE-DEVENSIAN LAKE DEPOSITS AT SKIPSEA WITHOW MERE

by S.J. Gale

INTRODUCTION

Symbols

D	Declination
I	Inclination
J	Intensity of magnetisation
J_0	Intensity of natural remanent magnetisation
0_{95}	A circle, centred on the mean, enclosing 95% of any Fisherian group of points on a sphere

If a detrital sediment contains magnetic particles, then during deposition, those particles will be acted upon not only by conventional sedimentological processes, but also by the aligning forces of the prevailing geomagnetic field. These aligning forces will continue to operate once deposition has occurred and prior to consolidation of the sediment; during this time magnetic particles may be free to rotate and hence to become realigned with the prevailing field (Irving 1957, Tucker 1980). The remanent magnetisation of detrital sediments may therefore provide an accurate record of the character of the geomagnetic field at the time of deposition. From a study of continuously-deposited sedimentary sequences, along with records of archaeomagnetic studies and geomagnetic observations, it has thus been possible to reconstruct the pattern of variations in the Earth's magnetic field for the last 15,000 years or more. Unfortunately, because the Earth's magnetic field does not constitute a simple dipole, but a dipole with a number of non-dipolar elements superimposed, these records of secular variations in palaeomagnetism only provide a record of geomagnetic changes within specific non-dipole fields. As a result, it has been necessary to attempt to reconstruct the pattern of secular variations in palaeomagnetism for a number of regions on the Earth's surface.

Given the foregoing, it has been suggested that the date of deposition of sedimentary sequences may be established by comparing their remanent magnetisation with the master curves of secular variations in palaeomagnetism established for each non-dipole field. The successful application of this approach in a limited number of studies (see, for example, Gale, Hunt and Southgate 1984 for an application in an archaeological context) encouraged the belief that the technique might be used to date part of the South Section at Skipsea. Since that part of the section investigated has been shown by biostratigraphic, lithostratigraphic and radiometric methods to be of Late-Devensian age (Chapters 5 and 6), it was considered that it might be possible to compare the palaeomagnetic results obtained at Skipsea with those of the large number of studies of secular variations in palaeomagnetism in Britain during the Late-glacial (Mackereth 1971, Creer, Mackereth, Molyneux and Thompson 1972, Thompson 1973, Creer, Gross and Lineback 1976, Thompson 1977). A composite curve of Late-glacial palaeomagnetism in Britain is shown in Figure 4.1.

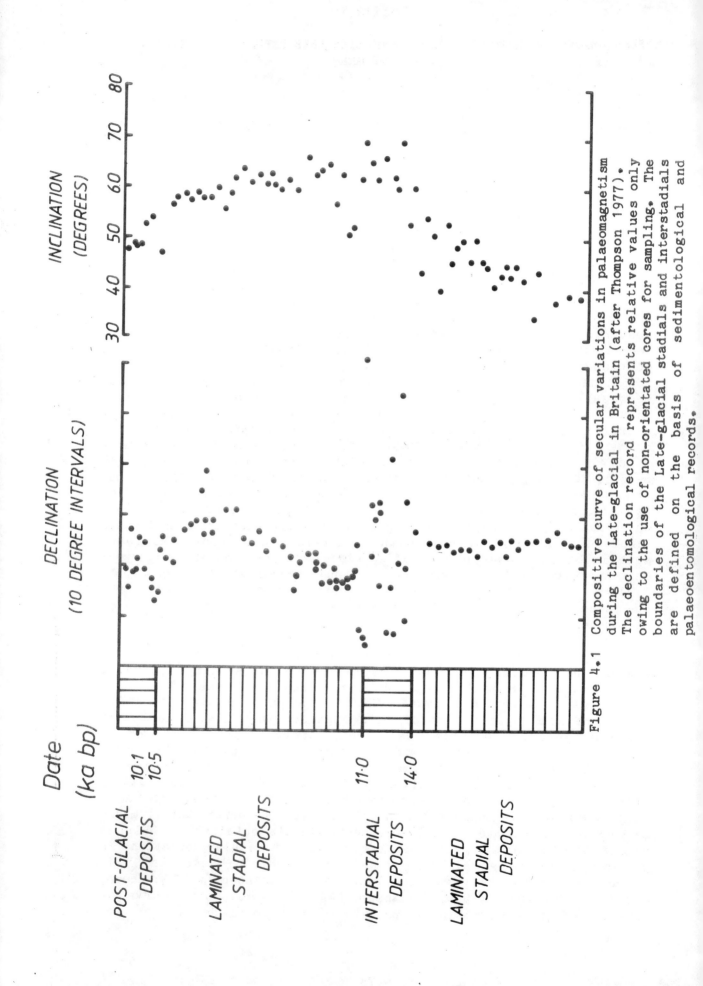

Figure 4.1   Compositive curve of secular variations in palaeomagnetism during the Late-glacial in Britain (after Thompson 1977). The declination record represents relative values only owing to the use of non-orientated cores for sampling. The boundaries of the Late-glacial stadials and interstadials are defined on the basis of sedimentological and palaeoentomological records.

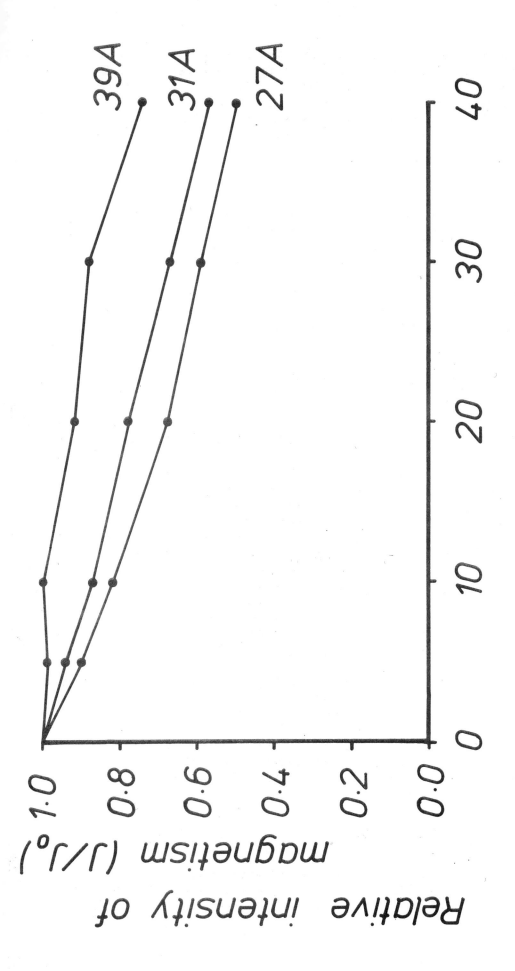

Figure 4.2 Relative intensity of magnetisation of specimens 27A, 31A and 39A during progressive stepwise demagnetisation in alternating magnetic fields.

SAMPLING

Palaeomagnetic sampling was confined to the central area (Section 5) at Skipsea (Figure 3.1). Sampling sites were established within the upper 20mm of beds 26, 27, 28, 29, 31, 35, 39 and 40 (Figure 3.7). At each site, four orientated specimens of 20mm depth x 20mm diameter (26A-26D, etc.) were taken, the sampling method following that suggested by Tarling (1983:79) for subaerially-exposed soft sediments.

MEASUREMENT

Three specimens, 27A, 31A and 39A, were selected from the top, middle and base of the sampled section respectively. The stability of the remanent magnetisation of these specimens was examined by progressive stepwise demagnetisation in alternating magnetic fields up to a maximum field strength of 60 mT. The direction and intensity of magnetisation after each demagnetisation step was measured using a Digico spinner magnetometer (Molyneux 1971) (Figures 4.2, 4.3). For all three specimens, the direction of magnetisation changed relatively little at demagnetisation steps between 5 mT and 30 mT. By contrast, the specimens exhibited variable changes in the direction of megnetisation during the initial demagnetisation step (5 mT), and erratic changes in direction of magnetisation after demagnetisation to levels higher than 30 mT. The initial change in magnetic direction can be attributed to the presence in the specimens of a viscous magnetic component of very low coercivity. On the other hand, the erratic behaviour at higher demagnetisation levels may be attributed to the acquisition by the specimens of either anhysteretic remanent magnetisation or rotational remanent magnetisation during magnetic cleaning. This is despite efforts having been made to minimise the acquisition of anhysteretic remanent magnetisation by cancelling the ambient magnetic field at the point of demagnetisation. Efforts were also made to take into account the possible acquisition of rotational remanent magnetisation by the use of the following procedure. After each demagnetisation step, the remanence of each specimen was measured. The orientation of the specimen was then reversed and it was demagnetised again to the same peak field value. A second measure of remanence was then made and the average value of remanence was then taken as the true value at that demagnetisation level.

It was assumed that the stable magnetic directions exhibited by the pilot specimens after demagnetisation in fields of 5-30 mT represented the primary magnetisation of the specimens. All the remaining specimens were therefore partially demagnetised in peak alternating magnetic fields of 20 mT to remove the viscous components of magnetisation and to isolate the primary component of remanence. The direction and intensity of magnetisation of the specimens was then measured in the magnetometer.

RESULTS

The measurements of direction of magnetisation obtained from each specimen were used to calculate site mean-direction and site O_{95}-direction values for each site. Similarly, the measurements of

Figure 4.3 Sterographic (equal angle) projections of directions of magnetisation of specimens 27A, 31A and 39A during progressive stepwise demagnetisation in alternating magnetic fields (peak alternating-field values given in millitesla). Solid circles on lowr hemisphere, open circles on upper.

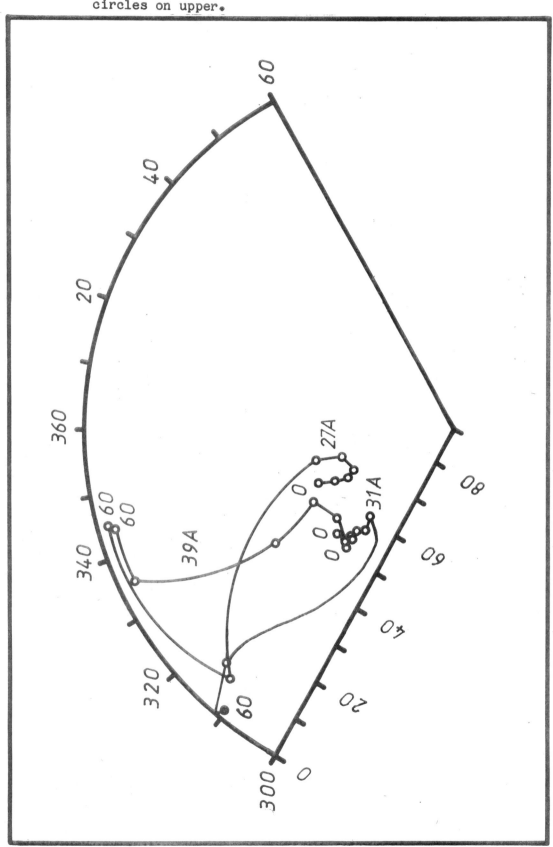

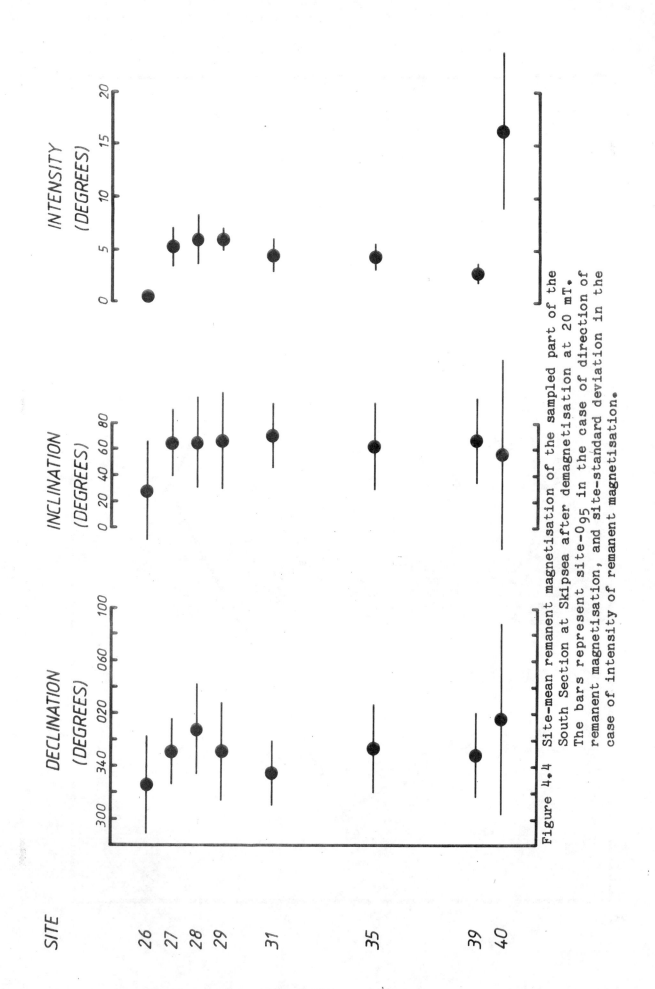

Figure 4.4 Site-mean remanent magnetisation of the sampled part of the
South Section at Skipsea after demagnetisation at 20 mT.
The bars represent site-O_{95} in the case of direction of
remanent magnetisation, and site-standard deviation in the
case of intensity of remanent magnetisation.

intensity of magnetisation obtained from each specimen were used to calculate site mean-intensity and site standard-deviation intensity for each site. The results are shown in Figure 4.4. It should be noted that specimens 26D and 28C were excluded from these calculations, since their cleaned magnetic directions (D = 200.7°, I = 35.7° and D = 303.2°, I = -46.9° respectively) suggested that they had experienced post-depositional disturbance.

DISCUSSION

Intensity

The intensity of magnetisation of the specimens at 20 mT was generally relatively low ($\sim 10^{-3}$ A m^{-1}), indicating a low magnetic mineral content in the materials sampled. The only exceptions to this were site 26 with very low magnetic intensities of $\sim 10^{-4}$ A m^{-1}, and site 40 with rather higher magnetic intensities of $\sim 10^{-2}$ A m^{-1}. These variations may indicate differences in the mineralogical or lithological nature of the deposits. The high median-coercivities (~ 40 mT) of the demagnetised pilot specimens (Figure 4.3) suggested the presence of haematite as the major magnetic constituent of the deposits (Dunlop and Stirling 1977).

Direction

Although the directions of magnetisation of each of the sites sampled displayed considerable scatter (Figure 4.4), the overall unit-mean direction of D = 349.5° and I = 61.3°, obtained by combining the mean values for each site, was close to that of the geocentric axial-dipole value at Skipsea (D = 360.0°, I = 70.0°). This suggested that the primary magnetisation of the specimens was largely a function of the direction of the ancient field, which tends, over periods as short as 2 ka, to approximate to a geocentric axial-dipole (Tarling 1983:190-194). The scatter of values may have been the result of post-depositional disturbance, particularly as the deposits can be seen to have undergone slumping and faulting (Figure 3.7). Alternatively, randomisation of magnetic directions in deposits such as these, composed mainly of silt, may have been a function either of the fabric of the sediment, which tends not to allow particles to realign themselves post-depositionally with the prevailing magnetic field, or of the movement of particles out of magnetic alignment as they were deposited in irregularities on the sediment surface.

Although the normal polarity of magnetisation of these beds excludes them from having been deposited during any of the magnetic excursions recorded during the Brunhes normal-polarity Epoch (Verosub and Banerjee 1977, Verosub 1982, Tarling 1983:211-215), it is impossible to establish any pattern of secular variation from the measurements made at Skipsea Withow. The magnetostratigraphic results therefore provide no firm evidence of the date of deposition of the beds. Nevertheless, the results obtained do not exclude the deposition of the beds from having taken place during pollen zone I of the Late-Devensian, as indicated by the palynological and molluscan evidence (Chapter 5).

CONCLUSIONS

Palaeomagnetic analysis of part of the South Section of the Upper Palaeolithic site at Skipsea, East Yorkshire, indicates that the direction of remanent magnetisation of the deposits largely reflects the direction of the ancient geomagnetic field. However, the results are only able to confirm that the deposits were laid down during the Brunhes normal-polarity Epoch, and not during one of the magnetic excursions recorded during that time.

CHAPTER 5

THE PALAEOBOTANY OF THE LATE-DEVENSIAN SEQUENCE AT SKIPSEA WITHOW MERE

by C.O. Hunt, A.R. Hall and D.D. Gilbertson, with contributions by Anne Blackham, Christine Williams and H.K.Kenward.

INTRODUCTION

Pollen analysis has been carried out on samples from sections 1, 7, 8 and 3 (Figure 3.1). The studies of section 7 are primarily concerned with the Flandrian and are discussed in Chapters 7 and 8. Plant macrofossil analysis was carried out on samples from section 8. Most of the pollen samples were split from the samples taken for molluscan analysis by D. Woodall and N. Thew (Chapter 6).

The plant macrofossils were separated from the samples from sections 8 and 1 used for molluscan analysis by N. Thew and D. Woodall respectively, see Figure 6.1 for details. Sample provenance is shown in Figure 3.7.

The pollen samples from sections 1 and 3 were prepared using hydrochloric and hydrofluoric acid and acetolysis. These techniques gave very sparse assemblages of poorly preserved pollen. More sophisticated techniques (Hunt 1984) were therefore used to prepare pollen from section 8. The samples were boiled in 5% potassium hydroxide , sieved from 120 micron and on 10 micron nylon sieves and 'swirled' on a clock-glass. 5ml samples were used and **Eucalyptus** pollen pills added so that pollen concentration in the sediment could be established, as summarised in Jones and Cundill (1978). It was later discovered that some of the pills contained no **Eucalyptus** pollen, so pollen concentration in the sediment could not be established for every sample.

Between 5 and 165 grains were identified from each sample in section 1, 100 grains were identified from each sample in section 3, and 5 to 720 grains were identified from each sample in section 8. Pre-Quaternary palynomorphs and Quaternary organic walled microfossils were also counted in section 8.

MICROPALAEONTOLOGY: TAXONOMIC NOTES

Pollen

The identification of pollen in general follows Moore and Webb (1978).

Organic-Walled Microfossils   (Figures 5.1, 5.2).

(a)   Pediastrum (Figure 5.1; 1). These algal microfossils are well-known, being illustrated by, for example, Cookson (1953).

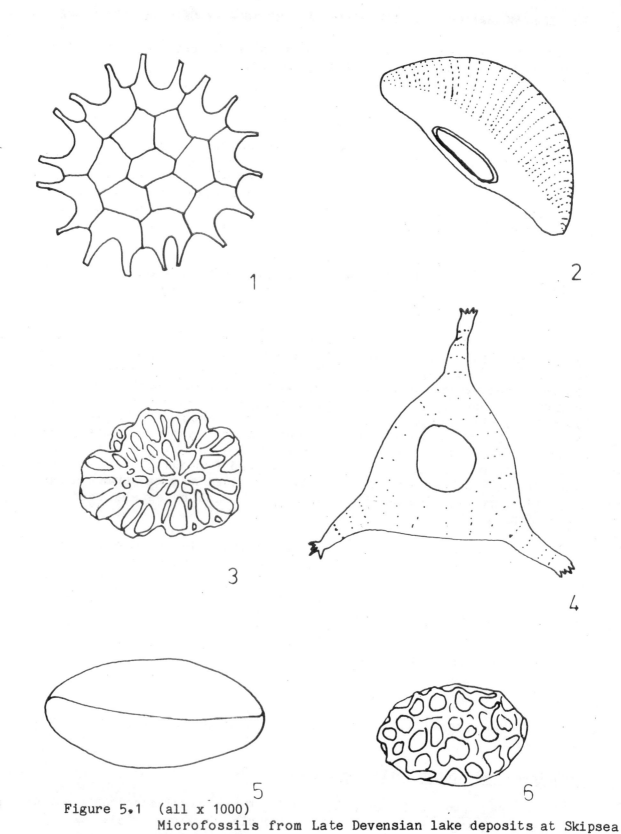

Figure 5.1   (all x 1000)
Microfossils from Late Devensian lake deposits at Skipsea
Withow.

1.   **Pediastrum** sp.
2.   **Cosmarium** sp. (Desmid)
3.   **Botryococcus** sp.
4.   **Staurastrum** sp. (Desmid)
5.   **Spirogyra** sp.
6.   **Zygnema** type

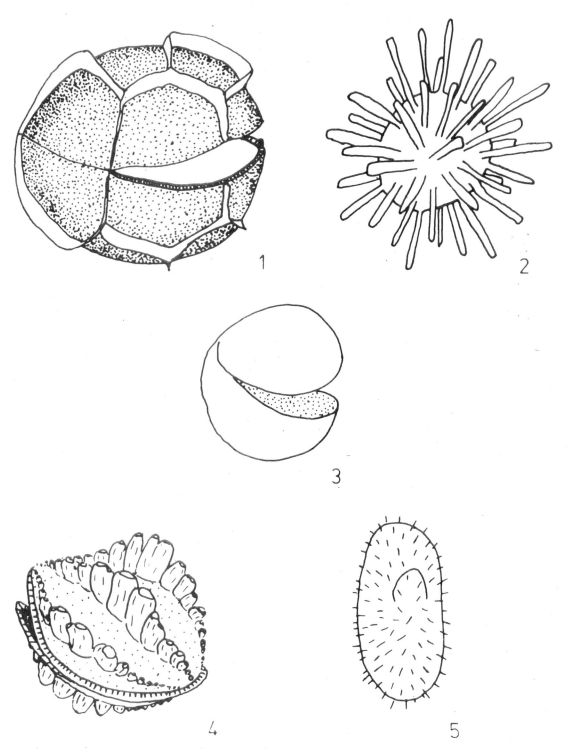

Figure 5.2 (all x 1000)
Microfossils from Late Devensian lake deposits at Skipsea
Withow.
1 - 5. Organic-walled microfossils, incertae sedis.

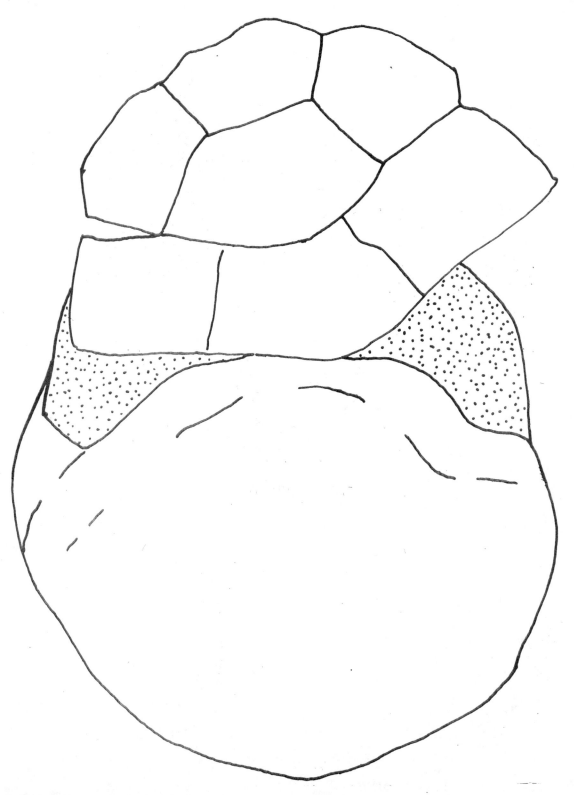

Figure 5.3 (x 2000)
          Microfossil from Late Devensian deposits at Skipsea
          Withow.
          Dinoflagellate cyst, redrawn from a scanning electron
          micrograph, showing cingulum, archaeopyle, and tabulation
          of the operculum.

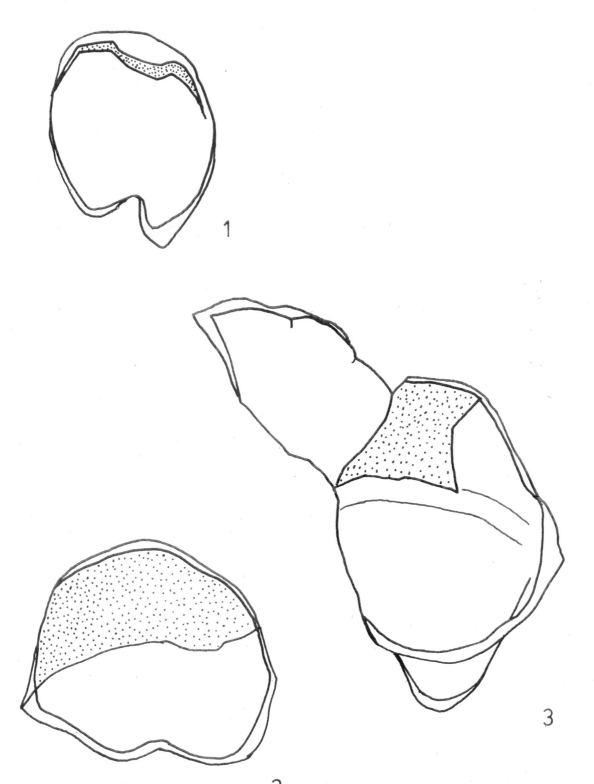

Figure 5.4 (x 1000)
Microfossils from Late Devensian deposits at Skipsea
Withow.
　　1.　Dinoflagellate cyst, showing incipient archaeopyle
　　　　formation across the apex of the cyst, dorsal view.
　　2.　Dinoflagellate cyst, showing archaeopyle, dorsal view.
　　3.　Dinoflagellate cyst, showing archaeopyle and attached
　　　　operculum, lateral view.

Figure 5.5 (x 1000)
Microfossils from Late Devensian deposits at Skipsea Withow.

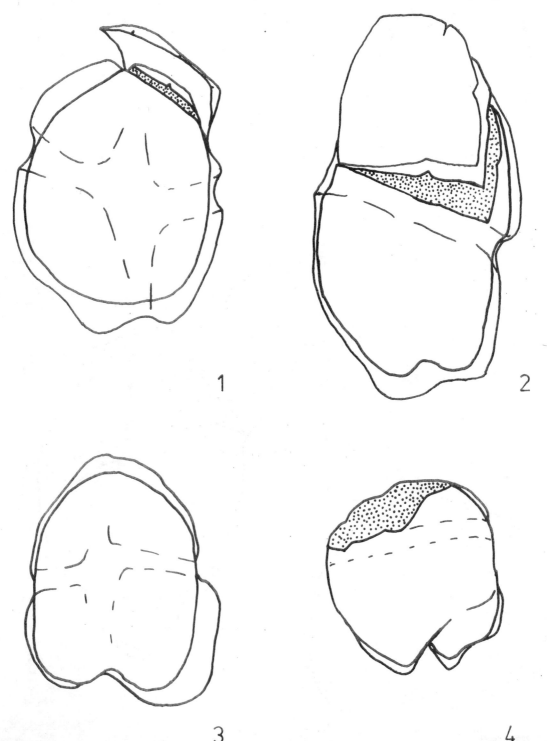

1. Dinoflagellate cyst, showing cingulum, sulcus and incipient archaeopyle formation at apex, ventral view.
2. Dinoflagellate cyst, showing archaeopyle formation and cingulum, dorsal view.
3. Dinoflagellate cyst, showing sulcus and cingulum, ventral view.
4. Dinoflagellate cyst, showing archaeopyle and cingulum, lateral view.

(b)   Dinoflagellate Cysts (Figures 5.3-5.5). One species of Pleistocene freshwater dinoflagellate cyst is present in the Skipsea section. Its distribution, preservation and morphology (there are no similar pre-Pleistocene species) strongly suggest that the cysts are not recycled from the underlying till. Similar cysts have been seen in fluvial deposits of the River Witham, Lincolnshire (C. Groves, pers. comm.) and in lacustrine deposits from the Morecambe Bay area (C.O. Hunt, unpublished).

The cysts are cornucavate to circumcavate, and peridinioid to ovoid in form. The inner wall is scabrate, and less than 0.5mm thick; the outer wall is also scabrate, and very thin. In most specimens, both the inner and outer walls show a rounded epitract and two very bluntly rounded antapical horns; in some specimens, however, the inner body is ovoid rather than peridinioid. The tabulation is indicated by the cingulum, archaeopyle and by very shallow grooves on the inner wall as 4' 3i 7" 5"' 2"". The cingulum is broad, laevorotary, and indicated by bulges in the outer layer and occasionally by very low (less than 0.25 microns) smooth-topped ridges on the outer layer. The archaeopyle opens by a transapical suture and a suture at the anterior edge of the girdle. On some scanning electron micrographs, tabulation on the operculum is indicated by irregularly-developed cracks. An archaeopyle tabulation of one apical, three intercalary and at least three precingular para-plates is indicated. A flagellar 'slit' can be seen under the scanning electron microscope; it is between 20 and 25 microns long and 1-2 microns wide.

The outer layer varies between 58 microns and 150 microns in length, averaging 91 microns (8 specimens measured), and 50 microns to 120 microns in breadth, averaging 68 microns (8 specimens measured). The separation of the anterior and posterior pericoels varies between 2 and 15 microns, alternatively the cysts may be circumcavate, with separation of the two wall layers of up to 25 microns.

These cysts are very similar to type D cysts of Norris and McAndrews (1970), differing only by being larger (type D cysts having a length of between 49 microns and 57 microns) and in having a slightly more peridinioid outline. The overall morphology of these cysts, together with the nature of the archaeopyle and the tabulation, suggests that they are cysts of a species of **Peridinium.**

(c)   Zygnemataceae (Figure 5.1, 5, 6). Most of the microfossils attributed here to the Zygnemataceae are similar to those attributed to **Spirogyra** spp. by Van Geel (1976) and Van Geel and Van der Hammen (1978). Rarer forms similar to those described as 'Type 58: Zygnemataceae' by Van Geel (1976) and '**Zygnema** - type' by Van Geel and Van der Hammen (1978) are also included; they are not differentiated in the diagram (Figure 5.8/9) since all the Zygnemataceae share common ecological requirements (references in Van Geel and Van der Hammen 1978) of shallow, stagnant, oxygen-rich fresh or slightly brackish water, which reaches temperatures of at least 10°C for at least a few months of the year.

(d)   Desmids (Figure 5.1; 2, 4). Most of the desmids recovered can be attributed to the biplex genus **Cosmarium.** Rare triplex forms attributed to **Staurastrum** spp. were also recovered.

SAMPLE	TAXON
SK6	Vaccinium type, Aster type, Galium, Circaea, Polygonum convolvulus
SK9	Rhamnus, Scilla type
SK13	Saxifraga granulata type, Mercurialis
SK17	Geum
SK18	Cirsium type, Meyanthes
SK19	Linaria, Vicia cracca
SK33	Glaucium, Ephedra
SK37	Dryas
LG5	Scabiosa columbaria
SK39	Mentha
A4	Polygonum convolvulus

Table 5.1   OCCURRENCE OF RARE POLLEN TAXA IN THE LATE-DEVENSIAN DEPOSITS
AT SKIPSEA WITHOW MERE, SECTION 8: Figure 3.1.

(e)   **Botryococcus**   (Figure 5.1; 3).   Colonies of a
Botryococcus species similar to those illustrated by Cookson (1953)
were recovered. For the purposes of this study, each colony of
Botryococcus was recorded as one individual. **Botryococcus** is a
planktonic alga of freshwater and brackish lakes and pools (Round
1973).

(f)   'Type 119'. Microfossils identical to those informally
named as 'Type 119' by Pals, Van Geel and Delfos (1980) were recovered
from three samples. These microfossils are characteristic of
slow-moving freshwater in the Netherlands (Pals, Van Geel and Delfos
1980).

(g)   Other organic-walled microfossils. A number of other
organic-walled microfossils of probable algal origin were seen. These
include:

(i)   a spherical psilate 'cyst' 15-25 microns in diameter,
       showing an equatorial suture (Figure 5.2; 3).

(ii)   an ovoid 'cyst' 15-20 microns long, 10-15 microns wide,
       bearing widely spaced (2 microns) baculate processes
       1.5-2 microns high and less than 0.5 microns thick,
       showing a semi-circular suture (Figure 5.2; 5).

(iii) a spherical (40-60 microns diameter), thick-walled (2-3
       microns) 'cyst', showing an equatorial suture, with a
       regular reticulum with straight-topped, narrow (less
       than 1 microns) lists, 2-4 microns high, enclosing
       polygonal lumina with rounded corners (Figure 5.2; 1).

(iv)   a flattened-ovoid (30-60 microns diameter) 'cyst', with
       an equatorial suture, with three to six lines of
       hollow, bulbous, open-topped processes, 2-10 microns
       high and 1-8 microns wide running down the longitudinal
       axis of each hemisphere (Figure 5.2; 4).

(v)   spherical 'cysts', 8-15 microns in diameter, bearing a
       dense ornament of baculate processes 4-10 microns long
       (Figure 5.2: 2).

Sponge Spicules

     Sponge spicules were recovered from sample 142, where they
occurred with an abundance of 0.4% of total pollen. The spicules are
hollow, acicular, up to 80 microns long and 10 microns wide. They are
similar to the spicules of many species of freshwater sponge, but their
morphology is too generalised to allow attribution to any particular
taxon.

air dried weight (kg)		7/M/16 upper 1.0	7/M/17 lower 0.5
depth		1.5-1.6m	1.6-1.7m

Taxon

Betula nana L.	fcs	1	-
Betula sp(p)	fcs	10	-
	fr	57	4
	mc	1f	-
Carex spp	n	4	3
Caryophyllaceae	s	2	-
cf. **Cretaegus monogyna** Jacq.	frst	1	-
Groenlandia densa (L.) Fourr.	pyr	1	-
Luzula sp.	s	2	-
Nymphaea alba L.	s	4	1
Populus sp.	bs	0	-
Potamogeton spp.	pyr	23	1
Potentilla palustris L.	a	2	1
Ranunculus subg.		-	-
Batrachium (DC.) A. Gray	a	3	1
R. sp. indet.	a	1	-
Rumex acetosella agg.	fr	4	-
cf. **Salix** sp.	bs	-	1
Schoenplectus sp.	n	57	1

Mosses, Algae

Aulocomnium palustre (Hedw) Schwaegr.	lf, sht	2	-
Bryum sp.	sht	1	1
Calliergon sp.	sht	-	1
Cratoneuron filicinum (Hedw) Spruce	sht	1	-
Sphagnum sp.	lvs, sht, tips	0	-
Chara sp(p)	oo	f	-

Key to abbreviations: Parts: a - achene(s); an - anther(s); b - bud(s);
        bs - budscale(s); car - carpel(s); fca - female cone axes;
        fcs - female catkin scale(s); fr - fruit(s); frst - fruitstone(s);
        lf, lvs - leaf, leaves; mc - male catkin; n - nut(let)s;
        oo - oospore(s); pyr - pyrene(s); sht(s) - shoot(s); w - wood.
        Elsewhere: f, ff - fragment(s); fr - frequent; imm - immature;
        o - occasional.

Table 5.2.   PLANT MACROFOSSILS FROM LATE-DEVENSIAN DARK GREY LAMINATED
            SILTS (UNIT 3c) AT SKIPSEA WITHOW: Section 7 (Figure 3.1).

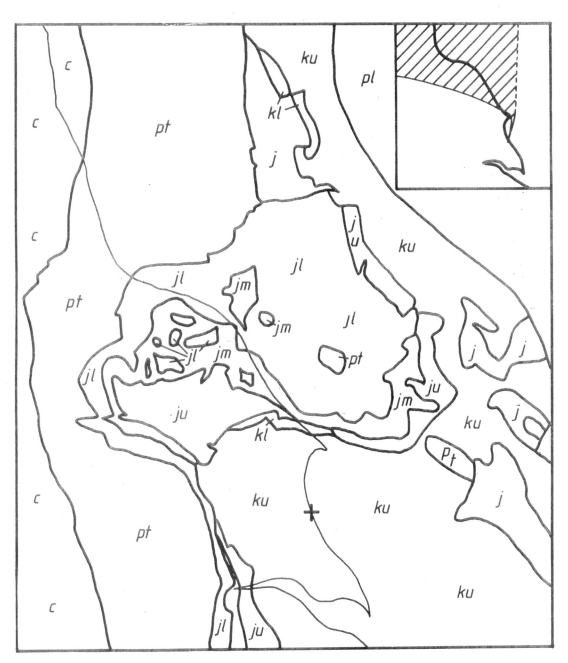

Figure 5.6 Source areas for pre-Quaternary palynomorphs recorded from
the Skipsea Till. Key - pl Pleistocene; ku Upper Cretaceous
kl Lower Cretaceous; ju Upper Jurassic; jm Middle Jurassic;
jl Lower Jurassic; j undifferentiated Jurassic;
pt Permo-Triassic; c Carboniferous; + Skipsea Withow Gap.

RESULTS

The results of the pollen and plant macrofossil analyses are shown in Figures 5.6-5.9 and Tables 5.1 and 5.3. The assemblages are divisible into three major units, corresponding to:

(i)   the basal till

(ii) the lacustrine silts and gravels

(iii) the overlying peats.

The results are discussed in detail below for each section studies - Nos. 1, 7 and 8.

The Till

The Till is only sparsely palyniferous, containing only 150 palynomorphs/cm^3. Only 8 grains/cm^3 (of **Pinus** and Gramineae) were seen in a state of preservation similar to the Quaternary pollen in the overlying lacustrine deposits. Other Quaternary taxa present included **Picea**, **Alnus**, **Tilia**, **Fraxinus**, **Pediastrum**, and marine dinoflagellate cysts, mostly **Spiniferites** spp. The palynomorphs in the till were present in the following proportions:

Pleistocene	11%
Lower - Middle Cretaceous	11%
Jurassic (mostly Lower - Middle)	58%
Triassic - Rhaetic	1%
Carboniferous	19%

The palynomorphs are mostly in very good condition, and show little evidence of weathering or corrosion. It is likely that the glacier which laid down the Skipsea Till passed over rocks of all these ages to entrain the palynomorphs. It is thus likely that the Skipsea glacier moved down the Northumberland - Yorkshire coast in a generally southerly direction, since this is the only direction in which formations of Cretaceous, Jurassic, Triassic-Rhaetic and Carboniferous age would be crossed (see Figure 5.6).

The Lacustrine Sequence: General Properties

In general, the lacustrine silts and gravels show a considerable uniformity in their pollen spectra, all samples having a 'cold-stage' aspect. Most samples contain high incidences of Cyperaceae and Gramineae. The sedges, and perhaps some of the grasses, were probably growing close to the sample sites, at the margins of the Skipsea Withow lake. The substantial representation of sedges in the plant macrofossil assemblages (Tables 5.2, 5.3) lends support to this argument. The high incidences of Cyperaceae and Gramineae derived from local vegetation obscures, to an extent, the fluctuations in the regional pollen rain.

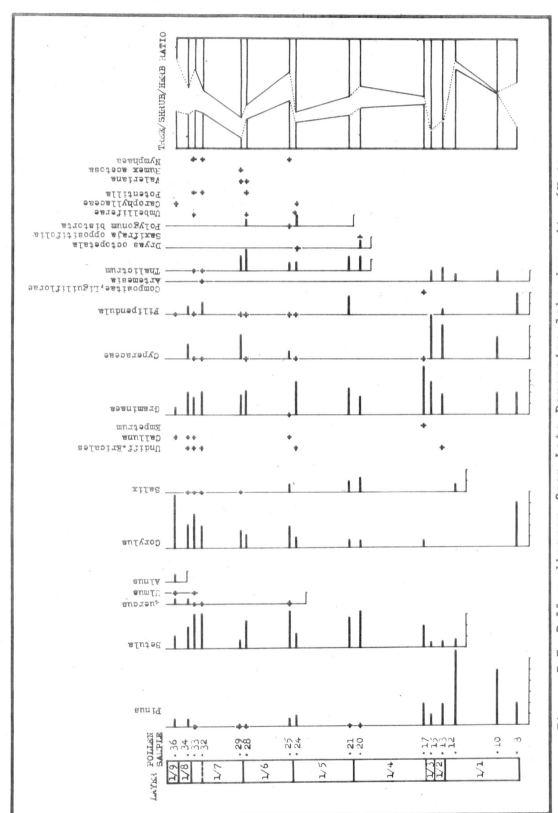

Figure 5.7 Pollen diagram from Late Devensian lake deposits (Unit 3/1/1-7, Units 4 and 5) from section 1 (Figure 3.1) at the northern margins of the former Skipsea Withow mere: analyses by Christine Williams.

The pollen profiles (Figures 5.7, 5.9 and 5.11) samples are also characterised by low but continuous incidences of **Pinus** and **Betula**. In sections 1 and 3, **Betula** pollen was not subdivided, but in section 8 most birch pollen was comparable with pollen of **Betula nana**. Leaf impressions and macrofossils of **Betula nana** are relatively abundant in the Late Devensian deposits (Plate 5.1, Tables 5.2, 5.3). **Pinus** is the most common tree pollen in most samples, but the absence of Pine macrofossils suggests that it may not have been locally present. Very low abundance of **Betula** cf. **nana**, tree birch and **Salix** are, however, accompanied by the occurrence of plant macrofossils, suggesting that these taxa were present. **Juniperus** and **Populus** are not represented at all by pollen, although plant macrofossils of both these taxa are present (Tables 5.2, 5.3).

Pollen of shrubs and dwarf shrubs is consistently present, particularly Ericaceae, **Helianthemum**, and the rarer **Hippophäe** and **Rhamnus**. The latter three taxa are, to varying extents, shade-intolerant; **Hippophäe** is also tolerant of considerable ground instability.

Herb taxa are represented by both pollen and macrofossils. Most are tolerant of, or characteristic of, open habitats, particularly the Compositae (**Artemisia**, Liguliflorae and **Anthemis** type, **Aster** type, **Serratula** type and **Cirsium** type), **Rumex acetosa**, **Rumex acetosella**, **Plantago** spp., **Thalictrum**, **Geranium**, Caryophyllaceae, Chenopodiaceae. Pollen of **Oxyria**, spores of **Botrychium** and macrofossils of **Dryas** represent three taxa particularly characteristic of montane and northerly habitats.

As in many other Devensian deposits known in Britain (Bell 1969, West 1977a,b; Pennington 1977), a group of taxa with a wide range of geographical and ecological preferences is often present. This group includes several taxa with present day northerly or arctic-alpine distributions, such as **Dryas, Linnaea, Empetrum**-type and **Betula** cf. **nana**, together with a group having modern southerly and easterly distributions, such as **Sanguisorba, Ephedra, Rhamnus, Scabiosa columbaria, Scilla** and **Helianthemum** (Fitter 1978). It was concluded by Bell (1969) that the combination of habitat availability and relatively high summer temperatures led to the development of this 'mixed' type of Devensian flora.

In general terms, the pollen and plant macrofossils suggest an open landscape dominated by a grass/herb/dwarf shrub vegetation on which open woodland occasionally developed. Marsh vegetation dominated the margins of the Skipsea lake.

Shifts in the plant macrofossil assemblages and pollen spectra allow the lacustrine sequence to be subdivided. Because the plant macrofossil assemblages and the pollen spectra show similar shifts at the same time, it is possible that they might reflect regional vegetational changes as well as changes in local sedimentary environments.

<u>NORTHERN EXPOSURES</u> (section 1, Figure 3.1).

<u>Plant macrofossils</u> (Unit 3/1/1-7). (A.H.)

Plant macrofossils are especially important in this context, providing valuable evidence on local presence or absence of a particular taxon.

The residues from Unit 3(1/1-1/7) were examined for plant macrofossils. These all yielded oospores of **Chara** and pyrenes of **Potamogeton** which were probably primary colonisers of the lake margin. However, Unit 3(1/2) also yielded other aquatic and water side taxa - notably **Hippuris vulgaris** and **Eleocharis** sp. A single female catkin of the dwarf birch **Betula nana** was also found. This slightly higher concentration of remains possibly reflects the results of inwashing from the nearby margins of the basin. The presence of dwarf birch suggests an open, possibly sub-arctic, climate.

<u>Insect assemblages</u> (by Harry Kenward)

The small assemblages from the samples in section 1 included some ants and beetles. Those of the latter that could be identified are indicative of open, treeless vegetation, perhaps short grass and moss.

<u>CENTRAL EXPOSURE</u> (Section 7, Figure 3.1)

<u>Plant macrofossils</u>

Two bulk samples 7/M/16 and 7/M/17 from Unit 3c were investigated for plant macrofossils. The results are set out in Table 5.2. These samples occurred at 0.2m (16) and 0.4m (17) at the base of the Flandrian peats radiocarbon dated to 9880 ± 60 b.p. (SRR 1944).

<u>Late Devensian Clays</u>

The lowest sample - No. 7/M/17, yielded a very small assemblage of plant macrofossils. These were in a poor state of preservation, such that it was not possible to distinguish fruits of dwarf birch, **Betula nana**, amongst those identified to the genus **Betula**: see also Plate 5.1. The other macrofossils are probably associated with aquatic or aquatic-marginal habitats and no doubt represent an early stage of colonisation of the lake at this site. The birch fruits, whether dwarf or tree birch (or both) represent early colonisation of the surrounding drier land by woody plants.

The next, upper sample (7/M/16) yielded a much larger assemblage of plant macrofossils. The bulk of these were fruits of birch (the majority were certainly tree birch, although a single female catkin of **Betula nana** was found), nutlets of **Schoenoplectus** (probably **Schoenoplectus lacustris**, the bulrush), pyrenes of **Potamogeton** spp., and oospores of **Chara**. The occasional bud-scales of **Populus** (probably **Populus tremula**) are of interest here, as are the leaves and shoot tips of **Sphagnum**. Whilst the former are

Plate 5.1 Leaf impressions of **Betula nana** from the Late Devensian lake silts (Unit 3) at Skipsea Withow mere: photograph by Trevor Corns.

consistent with the open-woodland vegetation indicated by the numerous birch fruits and abundant **Betula** pollen, the **Sphagnum** leaves (and spores in Figure 5.7) are less easily explained. The genus is recorded by Dickson (1973:69-72) from Late-Devensian deposits at several sites in Britain, although all are in the west. He discusses the possible habitats the moss might have occupied at this time, but it may be that some of the material from the present site is reworked from older (interglacial?) deposits. This is perhaps supported by the decline of **Sphagnum** in the spore record with decreasing mineral sedimentation. The tentatively identified hawthorn fruit (cf. **Crataegus monogyna**) recorded from sample 16, may likewise have originated in older sediments. The reworking of ?Ipswichian vertebrate remains into Devensian glacial deposits is well known in Holderness.

On the other hand, the leaf and shoot of **Aulocomnium palustre**, a frequent concomitant of certain **Sphagnum** spp. in wet, acid habitats, are less likely to be reworked. The moss is known from Late-Devensian deposits at Hooks, some 20km south of Skipsea (Dickson 1973:223) and has numerous other Late-Devensian and early Flandrian records.

The remainder of the assemblage from this sample included aquatic and waterside/marsh taxa, and four fruits of **Rumex acetosella**, a typical Late-Devensian weedspecies representing the disturbed soils caused by soil erosion and possibly mass movement.

CENTRAL EXPOSURES (Section 8)

The local plant assemblage biozones recognised in these exposures are defined below with their interpretation. The plant macrofossils are listed in Table 5.3, the results of the palynological studies are set out in Figures 5.8 and 5.9, and their stratigraphic distribution in the section is illustrated in Figure 5.10.

Biozone SKA

CHARACTERISTICS: Very restricted Quaternary palynomorph assemblages (5-29 grains/cm^3) together with abundant assemblage of pre-Quaternary taxa (up to 616 grains/cm^3). **Pinus**, Gramineae, Cyperaceae and herb taxa **Artemesia**, Compositae (Liguliflorae), **Rumex** spp., Chenopodiaceae, **Anthemis**-type, **Thalictrum**) dominate the assemblages. **Salix**, **Filipendula**, **Typha**, **Betula** cf. **nana**, **Helianthemum**, **Empetrum**-type and Coryloid are also present.

OCCURRENCE: Section 8, unit 2; Section 1, unit 3/1/1.

INTERPRETATION: **Pinus** and Gramineae are present in the underlying till; it is probable that they, together perhaps with the 'Coryloids', are recycled from the till, together with the pre-Quaternary palynomorphs. The residual pollen assemblages are dominated by herb taxa and some dwarf shrub pollen, with Cyperaceae becoming increasingly important.

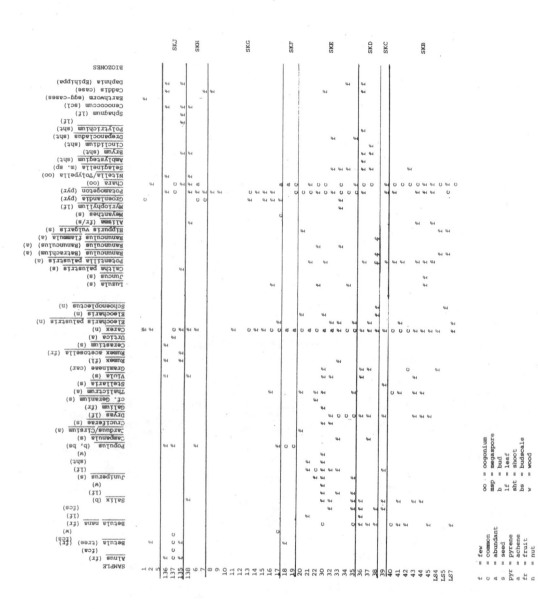

Table 5.3. Plant macrofossils from Late Devensian lake deposits
Central Exposures at Skipsea Withow: Section 8.

f = few   oo. = oogonium
c = common   msp = megaspore
a = abundant   b = bud
s = seed   lf = leaf
pyr = pyrene   sht = shoot
a = achene   bs = budscale
fr = fruit   w = wood
n = nut

98

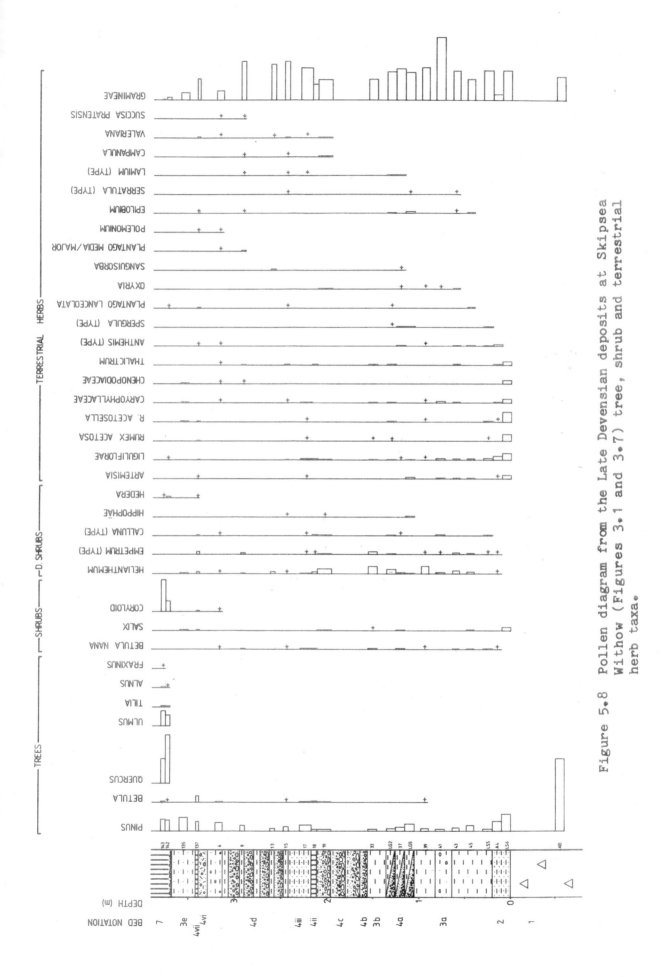

Figure 5.8   Pollen diagram from the Late Devensian deposits at Skipsea
Withow (Figures 3.1 and 3.7) tree, shrub and terrestrial
herb taxa.

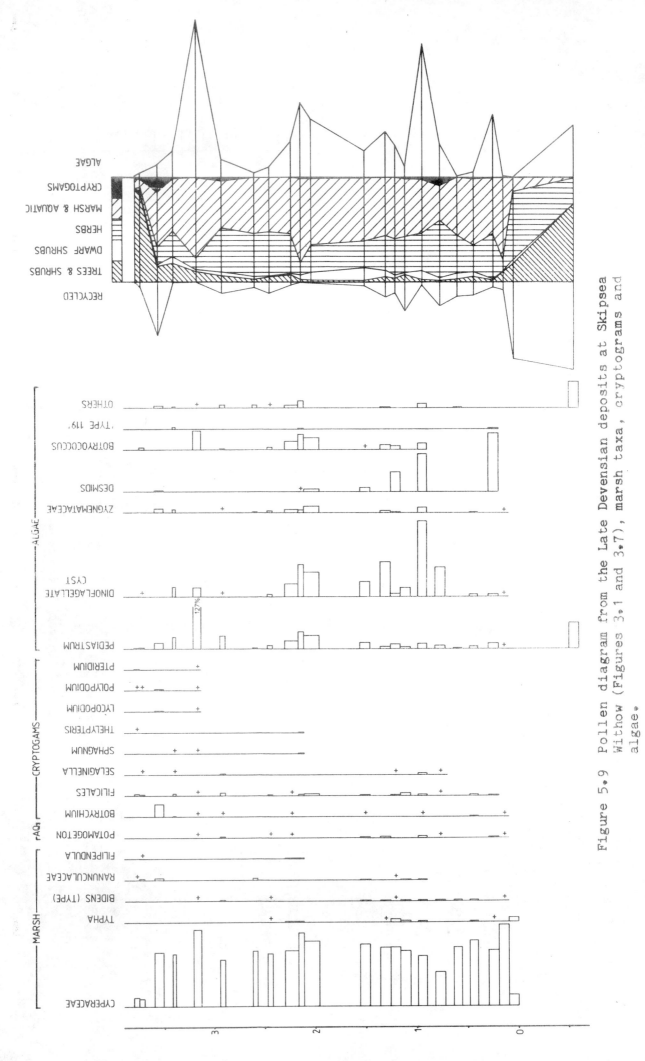

Figure 5.9 Pollen diagram from the Late Devensian deposits at Skipsea Withow (Figures 3.1 and 3.7), marsh taxa, cryptograms and algae.

The basal assemblage from section 8, dominated by **Salix**, **Artemisia**, **Rumex** spp., Caryophyllaceae, Chenopodiaceae and **Thalictrum**, is very similar to basal late-Glacial assemblages reported from Wales (Lowe 1980), the Lake District (Pennington 1977) and Scotland. These assemblages are thought to reflect a pioneer vegetation closely following deglaciation. The sedimentological evidence from unit 2 in Section 8 and unit 3/1/1 in Section 1 is not inconsistent with this interpretation: Unit 2 consists of cross-bedded sandy gravels with silt lenses and unsorted pebbly 'colluvial' silts, while unit 3/1/1 shows varve-like laminations (Chapter 4).

Biozone SKB

CHARACTERISTICS: Abundant Quaternary pollen (around 400 grains/cm^3) with low incidences of recycled palynomorphs. Plant macrofossils include **Betula** cf. **nana**, **Salix**, **Dryas**, **Thalictrum**, **Viola**, Gramineae, **Carex**, **Eleocharis palustris**, **Luzula**, **Juncus**, **Potentilla palustris**, **Ranunculus** **(Batrachium)**, **Hippuris**, **Alisma**, **Potamogeton**, **Chara** and **Selaginella**. The pollen assemblage is dominated by Cyperaceae, with lesser Gramineae and minor **Pinus**, **Betula** cf. **nana**, **Salix**, **Helianthemum**, Ericaceae, **Artemesia**, Compositae (Liguliflorae), **Rumex**, Caryophyllaceae, **Thalictrum**, **Anthemis**-type, **Spergula**-type, **Plantago**, **Oxyria**, **Epilobium**, Serratula-type, **Typha**, **Bidens**-type, **Potamogeton**, **Botrychium**, Filicales and **Selaginella**. The algal microflora includes rare **Pediastrum**, Zygnemataceae and 'Type 119' and occasionally common desmids and dinoflagellate cysts.

OCCURRENCE: Section 8, basal 0.8m of unit 3a; Section 1, units 3/1/2 and 3/1/3.

INTERPRETATION: During this biozone a lacustrine and lake-marginal flora of taxa such as **Potamogeton, Chara, Potentilla palustris, Bidens, Juncus,** Cyperaceae and algae developed. Dwarf shrubs (**Betula nana**) and herbs (**Plantago lanceolata, Dryas, Oxyria, Spergula**) immigrated into the already developing terrestrial flora. The decreased incidence of recycled palynomorphs probably reflects an increased vegetational cover and lessening erosion and mass-movement as the soil stabilised. A relatively complete ground-cover, dominated by grasses, herbs and dwarf shrubs, was thus present.

Biozone SKC

CHARACTERISTICS: Diverse Quaternary and low-incidence pre-Quaternary palynomorph assemblages: as SKB but containing the first occurrence of tree birch pollen and macrofossils of **Juniperus**; peaks in the thermophilous **Helianthemum** and **Sanguisorba** and in algal microfossils.

OCCURRENCE: Section 8, 0.8-0.9m in the upper part of unit 3a.

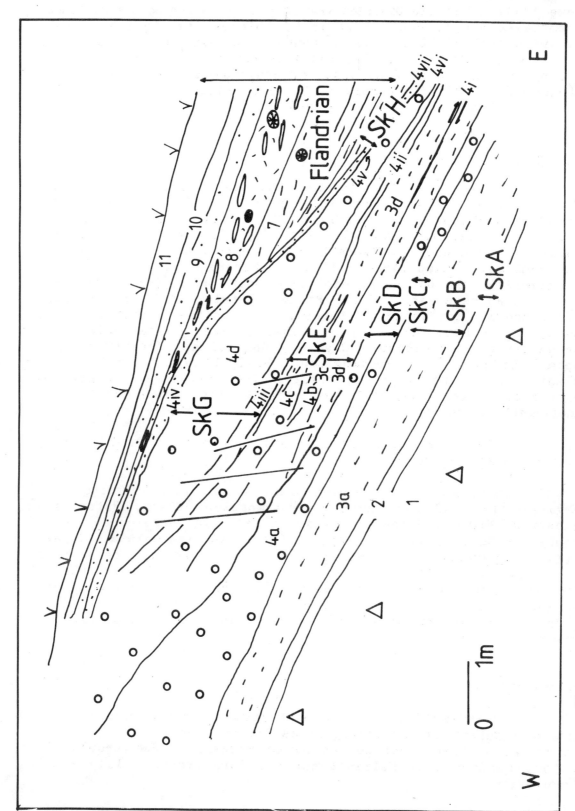

Figure 5.10 Distribution of the plant assemblage biozones (SK) in the central exposures at Skipsea Withow.

INTERPRETATION: This biozone marks the 'peak' of a ?climatic cycle, with the immigration of Juniper and perhaps tree birch and peaks in the abundance of thermophilous herbs and dwarf shrubs. The flora is similar to that of SKB in aspect, dominated by grasses, herbs and dwarf shrubs, with little sign of more than (perhaps) the occasional scattered tree-birch.

Biozone SKD

CHARACTERISTICS: Abundant Quaternary pollen, with higher incidences of recycled palynomorphs than in SKC. Pollen assemblages again similar to SKB, but with higher incidences of **Pinus**. Plant macrofossils include **Betula nana, Salix, Campanula, Dryas, Viola,** Gramineae, Cyperaceae, **Eleocharis, Schoenoplectus, Potentilla palustris,** Ranunculaceae, **Potamogeton, Chara, Selaginella** and mosses.

OCCURRENCE: Section 8, highest part of unit 3a and unit 4a.

INTERPRETATION: This biozone may reflect some type of climatic deterioration, since tree birch and Juniper disappear and other thermophiles, such as **Helianthemum** have low incidences. The higher incidence of **Pinus** and pre-Quaternary palynomorphs in this biozone probably reflect decreased ground-cover and accelerated erosion. A partial ground-cover of grasses, herbs and dwarf shrubs was, however, maintained, suggesting that the climatic episode was not of great severity.

Biozone SKE

CHARACTERISTICS: Diverse Quaternary and low-incidence pre-Quaternary palynomorph assemblages and diverse plant macrofossil assemblages. The flora is again broadly similar to SKB, but is characterised by the reappearance of **Juniperus** and relatively high incidences of thermophiles, such as **Helianthemum.** Macrofossils of **Dryas** disappear after the base of the biozone, to be replaced by taxa such as **Thalictrum, Galium, Geranium** and Cruciferae.

OCCURRENCE: Section 8, units 3b, 4b and the lower part of 4c.

INTERPRETATION: The reappearance of Juniper and peaks in the abundance of thermophiles suggests climatic amelioration. A diverse grassland flora developed, with some dwarf scrub present.

Biozone SKF

CHARACTERISTICS: Diverse and abundant Quaternary pollen and plant-macrofossil assemblages, recycled pre-Quaternary palynomorphs very rare. This biozone is characterised by the appearance of the pollen and macrofossils of tree birch, and of macrofossils of **Populus.** Aquatic, herb and dwarf shrub macrofossils and pollen are rare in this biozone. The marsh pollen and macrofossil assemblages and the algal microflora are diverse and abundant.

OCCURRENCE: Section 8, upper part of 4c and 4ii; section 1, unit 3/1/4.

INTERPRETATION: This biozone shows the 'peak' of the climatic amelioration also shown by SKE. Closed, or nearly closed, birch-poplar woodland developed in this biozone, which can be broadly equated with parts of Late-Devensian pollen zone II. On lithostratigraphic grounds, a major unconformity is present in this biozone, suggesting that lake levels fell at this time; this is mirrored in the pollen and plant macrofossil assemblages by the lack of characteristic aquatic taxa. High incidences of marsh taxa suggest that this part of the Skipsea lake basin was marshy, and the algal microflora contains several taxa which require at least seasonal standing water.

Biozone SKG

CHARACTERISTICS: High incidences of recycled pre-Quaternary palynomorphs and the occurrence of recycled pre-Quaternary megaspores, low incidences of low-diversity Quaternary pollen, algae and plant macrofossils. The assemblages are again broadly similar to SKB. Tree birch and poplar disappear, other thermophiles, such as **Helianthemum** are rare.

OCCURRENCE: Section 8, units 4iii and 4d; section 1, unit 3/1/5.

INTERPRETATION: The high incidences of recycled palynomorphs suggest accelerated erosion and an incomplete plant ground-cover. The disappearance of the tree species, together with the rarity of other thermophiles, suggests climatic deterioration, which probably set in at or below the base of unit 4iii. The incidences of tree birch and other thermophilous taxa in the basal part of this unit may result from several processes. The macrofossils of tree birch radiacarbon dated to 10,440+-80 (SRR 1943) and 10,710+-70 (Q-3035) are most likely to represent tree birch which survived into this cold stage, in sheltered habitats around the former lake. Sample SS4 has probably been introduced into its present sedimentary layer as a result of slumping and load casting. The palynological evidence of increased re-cycling of pre-Quaternary palynomorphs and hence accelerated soil erosion, suggests that some smaller macrofossils and microfossils (especially pollen) may have been re-cycled from materials laid down during biozone SKF.

The pollen, dominated by Cyperaceae and lesser Gramineae, with rare herb and dwarf shrub, together with the restricted algal pollen, suggests a low-productivity ecosystem typical of arctic conditions. A mosaic of open, disturbed ground and patches of poor grassland with occasional dwarf scrubs is suggested.

Biozone SKH

CHARACTERISTICS: High abundance, high diversity pollen floras, with the appearance of Coryloid and **Hedera**, the reappearance of tree-birch, and the disappearance of **Betula** cf. **nana**. Plant macrofossils of **Populus** and **Salix** also reappear. A diverse dwarf-shrub and herb assemblage, including **Helianthemum**, Ericaceae, Compositae (Liguliflorae), **Artemisia**, Caryophyllaceae, Chenopodiaceae, **Anthemis**-type, **Plantago**, **Polemonium**, **Epilobium**, **Valeriana** and **Succisa pratensis** is present. Incidences of Gramineae fall. Cyperaceae and other marsh and aquatic taxa are common, but the algal microflora, after a peak in the base of the biozone, shows a rapid fall.

OCCURRENCE: Section 8, units 4vi and 4vii; Section 1, unit 3/1/6 and the basal part of unit 3/1/7.

INTERPRETATION: The high incidence, high diversity pollen assemblages suggest a high-productivity ecosystem, made possible by climatic amelioration. The reappearance of tree birch, willow and poplar and the appearance of Coryloid and especially the thermophilous **Hedera** also suggest climatic emilioration. The fall in the incidence of Gramineae suggests that grassland was less extensive than in the lower biozones, but the occurrence of light-demanding taxa such as **Polemonium**, **Artemesia** and **Helianthemum** suggests that some areas of unshaded ground were still present. A vegetation of park woodland of birch, poplar-aspen and hazel, interspersed with areas of herb-rich grassland, is suggested.

Biozone SKJ

CHARACTERISTICS: Abundance of plant macrofossils and pollen of **Alnus** and **Betula**, together with common pollen of **Quercus**, **Ulmus**, **Tilia** and **Fraxinus**. Recycled palynomorphs and herb, marsh and aquatic pollen are rare. The basal sample of this biozone in section 8(1/3/7), contains a recycled Quaternary assemblage similar to those of biozones SKB-SKH. This assemblage is dominated by Cyperaceae, Gramineae, **Pinus**, **Helianthemum**, **Botrychium** and herb pollen, and can be differentiated by its weathered appearance and staining characteristics. An abundance of pre-Quaternary palynomorphs is probably the result of the same episode of recycling.

OCCURRENCE: Section 8, units 3e and 7; section 1, units 4 and 5.

INTERPRETATION: 'Full-interglacial' (i.e. Flandrian -Holocene) conditions and the presence of a local mixed-oak forest are suggested by the dominance of arboreal taxa (85-88% TP). The presence of **Quercus**, **Ulmus**, **Tilia**, **Fraxinus** and **Alnus** invites comparison with late pollen zone VI/early zone VIIa of Godwin (1975). The rarity of algal microfossils and plant macrofossils and pollen of marsh and aquatic taxa suggest rather dry conditions locally. A major unconformity at the base of this biozone is suggested on palynological grounds. This agrees with the lithostratigraphic evidence (Chapter 4). The 'dryness' of the flora suggests that the lowering of the lake level caused the unconformity. The lowering of the lake level may have been caused by higher evapotranspiration rates or lower rainfall in the early Flandrian.

SOUTHERN EXPOSURES (Section 3)

by Anne Blackham

The four samples from section 3:Figure 3.1, adjoining the flint blade, gave the pollen assemblages shown in Figure 5.11. Pollen was found to be sparse and often poorly preserved, yielding only a total of approximately 100 grains counted at each level. The tree pollen assemblage is dominated by **Betula** and **Pinus** with very small percentages of **Quercus** and **Alnus**. **Corylus/Myrica** pollen is represented by a single grain - SKIP25. Open ground land herbs are present in small numbers throughout - **Artemisia**, Compositae and the fern spores Filicales, **Pteridium**. The pollen indicates the environment at the period the blade was entrapped in lake sediment comprised the margin of an open lake, in an open, perhaps bleak, landscape.

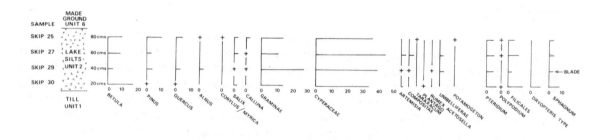

Figure 5.11 Pollen diagram from Late Devensian lake deposits (Unit 3a) at section 3 (Figure 3.1) southern exposures of the deposits of the former Skipsea Withow mere: analyses by Anne Blackham.

These pollen assemblages are broadly similar to those throughout the Late-Devensian sequence at Skipsea, but comparison with any of the detailed biozones differentiated in sections 1 and 8 does not yield any clear biostratigraphic correlation. Field mapping indicates a correlation with Skipsea biozone SKB.

COMPARISON WITH OTHER LATE DEVENSIAN DEPOSITS IN NORTHERN BRITAIN

The Late-Devensian deposits at Skipsea Withow display some similarities to and some differences from other Late-Devensian sections in northeast England. One other Late-Devensian section has been described from Holderness, at Roos Bog (Figure 7.5) (Beckett 1981). Elsewhere in Yorkshire, Late-Devensian pollen diagrams exist for Tadcaster (Bartley 1962), Seamer (Walker and Godwin 1954) and the Cleveland Dales (Jones 1977). Further afield, there are Late-Devensian pollen diagrams for Lincolnshire (Suggate and West 1959, Brown 1981), Durham (Bellamy, Bradshaw, Millington and Simmonds 1966, Turner and Kershaw 1973) and Northumberland (Bartley 1966, Bartley, Chambers and Hart-Jones 1976). Most of these sites lie in depressions in glacially-modified topography, mostly on glaciogenic deposits.

A common vegetational history can be seen at all these sites, subject to some local variation (see, for instance, the discussion in Bartley 1966, and Bartley, Chambers and Hart-Jones 1976). The sequence at Skipsea Withow seems to show the same vegetational succession, although there it is obscured by the high incidences of locally-derived pollen, especially from the lakeside flora of sedges and grasses, and by unconformities.

At Skipsea Withow and at other sites where deposition was initiated early in the Late-Devensian, there is an initial biozone with relatively high incidence of herb species such as **Artemisia**, **Thalictrum**, **Rumex** and Compositae (Liguliflorae), probably reflecting a colonising herb flora moving into the newly-deglaciated landscape.

This is succeeded by a minor peak of tree-birch, particularly at Tadcaster (Bartley 1962) and Roos (Beckett 1981) which must represent the initiation of colonisation by trees of a very open landscape. This colonisation seems, however, to have been interrupted, for the **Betula** peak is succeeded by a peak in the incidence of taxa such as **Helianthemum**, **Thalictrum**, **Artemisia**, and, at Roos, **Hippophäe**. Beckett (1981) suggested that climatic amelioration continued, to allow the expansion of the thermophilous **Helianthemum** and **Hippophäe**, but that a decrease in precipitation checked the advance of **Betula** woodland. At Skipsea, however, the rise in recycled palynomorphs suggests some climatic deterioration.

The succeeding biozone is characterised by high incidences of tree birch pollen and macrofossils. At some sites, such as Thorpe Bulmer (Bartley et al. 1976) and Tadcaster (Bartley 1962), the peak in **Betula** is preceded by a peak in **Juniperus**; at others, such as Bamburgh (Bartley 1966), Ronaldkirk (Bellamy et al. 1966), and Cranberry Bog (Turner and Kershaw 1973), the peaks of **Betula** and **Juniperus** approximately coincide. On Holderness at Roos (Beckett 1981) and at Skipsea, **Juniperus** pollen never became important, but macrofossils of Juniper appear at Skipsea some time before the appearance of tree birch. At all the sites, pollen of open-ground taxa continues to be present throughout the biozone, sometimes still at high incidences, suggesting that the woodland was never closed, and was locally replaced by herb-rich grassland. The occurrence of a significant poplar component in this woodland has not been recorded elsewhere in Yorkshire.

This biozone has been radiocarbon dated: at Aby Grange the middle of the zone gave a date of 11,205±120 B.P. (Suggate and West 1959) while at Roos Bog the biozone spanned the period 11,500±170 B.P. (Birm 318) to 11,220±120 B.P. (Birm 406) (Figure 7.2). The radiocarbon determination at Skipsea of c. 10,700 B.P. (Q 3035) falls beyond the end of the biozone; much of this biozone is missing at Skipsea Withow.

Following the **Betula** biozone lies a zone characterised by pollen of Cyperaceae, Gramineae, herbs, Birch and Pine, suggesting a treeless landscape with areas of sparsely vegetated, probably disturbed, ground. At Roos Bog this biozone ended at 10,120±180 B.P. (Birm 405), with the rise of regional Birch woodlands in the Flandrian.

The pollen diagram from Late-Devensian at Skipsea Withow is unusual only in the overwhelming dominance of the pollen of the Cyperaceae and Gramineae. This may, in large part, be ascribed to its unusual facies. The other Late-Devensian diagrams from northeast England are all from the centres of lakes, where much of the pollen rain is of regional origin. The lake-marginal position of the Skipsea Withow site means that the margin flora of the lake is relatively 'over-represented' by comparison with other pollen diagrams from the region, and the regional pollen rain is diluted, at times almost beyond recognition.

CONCLUSIONS

The palynology of the Skipsea Withow deposits suggests that lacustrine deposition was initiated early in the Late-Devensian, and continued, largely unbroken, except in Late-Devensian pollen zone II, until the early Flandrian, when there was a hiatus. Deposition recommenced relatively quickly in the more central zones of the current exposure and the evidence is discussed in Chapter 8. In the more marginal areas, the hiatus continued until peat deposits attributed to pollen zone VI of Godwin (1975) started to accumulate.

At Skipsea Withow the regional pollen rain was substantially diluted by pollen produced by the nearby lake-marginal vegetation, but is otherwise directly comparable with other Late-Devensian sequences in northeast England. The rapidity of sedimentation at Skipsea means that pollen concentrations are low, but that an unusually detailed sequence, divisible into seven local Late-Devensian assemblage-biozones, was generated and is now preserved.

CHAPTER 6

LATE DEVENSIAN MOLLUSCAN PALAEOECOLOGY OF HOLDERNESS

by N.M. Thew and D. Woodall.

INTRODUCTION

This chapter is concerned with summarising the results of molluscan studies carried out at the Withow mere site and then reviewing their significance - chronological, climatic and palaeoecological - for all of Holderness. Most of the new information presented here derives from the unpublished dissertations of Woodall (1981) and Thew (1983). Notes on the other animal groups found during this study, together with taxonomic and ecological notes on important molluscan taxa are given in the appendix to this book.

METHODS: PAST AND PRESENT

Field and laboratory

Phillips' (1829) early records of Mollusca from Holderness consist solely of qualitative assessments of a few large species visible to the naked eye, and are thus of limited use. Kennard's study (Boylan 1966), while not including detailed field notes, was made after careful laboratory extraction by washing and sieving, but its utility is now limited by the incomplete survival of the records of his counts, and no data survives as to original sample size or exact sampling location.

The laboratory processing techniques employed for the recent studies are described in detail in Woodall (1981) and Thew (1983). Though similar, Woodall sorted less than half of the oven dried (at 105°C) residue between 2mm and 0.25mm. He sorted all the residue greater than 2mm, while Thew sorted all the dried residue greater than 0.5mm as recommended by Sparks (1961 and 1964), thus introducing a numerical bias against the smaller species. Thew's method is outlined in Figure 6.1. One problem with this latter study, however, as that sample sizes varied considerably, and at an average of only 0.6kg, were well below the 1kg to 2kg recommended by workers, e.g. Sparks (1961, 1964). Molluscan nomenclature follows Waldén (1976) and Kerney (1976).

Analysis

Woodall and Thew both identified gastropods to species level using the reference collection of D.D. Gilbertson, and the standard guides produced by Ellis (1969 - land and freshwater), Evans (1972 -land), Macan (1977 [3rd edition] - freshwater) and Kerney and Cameron (1979 - land). Thew also attempted to separate slug plates (**Deroceras** spp.) with the aid of illustrations provided by Sparks (1957), although Kerney and Gilbertson (personal communication) have expressed doubts about the validity of such attempts due to the considerable morphological variability exhibited by these species.

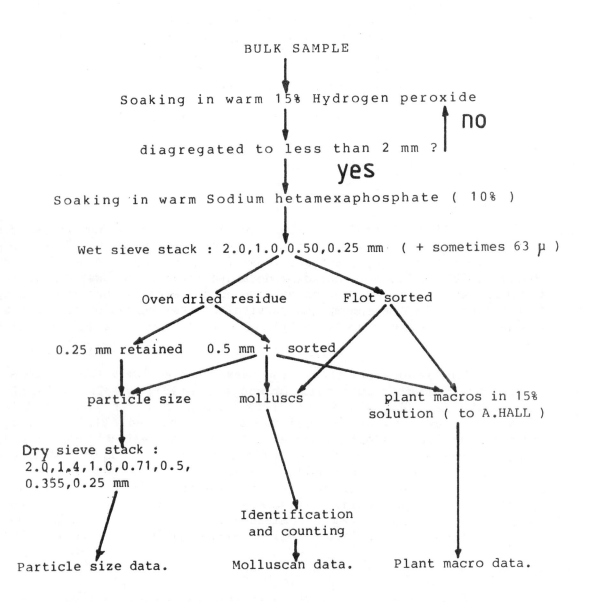

Figure 6.1 Laboratory procedures adopted by Thew (1983).

Table 6.1. LAND SNAIL COUNTS - THE CENTRAL MARGIN PROFILE SKIPSEA WITHOW MERE (SECTION 8)

SAMPLE	1	2	138b	135	136	137	5	6	7	8	9	10	11	12	13	14	15	16	23	17	24	25	18	19	20	21	30	22	32	33	34	35	LS7	36	37	38	39	40	41	42	43	44	45	LS4	LS5
Oxyloma cf. pfeifferi (Rossmässler)													1	2			1	1	1	1			6	1		9	7	1	3	4						1	1		1	1		1		1	
Succinea oblonga Draparnaud/ Catinella arenaria (Bouchard-Chantereux)																																													
Cochlicopa cf. lubrica (Müller)						1									1	1	1	2	1							3	1								1										
Vertigo genesii Gredler/ gejeri Lindholm																																											1		
Vertigo lilljeborgii (Westerlund)															1																														
Vertigo sp.															1	1		1	1	1						1													1	1		1		1	
Pupilla muscorum (L.)															5	6										5	2	2								1			1	1		1		1	
Vallonia pulchella (Müller)															4	2			1	1						10	2	1	1			1		1	1										
Punctum pygmaeum (Draparnaud)						1									13	8																		1	1										
Vitrina pellucida (Müller)																2										1									1			1							
Euconulus fulvus (Müller)																						1	1			1	1																		
Deroceras cf. agreste															3	1		2	1			1	1												1	2									
Cecilioides acicula - intrusive													1																																
Lymnaea truncatula (Müller)						1								1	7	5		3								3	1																		
Total land snails:						1							1	3	43	37	1	12	5	1	1	2	7	1		32	13	5	6	4		1		1	4	3	1	1	1	2		1	2	2	

112

Sample	1	2	138b	135	136	137	5	6	7	8	9	10	11	12	13	14	15	16	23	17	24	25	18	19	20	21	30	22	32	33	34	35	LS7	/36	37	38	39	40	41	42	43	44	45	LS4	LS5
Oxyloma cf. pfeifferi (Rossmässler)													3	3	20	17		1	1				11	1		16	12	2	5	7						2	2		2	3					
Succinea oblonga Draparnaud/																																													
Catinella arenaria Bouchard-Chantereaux																																													
Cochlicopa cf. lubrica (Müller)																2	2	2								5	2								2										
Vertigo genesii Gredler/																																											2		
geyeri Lindholm																																													
Vertigo lilljeborgii (Westerlund)																		1																											
Vertigo sp.															2	2		1	1	1	1					2														3					
Pupilla muscorum (L.)															9	12										9	3	4	3			2										2		2	
Vallonia pulchella (Müller)															7	4			1	1						13	3	2	2				2									2	2	2	
Punctum pygmaeum (Draparnaud)						2									24	16																		1	2										
Vitrina pellucida (Müller)																4																						2							
Euconulus fulvus (Müller)															4			2	2			2	2			2	2								2										
Deroceras cf. agreste															6	2		2	1			2													2	3									
Cecilioides acicula intrusive														1																															
Lymnaea truncatula (Müller)															13	10		3								5		2																	
Recalculated totals for land species						2							3	4	80	69	2	14	6	1	1	3	13	1		56	22	10	10	7		2		1	7	5	2	2	2	6		2	3	3	

N.B: Recalculated totals are the original totals recalculated to represent 1000 grammes of processed sample.

TABLE 6.2. LAND SNAIL COUNTS RECALCULATED TO REPRESENT A STANDARDISED 1000 GRAM SAMPLE – THE CENTRAL EXPOSURES (SECTION 8)

Sample	1	2	138b	135	136	137	5	6	7	8	9	10	11	12	13	14	15	16	23	17	24	25	18	19	20	21	30	22	32	33	34	35	LS7	36	37	38	39	40	41	42	43	44	45	LS4	LS5
Valvata cristata (Müller)																						59	233																					
Valvata piscinalis (Müller)													1	1			1	9	1	4	1	7	52	9	1	1	8	2	3	34	29			12	34	28	72	2	2	9	11	22	31	64	34
Bithynia tentaculata (apices) (L.)																	4	4	4	4	9	3	51	9																					
Bithynia tentaculata (opercula) (L.)														1[R]	3[R]	1[R]							170	21												1[R]									
Physa fontinalis (L.)																		2					1		1	1		1	1															
Lymnaea peregra (Müller)														1	7	2		4		1	1	2	8	10	1	15	26	5	9	12	1	2		6	36	4	40	29	7	16	16	69	2	17	16
Lymnaea sp. umbilicii *														1	9	4		6			2	3	8	8	4	19	32	17	5	5	4		1	2	17	12	28	45	16	14	19	56	2	26	24
Myxas glutinosa (Müller)																							1		1																				
Anisus leucostoma (Millet)														1	2											5	1	1		1	1														
Bathyomphalus contortus (L.)																		1				6	16	6		1	2	1		1															
Gyraulus laevis (Alder)																1	3					3				1	1			15	2				1	1	7		5	1	1			1	1
Armiger crista (L.)																		1				15	35	3		3	1	3		11							1							
Hippeutis complanatus (L.)																						5	5														1							
Total freshwater gastropods													1	3	9	3	8	21	5	9	11	102	521	49	4	27	39	13	13	74	33	2	1	18	71	33	121	32	14	26	28	91	33	82	51

(not inc. recycled operculae or L. sp. umbilicii, R and * respectively)

TABLE 6.3. ORIGINAL WATER SNAIL COUNTS - SKIPSEA WITHOW (EXPOSURE 8)

TABLE 6.4. WATER SNAIL COUNTS RECALCULATED TO REPRESENT A STANDARDISED 1000 GRAM SAMPLE - SECTION 8

Sample	1	2	13Bb	135	136	137	5	6	7	8	9	10	11	12	13	14	15	16	23	17	24	25	18	19	20	21	30	22	32	33	34	35	LS7	36	37	38	39	40	41	42	43	44	45	LS4	LS5
Valvata cristata (Müller)																						97	414																						
Valvata piscinalis (Müller)													3	1			2	9	1	4	1	11	92	13	1	2	14	4	5	57	49			16	55	47	115		3	26	19	37	52	110	58
Bithynia tentaculata (apices) (L.)														1[R]	6	2	8	5	5	1		5	91	13																					
Bithynia tentaculata (operculae) (L.)																		2		4	10	16	302	31												2[R]									
Physa fontinalis (L.)																		2					2		2	2	2	2																	
Lymnaea peregra (Müller)														1	13	4	5	5		1	1	3	15	15	1	26	44	10	15	20	2	3		8	58	7	64	60	12	46	27	115	3	29	27
Lymnaea sp. umbilicii														1	16	7	7	7		2	2	5	15	12	1	33	55	34	9	8	7		2	3	27	20	45	93	28	40	33	93	3	45	41
Myxas glutinosa (Müller)																							2			2							2												
Anisus leucostoma (Müller)													1		4								2		1	9	2	2	2	2															
Bathyomphalus contortus (L.)																		1				10	28	9		2	3			2							2								
Gyraulus laevis (Alder)																2		6				5				1		2		25	3			2	2	11		9	3	2				
Armiger crista (L.)																		1		1		25	62	4		2	2	6	2	19	2					2	2			3		2		2	5
Hippeutis complanatus (L.)																							10			2		2										2							
Recalculated total freshwater gastropods (not inc. recycled operculae)													3	4	16	6	16	23	6	9	12	167	996	73	5	48	67	26	22	128	56	3	2	24	118	55	199	66	24	75	48	152	55	141	88

N.B: Recalculated totals are the original totals recalculated to represent 1000 grammes of processed sample.

114

Bivalves were identified with the help of the same reference material, the standard work by Ellis (1979), an excellent set of illustrations provided by Kuiper (in Stelfox, Kuiper, McMillan and Mitchell 1972), and personal assistance provided by Dr. M.P. Kerney.

Most of the land snails consisted of apical fragments only, so the short guide by Preece (1981) on shell microsculpture proved most useful. Even so it proved impossible to separate **Cochlicopa lubrica** (Müller) from **Cochlicopa lubricella** (Porro), although the former is generally more common, while the **Succineidae** were attributed to **Oxyloma pfeifferi** (Rossmässler) only with the help of Dr. M.P. Kerney. Dr. Kerney also checked the identifications of the Vertiginidae, notably the rare specimen of **Vertigo lilljeborgii** (Westerlund). Other problems encountered with identifying the apical fragments of land species have been overcome with the help of Dr. R. Preece.

The freshwater snails proved to be much more straightforward except for the Valvatidae; these can be fairly variable and in the juvenile stage the flattened spire variety **alpestris** of the species **Valvata piscinalis** (Müller) can resemble **Valvata cristata** Müller and **Valvata macrostoma** Mörch (Fretter and Graham 1978 – with some useful SEM photographs).

The freshwater bivalves, however, proved much more difficult to identify as there are some dozen species of **Pisidia** known from the Late-Devensian, all superficially similar, and all subject to considerable morphological variation. Woodall's 1981 bivalve counts are reliable only in the separation of the distinctive **Pisidium amnicum** (Müller), **Pisidium obtusale** (Lamarck) and **Pisidium henslowanum** (Sheppard). Thew's (1983) **Pisidium** results are reliable only because of the considerable help received in checking identifications from Dr. M.P. Kerney. This latter study was also able to separate the fragile and much broken fragments of **Sphaerium corneum** (Linnaeus) by their larger size, except in samples where **Pisidium amnicum** was present, when shell microsculpture was examined.

Quantification

Reliable quantification of molluscan remains has always proved difficult due to the processes of sedimentological transport, deposition and compaction, which act differently on the various molluscan species causing considerable biases in patterns of survival and accumulation, and hence their ability to be extracted, identified and quantified by the analyst. Further taphonomic problems include erosion and recycling of more resistant elements like slug plates, the opercula of Bithyniidae, and the hinge fragments from mature individuals of the larger bivalve species like **Sphaerium corneum** or **Pisidium amnicum**.

In an attempt to combat one of these biases, the practice of separating Bithyniidae apex counts from valves for the opercula (Gilbertson 1980) has been followed. Both Woodall and Thew separated hinge fragments into their constituent four groups (LL, LR, RR, RL) and for all the Sphaeriidae counts were made of both right and left complete valves, and articulated specimens so as to give a crude MNI

PISIDIUM HIBERNICUM VAR. PORTENSA
RT. VALVE

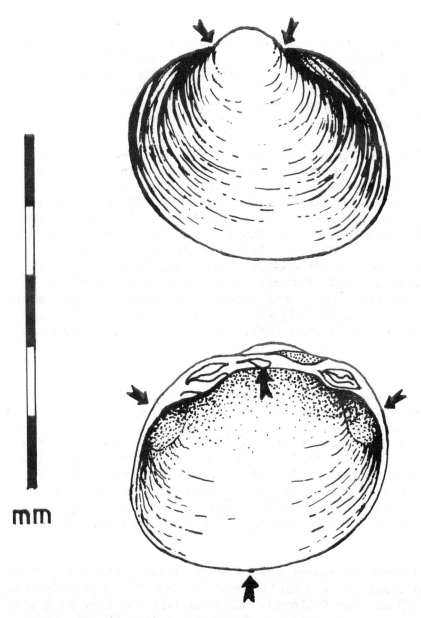

mm

Figure 6.2 Breakage patterns in bivalve molluscs, arrows indicate
characteristic loci of break.

value (Minimum Number of Individuals; crude because no attempt was made
to match up valves, the largest count of L or R being taken as the MNI
value) and a rough gauge of taphonomic loss (i.e. differences in count
values between L, R, and Whole). Thew also attempted to count both
apices and umbilicii of **Lymnaea peregra** (Müller) as a further
taphonomic indicator. No attempt was made to differentiate between
fresh and recycled molluscan remains, although a qualitative assessment
showed that only slug plates, Bithyniidae operculae, and large
bivalve hinge fragments were robust enough to survive recycling.

Kennard's counts include none of these refinements, and it is
not certain whether bivalve values refer to valve counts or halved
valve counts.

RESULTS

Results of the recent studies of profiles from the site will
be presented and discussed first, as these are the most detailed
records to date; earlier records will then be compared and contrasted.

Tables 6.1, 6.3 and 6.5 give the original counts for the land
and freshwater gastropods and bivalves from the central exposures
(section 8; Figure 3.7). **Lymnaea truncatula** (Müller) has been
included with the land species for the main central profile (section 8)
while Tables 6.2, 6.4 and 6.6 list these abundance values recalculated
to give the frequency per 1kg of sample (note: due to recalculation,
addition of species totals does not always exactly match total values
for each sample). Tables 6.9, 6.10 and 6.11 list original counts and
recalculated values for the northern profile (section 1; Figure 3.3)
while Tables 6.12 and 6.14 give the same data for the small,
unpublished counts made from different locations on the southern margin
(section 3; Figure 3.2). Finally, Table 6.13 details the additional
molluscan records made by Phillips and Kennard which cannot be
recalculated.

Tables 6.2, 6.4, 6.6, 6.9, 6.10 and 6.11 list the molluscan
totals for land species, freshwater snails, and freshwater bivalves for
all samples from the main central and northern profiles, in addition to
the number of species, and the land:freshwater and freshwater
gastropod: bivalve ratios (bracketed where not significant). Of these
indices, the number of species is probably least reliable as the data
set includes several species represented by small numbers which appear
only sporadically through the sequences, due to the relatively small
sample sizes and a stochastic element. The land:freshwater index is
similarly prone to fluctuations, possibly resulting from chance and
sample size. The freshwater gastropod:bivalve ratio is potentially
much more significant, however, as fluctuations seem to have some
statistical validity.

Taphonomy

As noted above, relatively few data were gathered on the
effects of fragmentation (Figure 6.2) and attrition caused by either
depositional processes or the disaggregation procedure which tends, as
Sparks observed (1961, 1964) to be rather brutal when dealing with

Species	Side	1	2	138b	135	136	137	5	6	7	8	9	10	11	12	13	14	15	16	23	17	24	25	18
Sphaerium corneum (L.)	L										1		1		2	25	8	1	6	10	12	6	11	57
	R												2		1	30	11		10	10	10	9	19	71
	W																							
	MNI										1		2		2	30	11	1	10	10	12	9	19	71
Sphaerium lacustre (Müller)	L																		1					
	R																							
	W																							
	MNI																		1					
Pisidium amnicum (Müller)	L																							
	R																							
	W																							
	MNI																							
Pisidium casertanum A (Poli)	L													1	1		3		1	1	1	1	5	3
	R														1		1		2	1	3	3	4	4
	W																							
	MNI													1	1		3		2	1	3	3	5	4
Pisidium casertanum B	L															1								4
	R															1			1					2
	W																							
	MNI															1			1					4
var.	L																							
	R																							
	W																							
	MNI																							
Pisidium casertanum var. ponderosa	L																							
	R																							
	W																							
	MNI																							
Pisidium obtusale (Lamarck)	L																1		1	1				1
	R																		1			1		2
	W																							
	MNI																1		1	1		1		2
Pisidium obtusale var. lapponicum	L																		1					2
	R																		1					5
	W																							
	MNI																		1					5
Pisidium milium Held	L														1								5	20
	R																						4	21
	W																							
	MNI														1								5	21
Pisidium subtruncatum Malm	L			1												6	2	1	24	22	1	24	2	28
	R		1													6	3	1	18	19	3	16	5	20
	W																		1					
	MNI		1	1												6	3	1	25	22	3	24	5	28
var.	L																							1
	R																1			1				1
	W																							
	MNI																1			1				1
Pisidium lilljeborgii Clessin	L																			2		3		2
	R																		3	3				3
	W																							
	MNI																		3	3		3		3
Pisidium hibernicum A Westerlund	L																							
	R																							
	W																							
	MNI																							
Pisidium hibernicum B Westerlund	L																		1	6	1	4		10
	R																			4	2	4		16
	W																							
	MNI																		1	6	2	4		16
var.	L																							1
	R																							
	W																							
	MNI																							1
Pisidium nitidum Jenyns	L														5	15	8	2	5	3	4	6	12	53
	R													1	3	21	7	3	6	3	3	4	11	43
	W																						2	1
	MNI													1	5	21	8	3	6	3	4	6	14	54
FRY	L															12	9	1	6	2	3	3	10	13
	R													1		16	13		2	2	3	2	14	19
	W																		1					1
	MNI													1		16	13	1	7	2	3	3	14	20
Hinge fragments	No.	1												1		2	9	2	14	25	15	23	34	196
— 4	MNI	1												1		1	3	1	4	7	4	6	9	49
Total bivalves	MNI	1	1	1							1		2	4	9	77	43	7	60	57	32	58	72	279

TABLE 6.5. ORIGINAL BIVALVE COUNTS – SKIPSEA WITHOW MERE (SECTION 8)

118

19	20	21	30	22	32	33	34	35	LS7	36	37	38	39	40	41	42	43	44	45	LS4	LS5
39	29	55	127	79	38									1					1	15	11
48	26	36	125	84	31				1			1		4						17	10
		1																			
48	29	56	127	84	38				1			1		4					1	17	11
1																					
1																					
	5	50	28	18	36	22	11	1		2	6		1		1						
	3	42	31	25	34	23	8			4	5		3	3	1						
		2									1										
	5	52	31	25	36	23	11	1		4	7		3	3	1						
3			4	2								1	27	14	18	3	5			4	11
1			5									2	26	14	19	5	5			2	19
3			5	2	1							2	27	14	19	5	5			4	19
			2	2								1	29	14	12	3	1				3
			2	2	1							1	24	11	8	2	1				2
																					3
			2	2	1							1	29	14	12	3	1				5
													2	2	4						
													1	2	3						
													2	2	4						
																					2
																					2
																					2
		1		1								1									
		1										1									
		1		1								1									
		1																			
				1			1														
		1		1			1														
		12	26	10	3	3							8	5	6						
1	2	11	22	12	2	4							5	9	6						
		4	3	1																	
1	2	16	29	12	4	4							8	9	6						
3	1	23	45	10	15	10						2	10	1	1	1	5			7	9
7	4	23	57	13	11	14							14	2	1	3	3			8	8
		2		1	2															1	
7	4	25	57	14	17	14						2	14	2	1	3	5			9	9
		1	1	1	2	2						1	1								
		1	1	1	1	2						1	1								
		1	1	1	2	2						1	1	1							
		4	1			2	1						2		2		1	6	5	23	1
		3				2	1								4			7	4	19	1
		4	1			2	1						2		4		1	7	5	23	1
			1				1				1							1	1	1	1
		1	1		2	2									2					1	1
		1		1	2	2					1				2			1	1	1	1
14	14	4	61	20	1		1						25	5	42	4	15	71	75	70	10
14	14	4	55	19	1		2						25	3	34	2	14	77	71	64	7
		4	1	13	1								1		1			6	1	1	
14	18	5	74	21	1		2						26	5	43	4	15	83	76	71	10
				6	6								7	2			1				
				3	5	1							7	4	1					1	
				6	6	1							7	4	1		1	1			
6	6	42	71	27	10	14	1				2	2	7	2	4		3	1	2	11	7
9	5	50	52	22	11	13					1	1	9	1	3		3		3	9	3
	6	4	3	3											1			3		1	
9	6	56	75	30	14	14	1				2	2	10	2	4		3	4	3	12	7
3	2	17	43	9	18	31						1	21	13	17	2	12	41	7	97	15
4	3	15	41	9	11	26							14	9	15	1	7	40	7	93	10
	1	6	6	2									1	1				2		6	
4	4	23	49	11	18	31						1	22	14	17	2	12	43	7	103	15
33	59	21	86	51	31	21	34					3	58	78	55	21	8	27	22	85	27
9	15	6	22	13	8	6	9					1	15	20	14	6	2	7	6	42	7
82	65	252	420	208	221	120	24	1	1	6	15	7	164	94	128	23	44	146	100	282	87

Note: L = Left valve, R = Right valve, W = Complete articulated bivalve

119

	1	2	138b	135	136	137	5	6	7	8	9	10	11	12	13	14	15	16	23	17	24	25	18	19	20	21	30	22	32	33	34	35	LS7	36	37	38	39	40	41	42	43	44	45	LS4	LS5
Sphaerium corneum (L.)															56	20	2	11	13	12	10	31	136	71	34	99	217	168	65				2			2		8					2	29	19
Sphaerium lacustre (Müller)																								1																					
Pisidium amnicum (Müller)																																												7	
Pisidium casertanum A (Poli)													3	1		6		2	1	3	3	8	8	4	6	92	53	50	61	40	19	2		5	3		45	29	33	14	9			7	33
Pisidium casertanum B															2												4	4	2								48	29	27	9	2				5
ditto variety																																					3	4	7						
total casertanum													3	1	2	6		3	1	3	3	8	15	4		12		10	3								96	62	60	23	10			7	38
Pisidium casertanum var. ponderosa																																											2		
Pisidium obtusale (Lamarck)																			1	1		2	4		2	2	2	2																	
Pisidium obtusale var. lapponicum																			1			2	10		2	2	2	2			2														
Pisidium milium Held														1								8	40	1	2	28	50	24	7	7						13	19		10		.				
Pisidium subtruncatum Malm	2	2													11		2	28	28	3	26	8	54	10	5	44	98	28	29	24						3	23	4	2	9	9			15	15
ditto variety																										2	1	2	3	4						2	2	2							
total subtruncatum	2	2													11	7	2	28	30	3	26	8	55	10	5	46	99	30	32	28						5	25	6	2	9	9			15	15
Pisidium lilljeborgii Clessin																		3	4		3		6		7	2	7	2	3	3	2		2	3		3		7		2	12	8		40	2
Pisidium hibernicum A Westerlund																						2							3		2		2	3							2	2		2	2
Pisidium hibernicum B																		1	8			25	31			31	10	126	36	2			3			43	10	74	12	26	138	127	122	17
ditto variety																						2					12	10	2							12	8	3	2		2		2	
total hibernicum																		1	8			26	32			31	24	140	42	2			3		2	54	19	79	12	26	142		124	19
Pisidium nitidum Jenyns											3	7	39	15	6	7	4	4	7	23	103	13	7	99	128	60	24	24	2				3		3	16	4	7	5	7	5		21	12
FRY											3		30	24	2	8	3	3	3	23	38	6	5	41	52	22	31	54	10	15				2	1	36	29	29	6	21	72	12	177	26
Hinge fragment M.N.I.			2																																2									72	12
Recalculated totals:	2	2	2								1	3	12	12	143	80	14	68	74	33	64	118	533	122	76	444	719	416	377	208	40	2	2	8	25	12	270	195	220	66	75	243	167	484	149

Note: Recalculated totals are the original totals directly recalculated to represent 1000 grammes of processed sample.

notes: P. casertanum   - A = Kuiper No. 2 in Stelfox et al 1972
                            B = Kuiper No. 1
                      B var = Kuiper No. 3

       P. subtruncatum   - = Kuiper No. 23
                         var. = Kuiper No. 22

       P. lilljeborgii - = Kuiper Nos. 25, 26, 28, 29 var. constricta

       P. hibernicum - A = Kuiper Nos. 7, 8, forma normalis
                     B = Kuiper Nos. 6, 9, 11, forma portensa
                 B var + Kuiper No. 10, form intermediate

TABLE 6.6. BIVALVE COUNTS RECALCULATED TO REPRESENT A STANDARDISED 1000 GRAMMES OF PROCESSED SAMPLE
SKIPSEA WITHOW (SECTION 8)

Sample	Land Snails Original	Land Snails Recalculated	Freshwater Snails Original	Freshwater Snails Recalculated	Freshwater Bivalves Original	Freshwater Bivalves Recalculated	Total Freshwater Original	Total Freshwater Recalculated	Total Molluscs Original	Total Molluscs Recalculated
1										
2					1	2	1	2	1	2
138b					1	2	1	2	1	2
135					1	2	1	2	1	2
136										
137	1	2							1	
5										
6										
7										
8							·1			
9					1	1	1	1	1	1
10					2	3	2	3	2	3
11	1	3	1	3	4	12	5	15	6	18
12	3*	4	3	4	9	12	12	16	15	20
13	43	80	9	16	77	143	86	159	129	239
14	37	69	3	6	43	80	46	85	83	154
15	1	2	8	16	7	14	15	30	16	32
16	12	14	21	23	60	68	81	92	93	106
23	5	6	5	6	57	74	62	80	67	87
17	1	1	9	9	32	33	41	42	42	43
24	1	1	11	12	58	64	69	76	70	77
25	2	3	102	167	72	118	174	285	176	288
18	7	13	521	996	279	533	800	1529	807	1542
19	1	1	49	73	82	122	131	194	132	196
20			4	5	65	76	69	81	69	81
21	32	56	27	48	252	444	279	491	311	548
30	13	22	39	67	420	719	459	786	472	808
22	5	10	13	26	208	416	221	442	226	452
32	6	10	13	22	221	377	234	399	240	409
33	4	7	74	128	120	208	194	336	198	343
34			33	56	24	40	57	96	57	96
35	1	2	2	3	1	2	3	5	4	7
LS7			1	2	1	2	2	4	2	4
36	1	1	18	24	6	8	24	32	25	33
37	4	7	71	118	15	25	86	143	90	149
38	3	5	33	55	7	12	40	67	43	72
39	1	2	121	199	164	270	285	470	286	472
40	1	2	32	66	94	195	126	262	127	264
41	1	2	14	24	128	220	142	244	143	246
42	2	6	26	75	23	66	49	141	51	147
43			28	48	44	75	72	124	72	124
44	1	2	91	152	146	243	237	395	238	397
45	2	3	33	55	100	167	133	223	135	226
LS4	2	3	82	141	282	484	364	625	366	629
LS5			51	88	87	149	138	237	138	237

*Cecilioides acicula is not included in the totals as it is probably intrusive

Table 6.7 ORIGINAL AND RECALCULATED MOLLUSCAN TOTALS AND DIAGNOSTIC INDICES – THE CENTRAL PROFILE (SECTION 8)

strongly cohesive fine sediments. Recycling was not quantified either. Some idea of pre-treatment depositional energy is given, however, by the frequency of articulated specimens of **Pisidium** and complete **Sphaerium** valves.

Sparks (1964) has discussed patterns of depositional attrition and most of his conclusions were confirmed by this study: **Sphaerium** spp. (especially the younger, smaller specimens prior to shell thickening) and thin-shelled **Lymnaea peregra** are particularly fragile, while among the Planorbidae, **Bathymophalus contortus** (Linnaeus) and **Hippeutis complanatus** (Linnaeus) are also extremely fragile. These species are extremely unlikely to have been capable of surviving recycling or energetic transport and deposition. By contrast, the apices of thick walled species like **Bithynia tentaculata** (Linnaeus) survived fairly well, although this snail was never found complete in its adult form. B. tentaculata operculae survived recycling but tended to split along the layers to form 'pseudo-operculae'; thus only the central portions of operculae should be counted, although this procedure was unfortunately not employed during either recent study.

Among the bivalves, hinge fragments of many species seem fairly resistant, but there was no evidence that any of these had been recycled except for fragments from the large adult specimens of **Sphaerium corneum** and **Pisidium amnicum**. **Pisidium nitidum** Jenyns is often recognised by its distinctive nepionic grooves on the umbo; these, however, seem prone to taphonomic removal although vestigial banding may still be seen if the shells are held up to a light source.

Of considerable interest was evidence among the freshwater molluscs of chemical weathering to the shells, which took the form of solution holes. Moreover, within many of the assemblages from the various sampled levels, differential patterns of solution weathering could be qualitatively observed, clearly indicating an element of post-mortem mixing of death assemblages before eventual deposition and burial.

Among the land species, the Succineidae survived fairly well, despite their extreme fragility, because of their extreme hygrophyllic habitat preference. Less water-loving species like the Valloniidae survived less well (although all the 'terrestrial' species were hygrophylic to some degree) with their distinctive aperture rarely retained by the shell, while the **Pupilla muscorum** (Linnaeus) specimens were all broken, and the Zonitidae only survived as apices. Slug plates, however, are extremely resistant, though the few specimens seemed fresh and free from the effects of recycling.

Juveniles

Juveniles were found in section 8 to be especially common among the land snail group, the freshwater Valvatidae and Sphaeriidae, but these were counted without distinction from the adults except for the genus **Pisidium**, where 'fry' values include all extremely small individuals too young to identify with confidence. In future work, however, account should be taken of the fact that different species produce young in greatly varying numbers annually, the death rate varying in direct proportion to the number of fry produced. Moreover, juveniles of species like **Sphaerium corneum** and **Lymnaea peregra** were not preserved because of their extreme fragility.

LOCAL MOLLUSCAN ASSEMBLAGE ZONES

Figure 6.3 represents a summary diagram for recalculated molluscan counts from the main central profile (section 8). Local molluscan assemblage zones are also shown, these having been delineated on the basis of the abundance and species composition for each sample. Tables 6.7, 6.8 and 6.9 list the criteria used to delineate local molluscan assemblage zones - main species, significant species, 'indicator species' - which when present have ecological or environmental significance, as well as abundance and ratio data.

THE CENTRAL PROFILE (Section 8)

Local molluscan assemblage zone LMAZ-A1: **Pisidium hibernicum - Valvata piscinalis - Pisidium casertanum - Lymnaea peregra - Pisidum lilljeborgii**

This assemblage presents an interesting dichotomy between the bivalves whose diversity indicates a fairly well developed level of habitat specialisation, and the gastropods which are represented only by three generalist taxa. This can be explained by reference to the freshwater gastropod:bivalve ratio; the low value indicates locally poor aquatic macrovegetation either due to deeper water, adverse conditions, or an early stage in the vegetational colonisation of a lake/pond margin habitat. The rationale for this assertion lies in the fact that most Sphaeriidae are bottom dwellers, being mostly filter feeders which breathe by absorbing dissolved oxygen while typically living burrowed in soft substrate (Boycott 1936, Meier-Brook 1969, Green 1971). On the other hand, gastropods tend to live on vegetation or in other shallow lake margin habitats. The pulmonate gastropods are lung breathers, which need to come to the surface regularly, except for **Lymnaea peregra** which can absorb dissolved oxygen in colder water, feeding by grazing on detritus, algae, etc. collecting on vegetation and stones. Prosobranch gastropods, such as the Valvatidae and Bithyniidae are gill breathers, which enable them to live at greater depths, feeding both by grazing or by filtration on either the vegetation or substrate (Boycott 1936, Young, M. 1975, Reavell 1980). In this case a low gastropod: bivalve ratio probably indicates either deeper water or poorly developed marginal macrovegetation.

Consideration of the species composition throws further light on the problem. Of the gastropods, **Valvata piscinalis** and **Lymnaea peregra** are the only two such species found at depths of up to 9 or 10 metres (Macan 1950, Fretter and Graham 1978); both, however, are also tolerant of poorly developed aquatic vegetation (Okeland 1969, 1979). **Gyraulus laevis** (Alder) is the only other gastropod present which is characteristic of poorly vegetated (successionally 'primitive') shallow lake margin habits (Boycott 1936, Norris, Bartley and Gaunt 1971, Stelfox et al. 1972, Kerney, Gibbard, Hall and Robinson 1982),

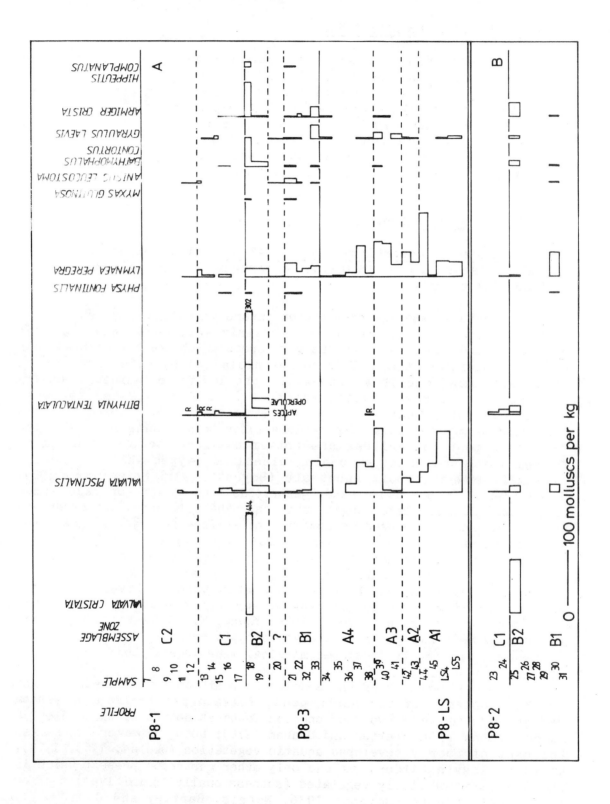

124

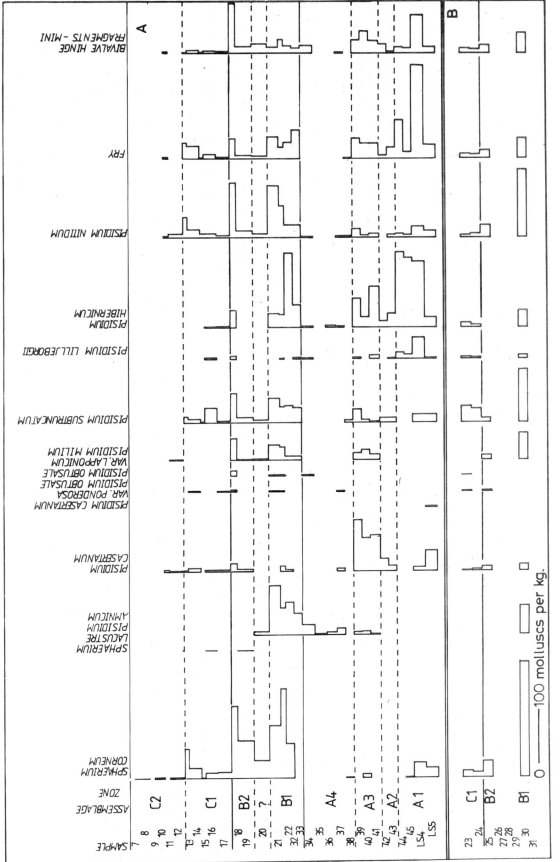

Figure 6.3 Frequency histograms for the recalculated molluscan studies from the Late Devensian deposits at Skipsea Withow mere (section 8: Figure 3.1).

125

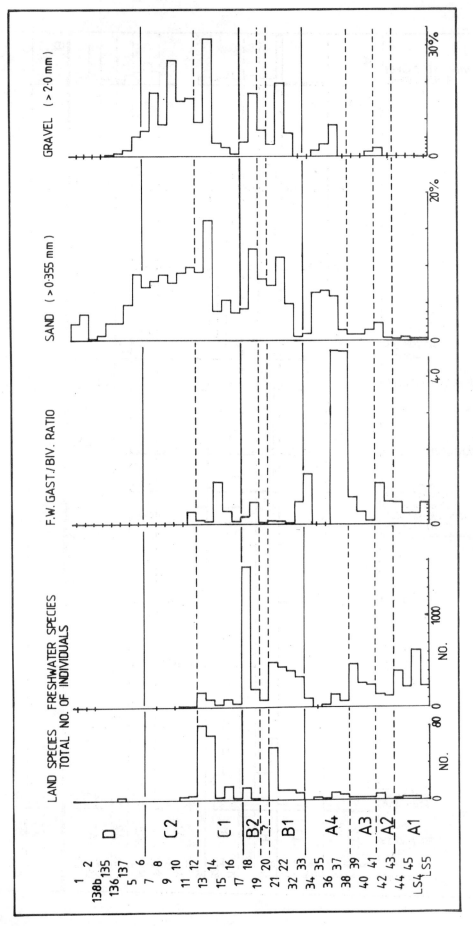

Figure 6.4 A comparison of the recalculated molluscan totals with the sample sand and gravel contents.

126

suggesting this as the most plausible explanation for the small numbers of gastropods present. **G. laevis** and **V. piscinalis** also prefer clean, eutrophic water conditions, with moderate dissolved calcium carbonate (Boycott 1936, Okeland 1969). **V. piscinalis** prefers a soft substrate, while the other two gastropod species are normally associated with stony bottoms.

The bivalves are all species tolerant of a poorly developed macrovegetation, none requiring much water hardness, although **Sphaerium corneum**, **Pisidium subtruncatum** Malm, **Pisidium lilljeborgii** Clessin, **Pisidium hibernicum** Westerlund and **Pisidium nitidum** all prefer clear, eutrophic water conditions. **P. lilljeborgii**, **Pisidium casertanum** (Poli), **P. nitidum** and **P. hibernicum** are very commonly associated in lowland, plateau lake settings (for example the Alpine Plateau (Jayet 1973), the Canadian Shield (Green 1971) and the Pyrenees), the first two preferring relatively deeper water and the latter two commonly in shallower conditions less than 4 metres deep (Meier-Brook 1969, Green 1971). In England, **P. subtruncatum** is often found with **P. casertanum** and **P. nitidum** in eutrophic lakes with **Sphaerium corneum** in addition to shallower locations (e.g. Paul 1976). **P. casertanum**, **P. nitidum**, and especially **P. lilljeborgii** (see appendix; ecological notes) all prefer fine organic mud substrates in low energy environments, while **P. hibernicum** and **S. corneum** are more commonly associated with coarser littoral locations among stones or vegetation (Meier-Brook 1969, Green 1971).

Pisidium lilljeborgii has very seldom been recorded from the fossil record, with only two published sites from the Late-Devensian (see taphonomic and ecological notes); this is probably due, however, not to an absolute rarity so much as a lack of previous malacological analyses of low energy lake margin locations such as the present Skipsea Withow mere exposures. Another rarity is **P. casertanum** var. **ponderosa**; this rare form is always found with normal **P. casertanum**, and Ellis (1962:42) claims that it is characteristic today of "specially favourable habitats such as large rivers". This would be its first record from the Late-Devensian, although M.P. Kerney when he examined the specimens indicated that they are not as robust as most typical **ponderosa** examples he has seen previously.

Taphonomically, the significant number of articulated bivalves indicates a fairly low energy depositional environment, while the large numbers of 'fry' present might indicate high infant mortality rates.

The land species are both typical of damp or marshy ground. The specimen of **Vertigo geyeri/genesii** suggests calcareous or neutral soils, while **Vallonia pulchella** (Müller) indicates grassland, with perhaps a lack of surrounding terrestrial tree/shrub vegetation.

Summary: The assemblage seems to comprise two contemporary faunas from adjacent shallower and deeper water habitats, the former being more littoral in character, possibly with a more stony substrate. In both locations the macrovegetation was poorly developed with eutrophic, possibly calcareous, water and a fairly low energy depositional environment.

Sample	LMAZ	Dominant species	Significant species	Indicator species (of climate and vegetational succession)
1 2 138b 135 136 137 5 6	D	Mo l l u s c s n o t p r e s e r v e d		
7 8 9 10 11 12	C₂	Sphaerium corneum Pisidium nitidum	Valvata piscinalis Pisidium casertanum	
13 14 15 16 23 17 24	C₁	Sphaerium corneum Pisidium subtruncatum Pisidium nitidum		Bithynia tentaculata Armiger crista
25 18 19	B₂	Valvata cristata Bithynia tentaculata	Sphaerium corneum, Valvata piscinalis, Pisidium nitidum, Armiger crista, Pisidium subtruncatum, Pisidium milium	Valvata cristata, Myxas glutinosa, Bithynia tentaculata, Armiger crista, Hippeutis complanatus, Physa fontinalis, Pisidium milium
20	?			
21 30 22 32 33	B₁	Sphaerium corneum, Pisidium milium, Pisidium nitidum Pisidium hibernicum Pisidium amnicum Pisidium subtruncatum	Lymnaea peregra	Physa fontinalis Myxas glutinosa Armiger crista Hippeutis complanatus Pisidium milium
34 35 LS7 36 37 38	A₄	Valvata piscinalis Lymnaea peregra Pisidium amnicum		
39 40 41	A₃	Pisidium casertanum Pisidium milium Pisidium hibernicum Lymnaea peregra	Pisidium subtruncatum, Gyraulus laevis, Pisidium nitidum, Pisidium amnicum, Valvata piscinalis	Armiger crista Pisidium milium
42 43	A₂	Lymnaea peregra, Pisidium hibernicum, Valvata piscinalis Pisidium casertanum	Pisidium subtruncatum	
44 45 LS4 LS5	A₁	Pisidium hibernicum Lymnaea peregra Valvata piscinalis Pisidium casertanum	Sphaerium corneum Pisidium subtruncatum Pisidium lilljeborgii	Pisidium casertanum var. ponderosa

Table 6.8   SPECIES CHARACTERISING THE LOCAL MOLLUSCAN ASSEMBLAGE ZONES FOR THE CENTRAL PROFILE (SECTION 8)

128

Sample	Land/F.W. Ratio	F.W. Gastropod/ F.W. Bivalve ratio	Number of Species: F.W. gastropod	F.W. bivalve	Total	Local Molluscan Assemblage Zone
1	(0)	(0)	–	1	1	
2	(0)	(0)	–	1	1	
138b	(0)	(0)	–	1	1	
135	–	–	–	–	–	D
136	–	–	–	–	–	
137	(00)	–	–	–	–	
5	–	–	–	–	–	
6	–	–	–	–	–	
7	–	–	–	–	–	
8	(0)	(0)	–	1	1	
9	–	–	–	–	–	
10	(0)	(0)	–	1	1	C_2
11	(0.20)	(0.25)	1	2	3	
12	0.25	0.33	3	4	7	
13	0.50	0.12	3	4	7	
14	0.80	0.07	3	5	8	
15	0.07	1.14	3	3	6	
16	0.15	0.35	6	7	13	C_1
23	0.08	0.09	2	7	9	
17	0.02	0.28	4	6	10	
24	0.01	0.19	3	6	9	
25	0.01	1.42	7	6	13	
18	0.01	1.87	9	8	17	B_2
19	0.01	0.60	5	6	11	
20	0	0.06	4	5	9	?
21	0.11	0.11	9	7	16	
30	0.03	0.09	6	8	14	
22	0.02	0.06	6	9	15	B_1
32	0.03	0.06	3	7	10	
33	0.02	0.62	6	6	12	
34	0	1.38	4	5	9	
35	(0.33)	(2.00)	1	1	2	
LS7	(0)	(1.00)	1	1	2	A_4
36	0.04	3.00	2	2	4	
37	0.04	4.73	3	5	8	
38	0.08	4.71	3	3	6	
39	0.004	0.74	6	7	13	
40	0.01	0.34	3	7	10	A_3
41	0.01	0.11	3	7	10	
42	0.04	1.13	3	3	6	A_2
43	0	0.64	3	5	8	
44	0.01	0.62	2	3	5	
45	0.02	0.33	2	4	6	A_1
LS4	0.01	0.29	3	6	9	
LS5	0	0.59	3	6	9	

TABLE 6.9. ABUNDANCE AND RATIO CRITERIA ALSO USED TO DELINEATE THE LOCAL MOLLUSCAN ASSEMBLAGE ZONES SET OUT IN TABLE 6.8; SECTION 8; SKIPSEA WITHOW MERE.

LMAZ-A2:   **Lymnaea peregra - Valvata piscinalis - Pisidium hibernicum - Pisidium casertanum**

        This zone is very similar to the one below, except for a marked decrease in overall numbers (accounting for the absolute decrease in **V. piscinalis, P. lilljeborgii** etc.), and a significant increase in the gastropod:bivalve ratio. This latter index change may be due to the partial destruction of suitable soft substrate bivalve habitats, as evidenced by an increase in the percentage of sand and fine grit within the matrix sediments. This change happened after the sharp decline in molluscan numbers. A more likely explanation involving general environmental deterioration may be suggested by the sharp decline in **P. hibernicum**, which prefers vegetated littoral locations (Meier-Brook 1969), and **S. corneum**, an indicator of 'goodness' of habitat, as it prefers to graze on macrovegetation (Boycott 1936). The loss of these species was contemporary with a marked rise in the numbers of **Lymnaea peregra**, an aquatic taxon of wide ecological tolerance and which thrives in competition-free environments.

        The land species are again indicative of marginal marsh or damp ground, both species being highly generalist and of broad ecological tolerance (Kerney and Cameron 1979).

        Summary: Ecologically, this zone is very similar to that below except for a probable decline in macrovegetation, and a general fall in habitat suitability with an increase in the energy of the depositional environment halfway through the zone, confirmed by an increase in sand deposited and an absence of articulated bivalves.

LMAZ-A3:   **Pisidium casertanum - Pisidium hibernicum - Lymnaea peregra - Pisidum milium**

        Ecologically, this zone is again fairly similar to those preceding, except for a very sharp rise and peak in molluscan species and numbers which may be indicative of a more favourable environment. The slight increase in the gastropod:bivalve index correlates with significant changes in species composition to indicate a considerable development in the abundance and diversity of aquatic macrovegetation. **Armiger crista** (Linnaeus) and **Bathyomphalus contortus** both appear, together with a few **Bithynia tentaculata** (as shown by the recycled operculae in the base of the zone immediately above) and a significantly large number of **Pisidium milium** Held. **A. crista, B. tentaculata** and **P. milium** all require a considerable development of macrovegetation (Macan 1950, Okeland 1969, Young, J. 1975, Dussart 1976, Fretter and Graham 1978). **P. milium** is unlike most **Pisidium** species because it lives on vegetation and not upon the substrate (Boycott 1936), Ellis 1962). **B. contortus** prefers abundant macrovegetation (Macan 1950). These three species also require a fairly high level of water hardness. **B. tentaculata** prefers moving water with a soft substrate (Fretter and Graham 1978). **P. milium** is often associated in slow moving rivers and well oxygenated lakes with **P. casertanum, P. subtruncatum, P. nitidum** and **P. amnicum**, and is commonly found with **P. lilljeborgii, P. nitidum, P. hibernicum** and **P. casertanum** in eutrophic 'plateaux' lakes (Alps - Jayet 1973, Canada - Green 1971, Pyrenees). In shallower eutrophic water locations, **Sphaerium corneum**

is also often associated with many of the above species. The
appearance of **P. amnicum** confirms the picture of hard water but this
species also prefers a fairly coarse substrate with a fairly energetic
water environment (Bass 1979).

The land species again tell us only that the margin of the
lake was marshy and damp.

Summary: Though ecologically similar to previous biozones,
the appearance of several new species with semi-specialist habitat
requirements involving hard water and abundant, diverse aquatic
macrovegetation, suggests how the state of ecological succession in the
lake had advanced notably. At the same time, the sharp rise in
molluscan numbers also indicates a more favourable environment.
Overall, a picture emerges of a eutrophic hard water body, with areas
of shallower, quiet, well vegetated water and more open stretches with
greater water movement. The presence of articulated bivalves,
contemporaneous with a slightly higher sand content relative to Zone A,
correlates well with this picture.

LMAZ-A4: **Valvata piscinalis - Lymnaea peregra - Pisidium amnicum**

This assemblage is really of a very different ecological
type, characterised by a very severe drop in molluscan numbers to few
more than zero in the middle of this zone. A much higher gastropod:
bivalve ratio may be due to the corresponding marked influxes of sand
and gravel at this level, which may indicate both lake shallowing and
the destruction of bivalve habitats. This conclusion is supported by
the relative increase in **Pisidium amnicum**, which prefers high energy
environments with a coarse substrate, and **Lymnaea peregra** which is
ecologically ubiquitous. The survival of **Valvata piscinalis** in all but
the middle of this zone, however, confirms the survival of some finer
substrate, probably in deeper water away from the thick gravel wedge
building up during this period at the southwest lake margin. The very
restricted fauna, low numbers and disappearance of all those species
characteristic of Zone A3 conclusively demonstrates a reversion to a
restricted level of aquatic vegetational development during this zone.

Despite the absence of articulated bivalves, the the low
number of Sphaeriid fry, taphonomic destruction cannot be invoked as
the major cause for the low molluscan abundance. This is because
Lymnaea peregra remains numerically significant, and these shells are
among the most fragile of molluscan species (Sparks 1961, 1964).

In addition to the normal marsh and damp ground species, the
relatively large number of terrestrial specimens introduced by the
active lake shore erosional processes included some interesting
varieties. **Vallonia pulchella** is indicative of open ground around
the lake, while **Deroceras** cf. **agrestre** (Linnaeus) also prefers
damp, relatively undisturbed, open ground conditions (Kerney and
Cameron 1979). The single specimen of **Pupilla muscorum** represents
the first true terrestrial species not necessarily associated with a
lake margin habitat, and is in keeping with the influxes of coarse
clastics from the erosion of the boulder clay surface surrounding the
lake.

Summary: The restricted, numerically poor fauna indicates a lake with a poorly developed aquatic macrovegetation with a highly energetic agrading lake margin with coarse substrate, with a finer muddy bottom in deeper water. The water was still calcareous. The land species indicate a simultaneously poorly vegetated surrounding terrestrial vegetation.

LMAZ-B1: **Sphaerium corneum - Pisidium nitidum - Pisidium subtruncatum - Pisidium hibernicum - Pisidium amnicum - Pisidium milium**

The return to high molluscan abundance, and a low gastropod: bivalve ratio and the overall species diversity of this molluscan assemblage zone indicate a return to more favourable ecological conditions, similar to those of assemblage zone A3, with the presence of **Armiger crista**, **Bathyomphalus contortus** and significant **Pisidium milium**, all demonstrating a return to a much more developed aquatic macrovegetation at the lake margin in terms of both abundance and diversity.

There are some notable differences, however, in species composition, with abundant **S. corneum**, **P. amnicum** and **P. nitidum**, and significant numbers of **P. subtruncatum**, all species requiring eutrophic, well oxygenated water. These replace the abundant **P. casertanum** and **Lymnaea peregra** of A3, both tolerant of a wide range of conditions. Whilst an increasing cover of macrophytes may account for some of these changes, other critical factors probably include variations in water depth, with the incoming bivalve species representing a shallower water facies than **P. casertanum**, and competition with the greater diversity of shallow water (but not lake margin) habitats encouraging a degree of bivalve specialisation which helped to exclude **L. peregra**. The new bivalve species are also tolerant of higher energy conditions than **P. casertanum** and **V. piscinalis**, which corresponds well with the significantly greater amounts of sand and fine gravel in the substrate in the matrix of this zone than in A3. Thus **S. corneum**, **P. amnicum**, **P. milium**, **P. nitidum** and **P. subtruncatum** are commonly associated today in slower British rivers rather than the more static, deeper lake assemblage of **P. casertanum**, **P. hibernicum** and **P. lilljeborgii** (Boycott 1936, Green 1971, Dussart 1976, 1979). **Myxas glutinosa** was found and confirmed by Dr. R. Preece in sample (21) from this zone, in keeping with the presence of **Pisidium amnicum** which also suggests hard, flowing water with coarse substrates occurred nearby. The specimen of **Hippeutis complanatus** found in sample 21, and the specimens of **Physa fontinalis** found in samples 21, 22 and 30 are noteworthy. Both these species require abundant vegetation in eutrophic calcareous water. Today these taxa are commonly found in slow, flowing water at lake margins or in rivers (Macan 1950, 1969, Okeland 1969, Young, J. 1975, Dussart 1976). They also suggest a milder, interstadial climate, perhaps akin to that of LMAZ B2.

The gravel-rich matrix probably derives from erosion of the gravel deposited in the previous period as a thick wedge at the lake shore; slumping into the lake would explain these coarse clastics, the relatively high proportion of land species, and the presence of a number of articulated bivalves and fragile 'fry' of **Pisidium** spp.

Among the damp and marsh terrestrial species are several juveniles of **Vertigo** spp., indicative of calcareous soils, while the **Pupilla muscorum** specimens seem to be of the 'wet-habitat' variety, as defined by Kerney (Kerney et al. 1964).

Summary: Once again there are indications of a favourable - ?milder interstadial - environment for molluscs, coincident with the reappearance of an abundant and diverse aquatic macrovegetation. Though still calcareous, the habitat seems to be in shallower, more moving water than in assemblage zone A3, with influxes of slumped, coarse, clastics providing a coarser substrate near shore.

LMAZ-B2: **Valvata cristata - Bithynia tentaculata**

Ecologically, this assemblage zone indicates a considerable shallowing with a very abundant assemblage typical of a well-vegetated shallow lake margin. **Valvata cristata, Physa fontinalis, Bithynia tentaculata, Armiger crista, Hippeutis complanatus** and **Pisidium milium** all require abundant, diverse vegetation in shallow, calcareous water. The general absence of **P. amnicum** might be explained therefore in terms of restricted water movement among this lake margin vegetation (abundant **Carex** fruits from the detritus peat near the top of this zone show it to be sedge-dominated). The continued influx of coarse sediment may therefore, result from mass movement rather than continuous, energetic lake margin erosion; this influx causing further shallowing until the detritus peat (Unit 4ii) near the top of the zone. Shallowing is confirmed by the very high gastropod:bivalve ratio, while reduced numbers of terrestrial species demonstrate reduced water energy, in keeping with the continued presence of articulated bivalves. The high number of hinge fragments associated with the detritus peat near the top of this zone is perhaps, therefore, an indication of a prolonged interval between death and burial. The very high numerical peak associated with the peat is, therefore, at least partly due to a higher mollusc:matrix accumulation ratio, the coarser detritus due to sudden episodes of mass wasting. The confirmed specimens of **Physa fontinalis** and **Myxas glutinosa** (18) confirm the impression given by **Hippeutis complanatus** of an interstadial climate with mild/warmer summers.

The small number of land specimens belong once again to hygrophilous marsh and damp species.

Summary: Continued shallowing in a favourable interstadial environment produced a typical well-vegetated shallow water lake margin assemblage (with hard eutrophic water) during this zone. The fauna of the detritus sedge peat (Unit 4ii) near the top of this zone indicates a near cessation of sedimentation in very shallow water. The continuation of coarse clastic deposition in a low energy environment suggests periodic mass wasting of the gravel-rich lake shore.

Also of note is the minor adverse fluctuations near the beginning of assemblage zone B2, where numbers decrease and the species like **P. milium**, which are strongly related to fairly rich vegetation, show a marked decline.

<u>LMAZ-C</u>:   **Sphaerium corneum - Pisidium subtruncatum - Pisidium nitidum**

        During this zone the very reduced number of molluscs, the marked reduction in the vegetation dependant species, and the coarse sedimentary matrix of alternating medium gravels and gravel-rich muds are indicative of ecologically harsher conditions, similar to those seen earlier in assemblage zone A4.   Vegetation-dependant species disappear except for a very few **Armiger crista, Bithynia tentaculata, Bathyomphalus contortus** and **Pisidium milium** present at the beginning of this assemblage zone; after a brief period, even these disappear totally.   The survival of **Sphaerium corneum, Pisidium subtruncatum** and **Pisidium nitidum,** however, suggests similar conditions of water chemistry and depth as before, being fairly shallow, eutrophic relatively slowly moving water.   It is a marked reduction in aquatic macrovegetation, therefore, which is most likely to explain the reversion to a fairly low gastropod:bivalve ratio, with only the hardy **Valvata piscinalis, Lymnaea peregra** and **Gyraulus laevis** eventually surviving of the gastropods (all the **B. tentaculata** opercula are presumed to have been recycled above sample 15).   A single specimen of **Physa fontinalis** from sample 16 shows the continuation of some aquatic vegetation at the start of this ecologically harsh assemblage zone.

        The coarse nature of the sediments confirms a situation of reasonably energetic erosion of the shore (made up of earlier gravels and boulder clay), these being deposited in locally thick wedges of gravel causing near-shore shallowing.   Mass movement was also a probable mechanism, as evidenced by the relatively large number of terrestrial molluscan species present within this zone before the maximum of the zone, when very adverse conditions and high energy, destructive deposition ensured the disappearance of molluscan material. Hence **Lymnaea peregra,** a very fragile but tolerant species, is rarely recorded during this zone.   Moreover, the coarse deposits prevented the survival of bivalve species like **P. lilljeborgii** and **P. hibernicum** which require relatively fine substrate.

        Among the enlarged collection of land snails deposited during this period are the usual common damp and marsh species, in addition to two oddities.   **Ceciloides acicula** (a burrowing snail) is undoubtedly intrusive; of much greater interest is a single specimen of **Vertigo lilljeborgii.   V. lilljeborgii** is very rarely found in the fossil record.   To date it has only been recovered from a handful of sites, indicative of calcareous damp conditions (Kerney and Cameron 1979). This species has only been found in upland locations in Flandrian contexts.   At this site, however, and a neighbouring Lincolnshire Late-Devensian sample, single specimens have been found in lowland contexts; a change in ecology is therefore a possibibility (R. Preece, pers. comm).   The presence of **Pupilla muscorum, Vallonia pulchella** and **Vertigo** sp. indicate lime-rich soils in a dry, open landscape around the lake.

        <u>Summary</u>:   During this period the water remain eutrophic. Macrovegetation declined sharply but did not entirely disappear and marked onshore erosion led to the deposition of locally thick, coarse clastics destroying bivalve habitats.   Around the lake, a dry, open,

"calcareous" landscape prevailed. The picture is therefore of considerable ecological adversity, causing the virtual disappearance of the molluscan population.

LMAZ-D: 'Not represented'

The amelioration at the start of the succeeding Flandrian stage is not represented in the molluscan record at section 8, although the banded silty sand (Unit 5a) capping the gravel is shown by pollen and plant macrofossil analysis to belong to zone IV of Godwin (1975) (see chapter 5), and the finer sedimentary nature of this layer is also indicative of ameliorating conditions (samples 5 and 6). The lack of molluscan material can be explained in terms of weathering, with acidic conditions beneath the overlying thin peat, and leaching due to soil formation above this peat.

The single specimen of **Pisidium subtruncatum** in the Flandrian blue silt beneath the main peat body is insufficient to comment on water conditions at this level, other than to say that they must have been eutrophic. The absence of molluscs is intriguing and may indicate an onset of post depositional acidity contemporary with the peat formation. Alternatively, this may represent a reworked deposit. The thin detritus peat beneath this blue silt only contained one specimen of the terrestrial species, **Punctum pygmaeum.**

The **P. subtruncatum** specimen in layer 9 is unexpected as this downslope-laminated sandy silt seems to represent a slope wash deposit -indeed this specimen seems to be recycled.

THE NORTHERN PROFILE (Section 1)

Tables 6.10 and 6.11 give the counts for molluscs from the clay-silt sequence on the north side of the Skipsea section analysed by Woodall (1981), while Table 6.13 lists counts made by Kennard from the top of the same deposit as recorded in Boylan (1966). These have been combined to give the assemblage zones for the sequence listed in Table 6.12.

The marked non-sequence between layers 3/1/4 and 3/1/5 previously noted (chapter 4) is confirmed by the molluscan evidence through the species represented, recalculated abundance figures and changes in the gastropod:bivalve ratios (Table 6.11). These data, therefore, when compared with the results of the main central profile (section 8) described, clearly point to layers 3/1/3 and 3/1/4 being correlatable with the local molluscan assemblage zones A1 to A3 (despite the sampling gap for the middle of layer 3/1/4), although the sequence of clay-silts is vertically compressed relative to the southern profile. Layer 3/1/2 would thus be seen as equivalent to this mixed deposit between the Skipsea Till and layer 3A of the central sequence (layer 2).

The molluscan faunas indicate 3/1/5 would appear to be contemporary with moluscan assemblage zone C, while layers 3/1/6 upwards represent the inferred succeeding Flandrian zone D, absent from the central profile due to weathering. The available pollen evidence

Table 6.10. MOLLUSCAN REMAINS NORTHERN MARGINS OF SKIPSEA WITHOW MERE (Section 1).

SAMPLE	1(2)	Unit 3/1 1(5)	2(3)	3(4)	4(6)	4(7)	5(40)	5(41)	6(42)	7(43)	7(44)	7(45)	7(26)	Unit 4 (46)	Unit 5 (47)
Gastropods															
Valvata piscinalis (Müller)				?1	27	35	18	26	64	65	155	266		185	
Valvata sp.														418	?1
Bithynia tentaculata (L)												9		10	
opercula											4	549		109	
Lymnaea peregra (Müller)			?7	7	5			6	6	31	5	790		17	
Lymnaea sp.			8			1	1	1	60	31	29	17			
Gyraulus laevis (Alder)			17	?3	2	35	6	53	20			2			
Armiger crista (L)				1				1	24	52	29	37		37	
Bathyomphalus contortus (L)										1		34		36	
Planorbis spp.					3							28		23	
Bivalves															
Sphaerium corneum (L)													P		
Sphaerium lacustre (Müller)			?1	3	1				4	1			P		
Pisidium amnicum (Müller)					1								P		
Pisidium obtusale (Lamarck)													P		
Pisidium subtruncatum (Malm)													P		
Pisidium casertanum (Poli)													P		
Pisidium lilljeborgii (Clessin)													P		
Pisidium hibernicum (Westerlund)													P		
Pisidium nitidum (Jenyns)													P		
Pisidium spp-undifferentiated		1	21	38	134	12	2	3	51	51	61	72	P	96	1
Sample air dried weight -g.	1102	1017	1151	549	1078	930	1100	882	936	723	840	871	1000	886	790

( ) = subsample number in layer

P = present

136

UNIT	SAMPLE	FRESHWATER GASTROPODS	FRESHWATER BIVALVES	TOTAL FRESHWATER	FRESHWATER GAST./BIV.	NO. OF GAST. SPECIES	L.M.A.Z.	
5	1/9 47	1	1	3	1.00	1	D_3	
4	1/8 46	201	1055	1256	5.62	7		
	1/7 45	125	1328	1453	10.61	6	D_2	
	1/7 44	79	236	314	3.00	3		
	1/6 43	178	236	415	1.33	5	D_1	
	1/6 42	43	221	264	5.18	4		Flandrian
	1/5 41	5	34	39	7.50	4	C	
3	1/5 40	3	59	62	21.67	4		Devensian
	1/4 7	85	41	126	0.48	3		
	1/4 6	264	71	335	0.27	3	A_1-A_3	
	1/3 4	193	51	244	0.26	4		
	1/2 3	18	7	25	0.38	1		transition
	1/1 5							lake with
	1/1 2							varved sediments

Table 6.11. RECALCULATED MOLLUSCAN TOTALS AND DIAGNOSTIC INDICES - NORTH MARGIN PROFILE (Section 1).

Table 6.12. SPECIES DEFINING THE MOLLUSCAN ASSEMBLAGE ZONES FROM THE NORTH MARGIN PROFILE (Section 1)

L.M.A. Zone	Dominant species	Significant species	Indicator species	Unit/Sample
D₃	Valvata cristata	Valvata piscinalis, Bithynia tentaculata	Valvata cristata, Bithynia tentaculata, Armiger crista, Bathyomphalus contortus	5 (47), 4 (46)
D₂	Valvata piscinalis, Bithynia tentaculata	Pisidium spp.	Valvata cristata, Bithynia tentaculata, Armiger crista, Bathyomphalus contortus	3/1/7 (45), 3/1/7 (44)
D₁ FLANDRIAN	Valvata piscinalis, Pisidium sp.	Armiger crista, Lymnaea peregra, Gyraulus laevis	Armiger crista, Bathyomphalus contortus	3/1/6 (43), 3/1/6 (42)
DEVENSIAN C	Valvata piscinalis	Gyraulus laevis	Armiger crista	3/1/5 (41), 3/1/5 (40)
A₁–A₃	Valvata piscinalis, Pisidium spp.	Gyraulus laevis	Armiger crista, Sphaerium lacustre	3/1/4 (7), 3/1/4 (6), 3.1.3 (4)
Transitional	Pisidium spp., Lymnaea peregra			3/1/2 (3)
Sterile				3/1/1 (5), 3/1/1 (2)

seems to confirm these cross-stratigraphic correlations; some indications of horizontal variation in species representation are thus available for the Late-Devensian.

LMAZ-LG: **No Mollusca**

The calcium carbonate content in layer 1/1/1 (Chapter 3) was too high to explain the total absence of molluscs in terms of chemical weathering. This absence can therefore be taken with the varved nature of the deposit to represent the product of a perennially frozen lake, with conditions being too severe for molluscs to survive. Alternatively, the absence of molluscs may be due to the delay necessary for colonisation upon the initial creation of the lake.

LMAZ-T: **'Transitional zone' - Lymnaea peregra - Pisidium spp.**

A small number of the most tolerant species are present in a silty-sand, overlying the varved silts, indicative of slope-wash from a bare, poorly vegetated boulder clay ground surface around the lake. This deposit may therefore represent a period of lake level lowering.

LMAZ-A1-3: **Pisidium spp. - Valvata piscinalis**

The high counts of **Pisidium subtruncatum** and **Pisidium** spp. indicate the extreme difficulty of identifying **Pisidium** species. **P. subtruncatum** is found in contemporary layers in the central profile, but so too are **P. hibernicum** and **P. casertanum**, which in the peculiar Late-Devensian morphologies represented at this site (Kerney, pers. comm) are in some ways similar to inequilateral **P. subtruncatum**.

In terms of gastropod species composition, however, this assemblage is ecologically similar to that of zone A1-3 on the central margins (section 8), with the tolerant **Lymnaea peregra**, **Valvata piscinalis** and **Gyraulus laevis**, together with single specimens of **Armiger crista** and **Sphaerium lacustre**. These last two species, coincident with relatively high abundance counts, suggest a significant development of freshwater macrovegetation. The gastropod: bivalve ratio suggests reasonably deep water. Moreover, **Pisidium amnicum** and **Pisidium henslowanum** both require moving calcareous water, while **P. subtruncatum** and **P. nitidium** also indicate clear, eutrophic water.

The decrease in abundance and the increased gastropod:bivalve ratio in the upper half of 3/1/4 correlate with the beginning of more severe conditions in zone A4.

LMAZ-B: **Not Present**

LMAZ-C: **Valvata piscinalis - Gyraulus laevis**

The presence of high numbers of **G. laevis** is significant. The specimen of **Armiger crista** is probably indicative of early colonisation by populations coincident with the beginning of renewed macrovegetation growth. This assemblage would therefore be seen as representing the end of zone C, after the most adverse ecological conditions have been replaced by a more favourable environment.

Woodall's (1980) identification of **Valvata macrostoma** in his 1981 report is probably mistaken; these instead being the variety **alpestris** of **V. piscinalis**, which have a flattened spire and are characteristic of lake habitats (Fretter and Graham 1978).

LMAZ-D1:   **Valvata piscinalis - Lymnaea peregra - Armiger crista - Gyraulus laevis - Pisidium** spp.

All these species are generalists except for **Armiger crista**, which normally requires fairly high levels of water calcium and relatively lush freshwater macrovegetation. The rise in numbers of the generalist species together with significant **Armiger crista** may be a characteristic feature of the earliest successional stages in this lake. The gastropod:bivalve ratios remain high, suggesting shallow water and plentiful macrovegetation for the lung breathing pulmonate gastropods. **Bathyomphalus contortus** also appears; this taxon also favours abundant vegetation (Macan 1950).

LMAZ-D2;   **Bithynia tentaculata - Valvata piscinalis**

This assemblage appears to represent the next successional stage to LMAZ-D1. There is a relative decline in importance of **Gyraulus laevis**. This taxon is characteristic of wild, vegetationally undeveloped habitats in modern Britain (Boycott 1936). **Armiger crista** and **Lymnaea peregra** also decline in relative importance. **Bithynia tentaculata** appears in large numbers, this taxon requiring both abundant vegetation and fairly calcareous water (J. Young 1975, Dussart 1976, Fretter and Graham 1978). **Valvata cristata** also appears in this zone; it is typical of abundant vegetation in shallow water with little movement (Fretter and Graham 1978). Moreover the very high gastropod:bivalve ratio also indicates very considerable shallowing, while the very high abundance figures for gastropods confirm the relatively high favourability of ecological conditions.

LMAZ-D3:   **Valvata cristata - Valvata piscinalis - Bithynia tentaculata - Pisidium** spp.

In ecological terms, this zone is fairly similar to D2 in terms of gastropod:bivalve ratio, abundance and species habitat preference. The relative changes in representation can, therefore, be attributed to this being the next successional stage in a well-vegetated, shallow, lake margin location during an interglacial stage.

Boylan's (1966) list of faunas from processed samples, taken from the same upper clay-silt horizons and analysed by Kennard in the 1930's, provide some interesting contrasts with these data. The very prominent counts for **Valvata piscinalis** and **Armiger crista**, together with significant numbers of **Valvata cristata, Bithynia tentaculata, Lymnaea peregra** and **Bathyomphalus contortus** and low **Gyraulus laevis** values place these three counts mid-way through zone D2: (Woodall sampled the top and bottom of this layer). In addition, however, **Hippeutis complanatus** is also present in significant numbers, while **Myxas glutinosa** (Müller) and **Physa fontinalis** (Linnaeus) are reported as significant in one of the three samples. **Bithynia leachii** (Sheppard), **Lymnaea stagnalis** (L) and **Planorbis**

planorbis (L) were also noted in small numbers. The absence of the small snail **H. complanatus** in this study in comparison with its finds in Kennard's study (Boylan 1966) may reflect the larger sieve size used in this study of the northern section.

Kennard's records of significant numbers of bivalves are important. He recorded numerous **Sphaerium corneum**, **Pisidum subtruncatum**, **Pisidium nitidum** with small numbers of **Anodonta cygnaea** (L), **P. amnicum**, **P. casertanum**, **P. personatum** (Malm), **P. milium** and **P. henslowanum**. This bivalve fauna confirms the ecological picture provided by the gastropods of a fairly shallow, well vegetated, eutrophic lake with moving calcareous water and a fine-grained substrate. Several new species arrive in this D2 zone. **Hippeutis complanatus** likes well vegetated, shallow lake margin habitats, with eutrophic, calcareous water (Okeland 1969, J. Young 1975). **Bithynia leachii** occupies similar calcareous locations to its relative, **B. tentaculata** (Fretter and Graham 1978). **Lymnaea stagnalis** prefers quieter, calcareous water, like that found among dense vegetation (Okeland 1969, Boycott 1936, Ellis 1969). **Myxas glutinosa** occurs in similarly quiet water with a fine substrate vegetation (Boycott 1936). **Physa fontinalis** dislikes both soft and very hard water, being commonly found with abundant vegetation (Macan 1969, Okeland 1969, J. Young 1975, Dussart 1976). **Planorbis planorbis** prefers hard, quiet water within small, confined water bodies (Boycott 1936, Ellis 1969, Dussart 1976). **Anodonta cygnaea** requires the presence of fish, which are essential to its life cycle, and a firm substrate with hard water (Boycott 1936, Ellis 1962). **Pisidium personatum** is a 'slum' species, found only in 'marginal' habitats such as marshes (Boycott 1936). It is also important to note that neither this study nor that of Woodall (1981) or Boylan (1966) recorded land species, in contrast to their continued presence in the Late-Devensian in the central exposure (section 8).

THE SOUTHERN PROFILES

A small fauna was recovered from section 3 (Table 6.14). The stratigraphic relationships of the samples and a flint blade are shown in Figure 3.2.

The molluscan fauna is entirely composed of species favouring large, open bodies of hard water: **Valvata piscinalis** in particular is a typical lacustrine species occurring in greatest number in quieter, deeper water at 1.5m to 2m in lakes or the more slowly moving parts (pools) of rivers (Okeland 1964). Species characteristic of rapid shallow flow - e.g. **Ancylus fluviatilis** - are absent. Similarly, no terrestrial taxa were detected. The fauna is impoverished compared to that noted in the central exposures or recorded in Boylan (1966). All the species are tolerant of a wide range of climatic conditions, ranging from temperate to arctic latitudes.

The species composition correlates well with LMAZ-A3 or A4 from the central profile in terms of low abundance, low gastropod: bivalve ratios and species representation. The two operculae of **Bithynia tentaculata** are especially interesting, these occurring in the central exposures from LMAZ-A3 on.

	S. side blue silt – ?pollen zone IV (Phillips 1829)	nekron mud ?pollen zone V (Phillips 1829)	N. side nekron mud pollen zone V (Godwin and Godwin 1933)	N. side marl: pollen zones IV – V: studied by Kennard, recorded in Boylan (1966).		
+Valvata cristata (Müller)				c	13	+
Valvata piscinalis (Müller)				c	153	+
+Bithynia tentaculata (L.)	c			c	32	+
*Bithynia leachii (Sheppard)						+
*Physa fontinalis (L.)				c		
+Lymnaea stagnalis (L.)	r				1	
Lymnaea peregra (Müller)				c	36	+
*Myxas glutinosa (Müller)				c		
+Planorbis planorbis (L.)					2	
Gyraulus laevis (Alder)				12	5	
+Armiger crista (L.)				c	132	+
Bathyomphalus contortus (L.)				c	23	+
*Hippeutis complanatus (L.)				c	19	+
*Acroluxus lacustris (L.)			c			
Total gastropods:				?	416	?
+Anodonta cf. cygnaea (L.)				2		
Sphaerium corneum (L.)	c	c		c		+
+Sphaerium lacustre (Müller)		c				
Pisidium amnicum (Müller)					–	
Pisidium casertanum (Poli)				1	–	+
*Pisidium personatum (Malm)				1	–	
+Pisidium milium (Held)					–	+
Pisidium subtruncatum (Malm)				c	–	+
Pisidium henslowanum (Sheppard)					. –	+
Pisidium nitidum (Jenyns)				c	–	+
Pisidium spp.					42	
Total bivalves				?	42	+

Note: bivalve counts are for valve numbers, not MNI.   Gastropod/Bivalve ratio = 9.90
+ thermophile group II;   * thermophile group III

Table 6.13. EARLIER STUDIES OF THE MOLLUSCAN REMAINS FROM SKIPSEA WITHOW MERE

Molluscs	Sample (1 kg)	103	105	106	107	108	Total
Valvata piscinalis (Müller)		3	2	2	4		11
Bithynia tentaculata (L) opercula				2	2		4
Pisidium amnicum (Müller)		2					2
Pisidium subtruncatum (Malm)			3				3
Pisidium henslowanum (Sheppard)			1				1
Pisidium nitidum (Jenyns)			25	1	7		33
Total		5	31	5	13	–	54
Plants –
Oospores of **Chara** spp.		109	91	15	–	–	

Table 6.14. MACROFOSSILS - MAINLY MOLLUSCAN - FOUND IN LAKE SILTS OF UNIT 3a AT SKIPSEA WITHOW (Section 3)

143

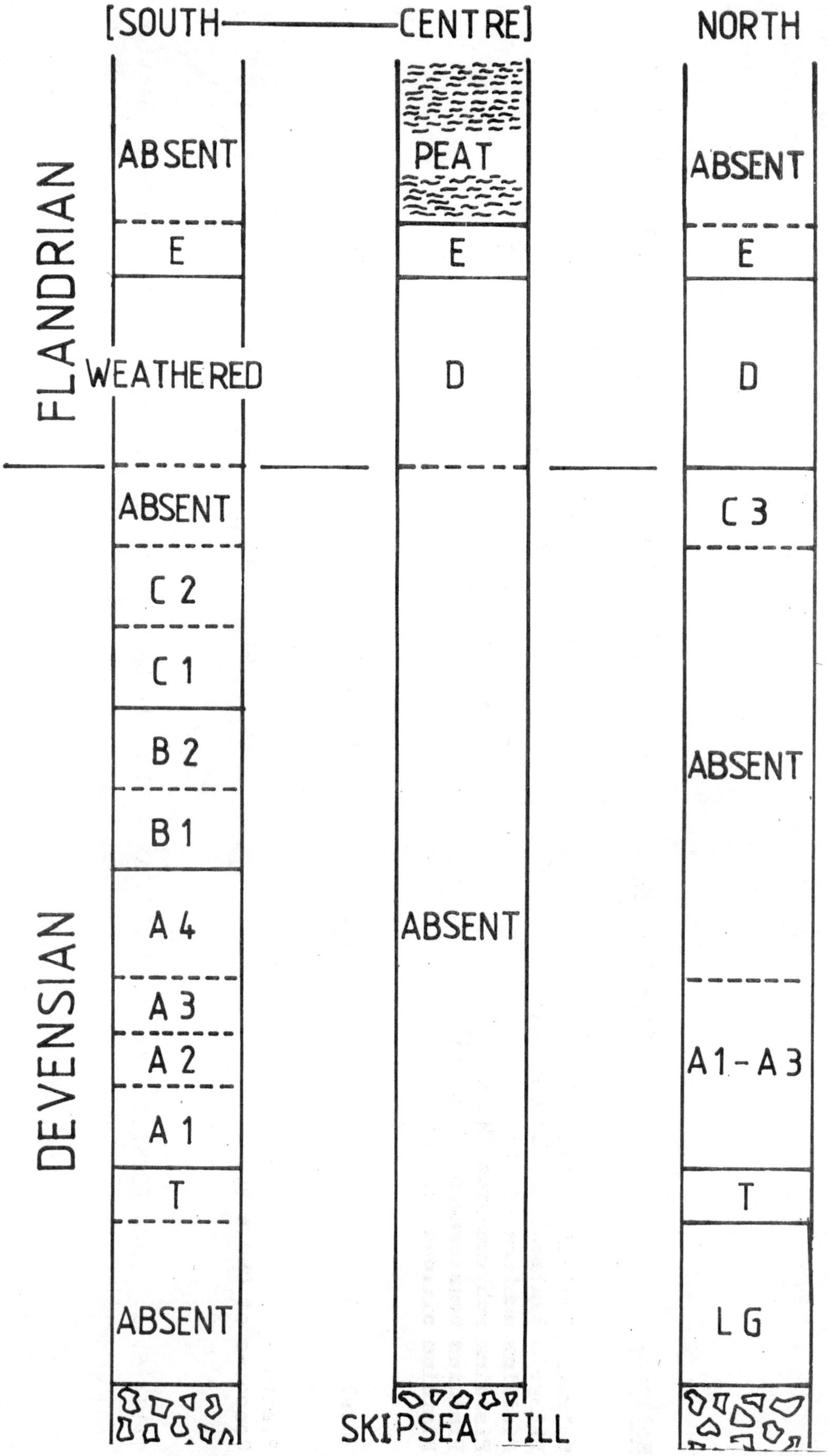

Figure 6.5 Molluscan assemblage zones at Skipsea Withow mere and their correlation across the Withow Gap exposures.

MOLLUSCAN BIOSTRATIGRAPHIC CORRELATION BETWEEN THE SKIPSEA WITHOW PROFILES

Figure 6.5 provides a composite picture of the various profiles discussed and illustrated from the various Skipsea profiles. Examination of these data suggests that after an initial sterile phase, evidenced by the mollusc-free varved silts of the northern exposure (section 3), there is a sequence through LMAZ-A to C that is without interruption in the central areas. However, there is a non-sequence, probably as a result of erosion of LMAZ-A4 to mid C in the northern sequence (section 3). At section 3, weathering appears to have removed the upper part of LMAZ C, whereas the Flandrian LMAZ-D appears to have been lost from parts of the southern sequence for the same reason. However, Flandrian LMAZ D is preserved in the top of the clay-silts of the northern exposure (Unit 4). Erosion and acid conditions have caused the loss of molluscs in the overlying (very late) Late-Devensian and Flandrian deposits in the central exposures.

The importance of these data lies in the extent to which a clear and useful molluscan biostratigraphy has emerged. Second, there is abundant evidence of local environmental change - especially fluctuations in water level/erosion/sedimentation - and of climate.

PREVIOUS STUDIES AT SKIPSEA WITHOW

Phillips (1829)

The earliest molluscan records obtained from Skipsea Withow mere by Phillips in 1826 (published 1829) are given in Table 6.13. The stratigraphic record made at that time is summarised in Figure 1.7. Significantly, his log shows that the Late-Devensian sequence was completely lost about 240m further east towards the centre of the mere, where his notes were made prior to coastal erosion. A notable period of erosion is evidenced. This episode was probably contemporary to that early in the Flandrian seen in both the main central and northern profiles prior to the beginning of peat deposition; indeed the sequence recorded by Phillips with a thin (0.3m) gravel overlain by blue clay under peat, is identical to that logged in the central profile subsequent to the erosional episode. The blue clay is recorded as having **Sphaerium** spp., while an additional 'yellowish clay' representing a nekron mud between the clay and overlying peat was said to contain abundant **B. tentaculata, S. corneum** and **S. lacustre** (Müller), with a few **Lymnaea stagnalis.** In general, this record is very similar to that from the early Flandrian LMAZ D of the northern profile.

The **Ancylus** faunas

Both Armstrong (1922) and Godwin and Godwin (1933) referred to an **'Ancylus'** fauna in nekron mud recorded as a brown organic silt between the silty clay marls and main peat deposit. By comparison with other known records of mere deposits in the Holderness area, (Table 6.13) and a consideration of their comparative ecological preferences, this record of **Ancylus** must refer to **Acroloxus lacustris** (formerly **Ancylus lacustris**) which prefers quiet water, hard or soft, among abundant vegetation to which it can cling; being resistant to organic acids it can tolerate fairly peaty water.

LATE QUATERNARY MOLLUSCAN FAUNAS OF HOLDERNESS

Table 6.15 lists all previously published molluscan records from Holderness.

Late-Devensian

Reid (1885) makes vague references to shells being derived from "?pro-glacial varved silts" contemporary with the Withernsea Till ice. Only **Lymnaea peregra** is clearly identified as coming from outwash gravels at Bridlington (Reid 1885). The status of these specimens is unclear - whilst ubiquitous taxa like **Lymnaea peregra** might represent early colonisers, the type of glacial derivation and reworking suggested for the Kelsey Hill Gravels (chapter 2) may apply here. Otherwise in all current coastal exposures of lacustrine texturally-varved silts identified in the area, no non-marine Mollusca have been recovered. This sterile period would correspond with Skipsea LMAZ-LG. Records of sterile varved silts have been made for Bridlington (Reid 1885), Barmston (Bridger in Catt 1977), Horsea (Etheridge 1875, Reid 1885), Kilnsea and Easington (Reid 1885).

The earliest colonisers of the lakes which developed on the Late-Devensian tills recorded elsewhere in Holderness appear to be **Lymnaea peregra** identified by Reid (1885). The same species, together with a few specimens of **Pisidium**, are the earliest colonisers at Skipsea.

Sites of 'probable' Late-Devensian age at the following Holderness locations have yielded non-marine molluscs at:

Barmston (**Valvata piscinalis, Sphaerium** spp. Catt 1977);

Holpton (**Planorbis** spp., **Lymnaea peregra, Sphaerium corneaum, Pisidium** spp. - recorded by Reid in 1885 - and additionally **Bithynia tentaculata** recorded by Phillips in 1829);

Bridlington (**Valvata** sp., **Lymnaea** sp., **Sphaerium** sp., **Pisidium** sp.).

The faunas are essentially similar to those of the Late-Devensian at Skipsea Withow.

EARLY FLANDRIAN FAUNAS IN HOLDERNESS

Freshwater faunas.

        Records for early Flandrian lake deposits are rather more
informative. In general terms, they confirm the successional pattern
established at Skipsea Withow, with most records belonging to marls or
clay silts immediately beneath the thick peat deposits that predominate
in the Flandrian mere deposits along the Holderness coast.

        Most records are unsystematic, with specimens picked by eye,
explaining the over-representation of the large **Anodonta** sp. in most
of the marls. The best data comes from Hornsea, where Sheppard (1906)
listed a considerable number of species recovered from the Hornsea 'Old
Mere' deposits sectioned by the cliff retreat. Most species were found
in the majority of bands of marls beneath and within the base of the
main peat body. The long list of taxa includes several not seen at
Skipsea in LMAZ D (including **Segmentina nitida**, **Gyraulus albus**,
Anisus vortex, **Lymnaea auricularia** and **Anodonta anatina**).
Sheppard (1906) also listed the molluscan species living in the present
Hornsea mere at the start of the twentieth century. The modern fauna
is seen to be more species rich, and includes late colonisers such as
Planorbis carinatus (Müller), **Planorbis corneus** (L), **Lymnaea
palustris** (Müller) and **Lymnaea glabra** (Müller) - (see Boycott
1936). The modern fauna lacked **Gyraulus laevis.**

        Boylan (1966) provides a detailed account of a molluscan
fauna from lake silts at Barmston. This is attributable to Kerney's
1977 molluscan biozone 'd', since it contains the terrestrial mollusc
Discus rotundatus. This equates with Flandrian pollen zones VI to VIIa
of the Godwin 1975 scheme - as illustrated in Table 2.1 here. The
species diversity present lies midway between the very early Flandrian
and modern faunas noted by Sheppard (1906) at Hornsea Old Mere. The
Barmston fauna lacks **Gyraulus laevis** - this species' disappearance is a
regular feature of interglacial succession in lakes. It is consequently
of interest that this taxon is known from stream marls at Burton
Salmon, West Yorkshire, which are attributed to pollen zones VI to VIIb
of the Godwin scheme (Norris et al. 1971).

        The Barmston record provides useful quantitative data which
indicates that a distinct molluscan assemblage was present:

        **Valvata cristata - Pisidium casertanum - Lymnaea
        peregra - Pisidium personatum - Ancylus fluviatilis;**

with small numbers of:

        **Valvata piscinalis, Bithynia tentaculata, Bathyomphalus
        contortus, Acroloxus lacustris** and **Pisidium amnicum.**

        This assemblage indicates a well vegetated water body, with
sluggish reaches and areas of more agitated water.

	Bridlington zone T. gravel (Reid 1885)	Bridlington zone B (IIa) marl (Phillips 1829)	Barmston zone B (IIa) marl (Catt 1977)	Holmpton zone B (IIa) marl (Reid 1885)	Hilston zone C or D (III) IV marl (Reid 1885)	Sand-le-Mere zone D IV-V marl (Phillips 1829, Reid 1885)	Hornsea zone D: IV-V marl (Sheppard 1906)	Skipsea Low and Bail meres zone D marls (Smith 1911)	Barmston zone E (VI) marl (Boylan 1966)	Owthorne zone E (VI) peat (Reid 1885)	Hornsea zone E (VI) peat (Beckett 1981)	Hornsea zone F. Today's lake (Sheppard 1906)
PROSOBRANCHIA												
*Theodoxus fluviatalis (L.)									13			
*Valvata cristata (Müller)							+	+	1245			+
Valvata piscinalis (Müller)		+	+				+	+	355			+
×Bithynia tentaculata (L.)					+			+	290			+
*Bithynia leachii (Sheppard)									50			+
PULMONATA												
*Aplexa hyporum (L.)												+
*Physa fontinalis (L.)									5			+
*Lymnaea truncatula (Müller)							+		1			+
*Lymnaea auricularia (L.)							+					+
×Lymnaea palustris (Müller)									1			+
×Lymnaea stagnalis (L.)					+				22			+
*Lymnaea glabra												+
Lymnaea peregra (Müller)	+	+		+			+		900			+
×Planorbis planorbis (L.)							+		4			+
*Planorbis carinatus (Müller)												+
Anisus leucostoma (Millet)							+		18			+
*Anisus vortex (L.)							+					
Gyraulus laevis (Alder)							+					
*Gyraulus albus (Müller)							+		46			+
×Armiger crista (L.)							+		46			+
×Bathyomphalus contortus (L.)							+		272			+
*Planorbarius corneus (L.)												+
*Hippeutis complanatus (L.)												+
*Segmentina nitida							+					+
*Acroluxus lacustris (L.)									107			+
×Ancylus fluviatalis (Müller)												
Planorbis spp.					+							
BIVALVIA												
×Anodonta cygnea (L.)							+					+
×Anodonta anatina (L.)						+	+	+		+	+	+
Sphaerium corneum (L.)		+	+	+		+	+					+
*Sphaerium rivicola												+
×Sphaerium lacustre (Müller)												+
Pisidium amnicum (Müller)									157			
Pisidium casertanum (Poli)							+		1250			+
*Pisidium personatum (Malm)						+	+		560			+
×Pisidium milium (Held)							+		23			+
Pisidium subtruncatum (Malm)												+
Pisidium henslowanum (Sheppard)												+
Pisidium nitidum (Jenyns)							+					+
Pisidium spp.		+		+								

Note: ×thermophile grade II   *thermophile pollen zone III or IV - see text for explanation.

All bivalve values are for valve counts.

Table 6.15. MOLLUSCAN DATA FROM OTHER HOLDERNESS MERES - WITH SUGGESTED CORRELATIONS WITH SKIPSEA WITHOW MERE LOCAL MOLLUSCAN ASSEMBLAGE ZONES AND GODWIN'S (1975) POLLEN ZONES.

Land Species

Unfortunately, land species of Late-Devensian age are not known from other Holderness sites. The concentration in the area of slumping and mass movement only at one sector of the former Late-Devensian Skipsea Withow mere lake shoreline emphasises the extent to which 'normal' studies of lake deposits may fail to yield direct molluscan evidence of the character of the former land surface around the lake. This phenomenon was noted long ago by Sparks (1956) in his studies of the lake-centre facies at Hoxne, Suffolk.

THE EFFECTS OF BIOLOGICAL SUCCESSION AND DISPERSAL AMONG MOLLUSCAN FAUNAS

A simple model of succession and habitat change after deglaciation might be that an ameliorating climate allows newly arrived organisms to colonise an area from which they might have been previously excluded by too harsh conditions. While the climate is severe, vegetation is stunted and with few species, and the molluscan faunas are similarly low in numbers and species diversity. The species of molluscs present will be 'generalists' capable of withstanding a wide range of conditions, both ecological and climatic, and a few species which specialise in inhabiting poor habitats avoided by other molluscs. As the climate improves, vegetation will increase in abundance and diversity and so will the associated molluscan faunas. As the vegetational communities build up and become more complex, so the environment becomes increasingly modified and improved from the molluscan point of view, with a larger number of ecological niches with decreased niche width. In consequence, 'generalist' species are replaced by 'intermediate' species, which are in turn succeeded by 'specialist' species, as polyclimax vegetation develops and 'succession' occurs, with the ensuing specialist communities being adapted to specific ecological conditions and to competition with other species; the generalist species often decrease in numbers as a result of such competition.

The order and speed at which species invade is also related to their dispersal capabilities. Molluscan dispersal is influenced by the distance between suitable habitation sites, the diversity of the receiving area (dictating the number of adequate habitats) and the adaptability of the species being dispersed (Boycott 1934, 1936, Valovirta 1977). Dispersal is also dependant on suitable carriers, these most commonly being insects and birds (Boetters 1979, 1982, Boycott 1926, Okeland 1969, 1979) and occasionally mammals for land species; the greater the diversity of the reception area, therefore, the greater the likelihood of colonisation.

Successional developments in the Skipsea Withow Molluscan faunas

Table 6.16 includes an assessment of the successional stage reached by the associated vegetation as revealed by the molluscan faunas. Stage I is thought to be 'primitive' with little vegetational diversity. During LMAZ A, vegetation seems to have been reasonably abundant and capable of supporting a fairly abundant molluscan fauna,

L.M.A. Zone	Successional stages/Vegetation	Climate/Species with temperature defined distributions
Oldest		
A_1	Probably reasonably abundant, but not very diverse and successionally "primitive" stage I	*(?)Pisidium casertanum var ponderosa: only from interglacial and interstadial assemblages. (? becoming milder)
A_2	Less abundant, still "primitive", stage I	(cool)
A_3	Abundant and diverse, but successionally stage II developed.	Bithynia tentaculata: 66°-67°N in FennoScandia Armiger crista: 66°N in FennoScandia Pisidium milium: 66°-67°N in FennoScandia (becoming milder)
A_4	At centre of this zone vegetation is very poorly developed.	Armiger crista: appears at end of this zone (mostly very cold - stadial)
B_1	Vegetation very abundant and diverse reaching successional stage II/III	*Physa fontinalis: c. 63°N in FennoScandia *Myxas glutinosa: 63°N in FennoScandia Armiger crista *Hippeutis complanatus: 63°N in FennoScandia Pisidium milium (mild)
B_2	Vegetation very abundant and diverse; successionally developed, stage III	Valvata cristata: 65°N in FennoScandia Bithynia tentaculata *Physa fontinalis *Myxas glutinosa Armiger crista *Hippeutis complanatus Sphaerium lacustre Pisidium milium (mild)
C_1	Vegetationally poor; stage I-II	Few Bithynia tentaculata, Armiger crista, Sphaerium lacustre, Pisidium milium
C_2	Vegetationally extremely poor.	
C_3	Vegetationally poor; stage I-II	Molluscs weathered and lost and possible non-sequence (C_1 - C_3 mostly very cold - stadial)
D_1	Vegetation abundant and diverse, successionally developed stage II	Molluscs weathered out (WARM INTERGLACIAL)
D_2	Vegetation abundant and diverse, successionally developed stage III	NOT PRESENT IN SECTIONS STUDIED
D_3	Vegetation very abundant and diverse; successionally very developed stage IV	
		(WARM INTERGLACIAL)
E (nekron mud)	Vegetation very abundant and diverse stage IV	Bithynia tentaculata) recorded by Lymnaea stagnalis) Phillips 1826 Sphaerium corneum) (published 1829)
Youngest		

note: * indicates thermophile class III; those not so designated are thermophile class II: for explanation see text.

Table 6.16. INFERRED SUCCESSIONAL/VEGETATIONAL AND CLIMATIC CONDITIONS ACHIEVED DURING EACH LOCAL MOLLUSCAN ASSEMBLAGE ZONE AT SKIPSEA WITHOW MERE - CENTRAL EXPOSURES (SECTION 8). THE SUCCESSIONAL STAGES I - IV ARE DEFINED IN THE TEXT.

but it was successionally 'primitive' lacking sufficient ecological complexity to support species like **Armiger crista** and **Pisidium milium** which are both easily dispersed (Boycott 1936). Local molluscan assemblage zones A4 and C, however, seem to have had both low abundance and diversity as the associated molluscan faunas were very poor. By contrast, LMAZ A3 and B1 show signs of some successional development, with **Armiger crista**, **Bithynia tentaculata**, and **Pisidium milium** present in varying quantities, all three requiring a developed vegetational community. **Myxas glutinosa** which favours stony rather than muddy substrates and will tolerate the poor macrovegetation of early successional stages has also arrived by this stage. LMAZ B2 has evidence of even greater successional development, with **Valvata cristata** and **Hippeutis complanatus** also being present.

LMAZ D shows similar complexity to B2. However, it was only in LMAZ D2 of the Flandrian that a sufficiently mature vegetational community was well enough established to permit specialist vegetational species like **Bithynia leachii**, **Physa fontinalis** and **Acroloxus lacustris** to appear, in addition to more slowly dispersing taxa such as **Lymnaea stagnalis**, **Myxas glutinosa**, **Planorbis planorbis** and **Anodonta cygnaea**.

DISTINGUISHING CLIMATIC INFLUENCES ON MOLLUSCAN ASSEMBLAGES

Habitat conditions are also obviously extensively influenced by the more regional climatic factors, such as temperature, rainfall and insolation. Climatic variation can thus be used to explain both spatial distribution patterns, given similar local hydrological regimes, and changes in species representation through time in freshwater localities; as occurred through the Late-Devensian at Skipsea Withow mere.

For example, temperature increases are matched proportionately by larger concentrations of dissolved calcium carbonate (required by most mollusc species for shell formation, and a limiting factor to some species called 'calciphiles' by Boycott 1936) and trophic status (i.e. increased bacterial activity promotes more rapid breakdown of organics into detritus, which forms the majority of most mollusc species' diets, food availability being the primary limiting factor - Reavell 1980), while the amount of dissolved oxygen absorbed from the atmosphere decreases. Temperature also acts indirectly through its very great influence on both the quantity and quality (diversity) of aquatic macrovegetation. Sunlight is also an important factor in macrovegetation growth, while rainfall regimes (i.e. quantity and seasonal distribution) affect the supply of water and minerals to a freshwater habitat and thus influence molluscs directly, and indirectly via macrovegetation.

These three factors of temperature, sunlight and rainfall regime vary spatially with latitude, altitude, regional topography (i.e. proximity to areas of high altitude) and continentality (i.e. position of site relative to the coast and to wind currents blowing inland from maritime sources). While rainfall and sunlight are important indirect influences on molluscan distributions, however (mostly through their control of macrovegetation), only temperature acts directly as a limiting factor to molluscan survival, given reasonably stable hydrological conditions.

The degree of influence that temperature exerts on the different molluscan species depends largely on genetic characteristics, (relating to life-span, reproductive method and their breeding-life cycle). During the winter, after the summer breeding season half-grown juveniles must survive colder water temperatures; most bivalves and prosobranch gastropods breathe diffused oxygen and tend to burrow into the substrate to hibernate, affording them considerable protection from the cold; pulmonate gastropods, however, are lung breathers which have to remain near the surface (except for a few species like **Lymnaea peregra** that can absorb dissolved oxygen where concentrations are high enough). Water has a higher specific heat capacity than the land, ensuring higher winter temperatures due to slower cooling; it follows that the shallow water inhabited by pulmonate gastropods is less insulated than the deeper water surrounding the prosobranchs and bivalves which also have the benefit of a substrate covering.

A review of the literature suggests that despite these habitat differences during the colder winter months, however, summer temperatures seem to be the more important limiting factor upon molluscan populations, because as Boycott points out (1936:168):

> "Generally speaking, our Mollusca are active, grow and breed only in summer, and within the range of our (British) climate the hotter it is the better."

Moreover,

> "cold such as we experience does no perceptible harm...and like other fresh-water animals snails can be frozen into ice for a good long time without being killed;"

while

> "some of the southern (British) species...in Scandinavia and Siberia live through far more severe winters than we have anywhere" (Boycott 1936:170).

The clear implication is that molluscs are at their most vulnerable in the summer months, when breeding occurs producing young which are at their most fragile in the weeks immediately following birth. Thus so called 'warmth loving' southern British species may survive in Siberia, where the continental climate provides warmer summer temperatures than much of northern England and Scotland (up to +15°C), despite far colder winter temperatures (as low as -14°C). It follows, therefore, that it is no surprise that in areas with cold summers, relatively few species of shallow water pulmonate gastropods survive in comparison with the "deep-water" and substrate-dwelling prosobranchs and bivalves.

Detecting the influences of climate on molluscan assemblages at any one freshwater location through time must depend, therefore, on distinguishing both indirect and direct climatic influences. Of great importance are climatic controls on the critical ecological factors of the abundance and diversity of aquatic macrovegetation, in addition to influences on dissolved calcium carbonate and trophic status of the water body. Temperature has a direct influence, however, on many pulmonate gastropod species, as well as some viviparous prosobranchs (a genetic adaptation conferring competitive advantage with separate males and females in favourable ecological conditions, unlike most species which are hermaphrodites - Calow 1981), these having northern and continental limits defined by summer temperatures. Consideration of these limits allows an assessment of changes in temperature regime should the numerical representation of such species vary significantly over time within fairly hydrologically constant water bodies.

Climatic Influences and the Skipsea Withow Molluscan assemblages

The preceding section describing localised ecological conditions, describes in detail the approximate changes in the abundance and quality of aquatic macrovegetation as revealed by fluctuations in species abundance and relative composition (e.g. species like **Armiger crista**, **Bithynia tentaculata**, **Valvata cristata** and **Pisidium milium** which require abundant macrovegetation). This indirectly provides evidence on environmental favourability but also includes elements of successional change in both molluscan and plant populations which can perhaps mask climatic variations.

Table 6.16 gives a qualitative assessment of the richness of macrovegetation based on abundance figures and species composition for all the molluscan studies. It also lists details of species present within each sample, which give direct inferences on temperature regimes through their northern and continental tolerance limits with regard to summer temperatures. This table includes two qualitative notations which need explaining: an index of the successional stage achieved by vegetation in the mere (explained in the next section), and an index of the extent to which the molluscan species recovered at Skipsea are thermophilous. These ideas derive from those of Sparks (1961, 1964).

Molluscan species referable to thermophile class I include all those that have distributions extending considerably north of the Arctic Circle; these animals have developed a high degree of tolerance to summer and winter cold and thus provide little data of palaeo-climatic significance. They are not shown on Table 6.16. Species belonging to thermophile class II are found as far north as the Arctic Circle (66°N) but not beyond; in other words, while being extremely tolerant of cold conditions, they are not capable of surviving extreme summer cold when the young are produced. Their presence in the Skipsea Withow samples indicates that in the contexts of the Late-Devensian in Britain, conditions were not bad enough to warrant the term 'stadial', although if the climate was very continental as in modern Siberia, winters may have been extremely cold. Species belonging to the class III are only found today in southern Scandinavia (up to c. 63°N); although the winters here may be cold (some of these species are found in milder regions of Siberia today) summer temperatures must be in the order of +14° to 16°C. Given that the climate in northeast Britain seems never to have been as continental as the huge plateau expanse of modern Siberia (although with a considerably lower sea level, palaeo-temperature regimes in Holderness would have been far more variable than today) it would seem safe to suggest that, where present in the Skipsea sequence, climate would have been of a "milder" nature.

From this assessment of 'indicator species' and an appreciation of the evidence for vegetation development, it can be concluded that LMAZ D represents the start of the present Flandrian interglacial, and LMAZ B seems to represent a "milder" episode. Conversely, the extremes of LMAZ A4 and C clearly suggest 'stadial' type conditions with very limited floras and faunas present. A1 and A3 are in several senses intermediate in status.

The Climatic Significance of other Holderness Molluscan Assemblages

Little can be said of the climatic significance of the few Late-Devensian records other than the fact that their faunas are in keeping with the stratigraphically ascertained zonal assignations reported in here. In Table 6.16, species marked with an asterix belong to thermophile groups III or IV (IV is not represented at Skipsea Withow but includes species like **Segmentina nitida** which is not found north of 61ºN but is still known from Siberia - Sparks 1957). This table usefully demonstrates how much higher is the proportion of pulmonate gastropods among the III-IV thermophile group, most of the others being within group II (marked with a cross). This is in sharp contrast with the hardy bivalve species. Not surprisingly, all the LMAZ E peat and silt assemblages contain many representatives of the thermophilous species associated with a very rich and abundant vegetation which is successionally advanced.

The Wider Climatic Significance of the Skipsea Withow Molluscan Sequence

Nazeing

Unfortunately, very few published records exist from other freshwater Late-Devensian deposits. A useful study comes from Nazeing in the Lea Valley near London (Allison, Godwin and Warren 1952) belonging to pollen zones I to IV on the Godwin (1975) chronology. In this study, land and marsh species comprise between 30-100% of the faunas, preventing a direct comparison of ecological facies change with that at Skipsea Withow. The assemblages do, however, permit potentially useful comparisons of species presence and absence in the Late-Devensian with reference to climatic variation. Of the class III thermophiles seen at Skipsea, only **Hippeutis complanatus** was found in Godwin's (1975) pollen zone IV onwards at Nazeing; **Myxas glutinosa** only in pollen zone II, and **Acroloxus lacustris** only from pollen zone IV onwards. Of the species belonging to the group II thermophiles at Nazeing, **Valvata cristata** was only present from pollen zone IV onwards, **Bithynia tentaculata** was found in pollen zones II and IV onwards, **Armiger crista** was present in pollen zones I, II and IV onwards, and **Pisidium milium** only from final pollen zone III onwards. Interestingly though, **Lymnaea stagnalis**, **Lymnaea palustris** and **Planorbis planorbis** which are also normally assigned to group II thermophiles were found in pollen zone III.

Sturton, Lincolnshire

At Sturton, north Lincolnshire, **Pisidium milium** has been found from deposits dating from the end of the Late-Devensian, which also contain a land and marsh molluscan fauna similar to that seen at Skipsea Withow mere in LMAZ-C, at the top of the Late-Devensian sequence (Preece and Robinson, 1984).

Berkshire valleys

A recent series of studies of river valley deposits in Berkshire has revealed more faunas dating from the very end of the Late-Devensian. In addition to a restricted land assemblage, freshwater species included **Anisus leucostoma**, **Ancylus fluviatilis**, **Pisidium obtusale**, **Pisidium subtruncatum** and also, importantly, a few **Valvata cristata** and **Bathyomphalus contortus** (Holyoak 1983). It seems, therefore, that at these two locations, as at Skipsea Withow, the end of the Late-Devensian is marked by an amelioration in summer temperatures, allowing the influx of grade II thermophiles like **Valvata cristata**, **Armiger crista** and **Pisidum milium**. Interestingly, at the Berkshire sites, the accompanying flora still retains the Gramineae-Cyperaceae dominance typical of the rest of the Late-Devensian Loch Lomond stadial.

Staines, West London

Although not of direct climatic relevance, a study of freshwater Mollusca from near Staines provides a very useful early Flandrian fauna (Preece and Robinson 1982) comparable with the Flandrian material at Skipsea Withow.

Leven Valley, Cleveland, north Yorkshire.

A late Devensian/early Flandrian molluscan fauna has been reported from Kildale in the Leven Valley by Keen, Jones and Robinson (1984). This fauna has many similarities to that at Skipsea. A fauna attributed to pollen zone III is dominated by lake taxa - especially **Lymnaea peregra** and **Pisidium hibernicum**. It is generally species-poor when compared to the Skipsea site, but this feature may also reflect the location of the Kildale sampling site within the palaeo-lake's geography. The bivalves **Pisidium personatum** and **Pisidium obtusale** were noted. These taxa have not yet been detected at Skipsea. The transition to the Flandrian at Kildale was marked by the local colonisation by terrestrial snails and the demise of freshwater taxa. This reflects the infilling of this small lake - a fate which also befell many of the smaller lakes of Holderness.

Seamer Carrs

Of greater future importance is the molluscan palaeoecological study currently being carried out of Late-Devensian and early Flandrian deposits at Seamer Carrs, north of Holderness and the North York Moors, in the bed of a former 'Lake Pickering'. The lithological and geomorphic properties of these deposits have many similarities with those from Skipsea Withow mere. At present, the study is only in its early stages (J.G. Evans and R. Coles, pers. comm).

<u>White Bog, Co. Down, Northern Ireland, and the island of Sjaelland,</u>
<u>Denmark.</u>

Two other major published records of Late-Devensian freshwater molluscan faunas are those from the 'White Bog', Co. Down, northeastern Ireland (Stelfox <u>et al</u>. 1972), which covers pollen zones II and IV to VI (ascertained by pollen and plant macrofossil analysis), and that from lake deposits at Sjaelland, Denmark (Marcussen 1967).

The White Bog site is a lake deposit, affording more direct comparison with Skipsea Withow mere. Pollen zone II at White Bog is characterised by **Valvata cristata**, **Gyraulus laevis**, **Armiger crista**, stunted **Lymnaea peregra** and one **Acroloxus lacustris** specimen. There are eight species of **Pisidium**, dominated by **Pisidium nitidum** and **P. hibernicum** and also including **P. milium**. The early Flandrian assemblage included **Bithynia tentaculata**, **Gyraulus albus**, **Planorbis carinatus**, and **Lymnaea auricularia**, these last three species being class III thermophiles.

The Sjaelland site is broadly similar to the White Bog and Late Devensian at Skipsea Withow mere. The molluscan fauna is dominated by **Valvata cristata**, **Valvata piscinalis**, **Bithynia tentaculata**, **Lymnaea peregra**, and **Pisidium nitidum** As at Skipsea, **Physa fontinalis** and **Armiger crista** occur in these deposits of a medium sized lake.

<u>Early and Mid-Devensian Molluscan Faunas</u>

Although there are few sites with freshwater molluscan assemblages published from the Late-Devensian, there are a considerably greater number available from the Early and Middle Devensian, and from earlier glacial periods. A literature survey confirms conclusions made by Holyoak (1982) that class II thermophiles are very rarely found in stadial deposits, being occasionally present at the end or beginning of these severe climatic periods, while class III thermophiles are exclusively confined to Devensian interstadials. In deposits where class II thermophiles are present, vertical changes in molluscan abundance figures normally separate the stadial from interstadial or intermediate-type climatic zones. This palaeoecological data from the reservoir of published Early and Middle Devensian sites supports the sequence of climatic events listed in Table 6.16 for the Skipsea Withow site.

<u>FUTURE PROSPECTS</u>

If this Skipsea Withow sequence is accepted as valid, and it is equally accepted that the sequence is fairly complete, then it might be worthwhile trying to match these molluscan data to conclusions on climatic events, reached on the basis of other environmental indicators. As it stands, it might be suggested that LMAZ-A4 may be equivalent to pollen zone Iz (of Godwin 1975) which is traditionally seen as a severe stadial, the 12,000 to 12,200 colder episode described in Coope and Pennington (1977) and Beckett (1981). LMAZ-C may be equivalent to the established pollen zone III, the Loch Lomond stadial.

Similarly, LMAZ-B might be seen as equivalent to the pollen zone II, often referred to as the Allerød interstadial, while LMAZ-A1 and A2 may represent pollen zone I1. If these associations were shown to be reliable by future study, then the Skipsea Withow site would provide an interesting comparison with the picture in the west of Britain where pollen zones I and II have been abandoned in favour of the single Lake Windermere Interstadial (Coope 1977, Pennington 1977).

CHAPTER 7

CHAPTER 7

THE FLANDRIAN VEGETATIONAL HISTORY OF THE MERES OF HOLDERNESS

The first two parts of this account describe and interpret the Flandrian vegetational history of Skipsea Withow mere. The final part introduces new pollen diagrams from the other meres of Holderness and describes the vegetational history of the region. Micro- and macrofossils have been examined from the Flandrian deposits at Skipsea Withow mere. The pollen diagram encompasses the upper part of the Late-Devensian sequence at section 7 (Figure 3.1). Plant macrofossils of these cold stage deposits were reported in chapter 5.

A POLLEN ANALYTICAL STUDY OF THE FLANDRIAN VEGETATIONAL HISTORY AT SKIPSEA WITHOW

by Anne Blackham and J.R. Flenley

The first pollen analysis of Skipsea Withow was carried out by Godwin and Godwin (1933). Since that time there has been considerable erosion of the coast so that the exposed stratigraphy has changed. In addition, palynological techniques have advanced: far more pollen types can be recognised, and pollen can be extracted from sediments previously considered intractable. These factors combine to make a new study of the deposits worthwhile.

TECHNIQUES

The exposed face in the cliff was cleaned and samples were removed directly from it. The sample at 2.63m was obtained from the beach at low tide. The pollen was extracted in the laboratory by standard procedures (Faegri and Iversen 1975). Pollen was counted under high power of a Vickers Phase Contrast microscope (x 500-1200). The collection of over 5000 reference pollen slides at the University of Hull was available for comparison, but identification was also aided by keys and photographs (Faegri and Iversen 1975, Moore and Webb 1978, Erdtman, Berglund and Praglowski 1961).

RESULTS

As both tree-dominated and non-tree-dominated pollen spectra were present, the results were expressed as percentages of total pollen and spores, and are shown in Figure 7.1. For comparison with the work of Godwin and Godwin (1933) the tree (+ **Corylus**) pollen counts have also been expressed as percentages of total tree pollen, and these are shown in Figure 7.2.

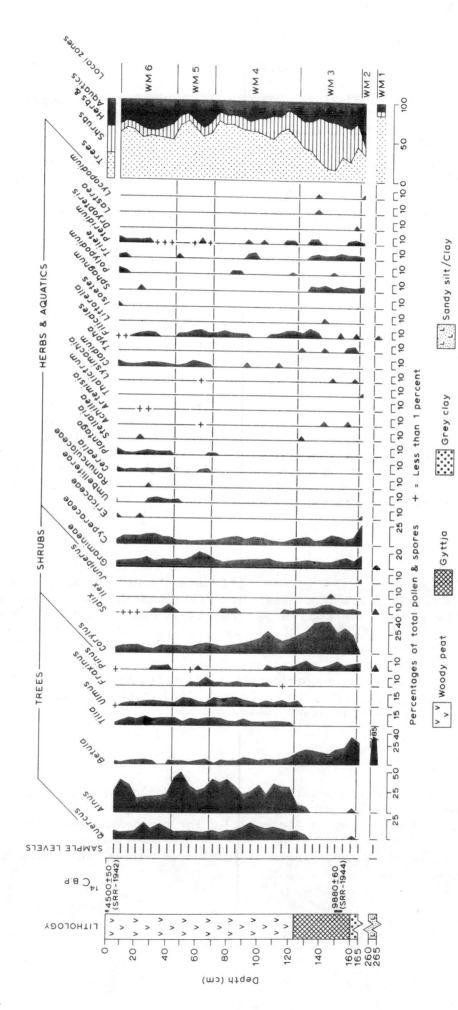

Figure 7.1 Pollen diagram from Skipsea Withow Mere; analysis by A. Blackham. Values are percentages of total pollen and spores.

160

DISCUSSION

Zonation of the pollen diagram

For ease of discussion, the pollen diagram has been divided into six local pollen assemblage biozones. These are numbered, with the prefix WM for Withow Mere. An attempt to allocate them to regional pollen assemblage zones will be made in the next section. Dating will also be considered in the next section, although some preliminary suggestions may be made here.

A brief description of the zones is presented here.

Zone WM1 (2.65m) Dominated by **Betula** pollen. Small values for **Pinus**, **Salix** and Gramineae. Possible date: Late Devensian (before 10,000 b.p.).

Zone WM2 (1.65m) High values for **Betula**, Gramineae and Cyperaceae. Possible date: Late Devensian (before 10,000 b.p.).

Zone WM3 (1.62-1.22m) Dominated by **Betula** and **Corylus** pollen. **Pinus** reaches a peak value as % AP on Figure 7.2. **Quercus** and **Alnus** appear at the end of the zone. Possible date: Early Flandrian (c. 10,000 b.p. to c. 7,000 b.p.). This does not conflict with the ^{14}C date of 9880+60 (SRR 1944) at 1.50-1.55m.

Zone WM4 (1.22-.67m) **Alnus** is dominant. **Quercus**, **Ulmus** and **Tilia** are also present. **Fraxinus** appears and **Pinus** disappears during the zone. Possible date: Flandrian (c. 7000 b.p. to c. 5000 b.p.).

Zone WM5 (.67-.42m) There is a reduction in total tree pollen percentage, followed by a recovery. The trees most affected are **Alnus**, **Ulmus** and to a lesser extent, **Tilia**. Gramineae pollen reaches a peak. Cereal and **Plantago** pollen is present. Possible date: Flandrian (after c. 5000 b.p.).

Zone WM6 (.42-.02m) There is another reduction in total tree pollen percentage, and recovery this time is only partial. The trees chiefly affected are **Alnus** and **Ulmus**. Cereal and **Plantago** pollen are continuously present. Possible date: Flandrian (after c. 5000 b.p.). The ^{14}C date of 4500+50 b.p. (SRR 1942) at 0-.02m does not conflict with this, but seems rather old.

Correlation with the pollen diagram of Godwin and Godwin (1933)

The two diagrams are shown for comparison in Figure 7.3. It seems possible to correlate them at two points. The rise of **Alnus**, (Zone WM3-4 boundary), marking the well-known Boreal-Atlantic transition, is clear at about 1.22m on Figure 7.2 and at about 2.11m on Figure 7.2a. The decline of **Ulmus**, (Zone WM4-5 boundary), the equally well-known elm decline, occurs at about .67m on Figure 7.2a and at about 1.42m on Figure 7.3.

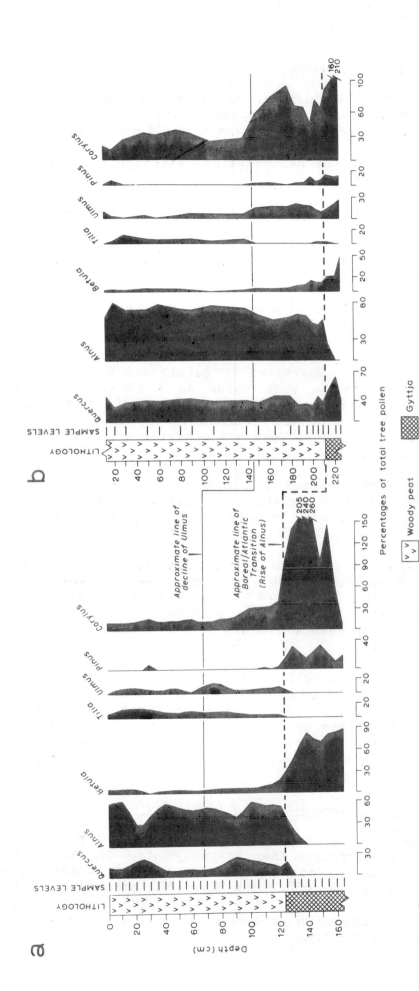

Figure 7.2a The pollen diagram from Figure 7.1 recalculated as percentages of total tree pollen; only selected taxa are shown.

Figure 7.2b The pollen diagram of Godwin and Godwin (1933) for comparison.

162

It is clear that the lower part of Figure 7.2a is unrepresented on Figure 7.2b; in other words, the new diagram goes back to an earlier stage than the diagram published in 1933. Correlations above the elm decline are not clear, and it is uncertain which diagram has the greater temporal coverage at this period.

The development of Skipsea Withow Mere

Although the evidence is rather slight, the following account of the development of the mere may be advanced from pollen analytical evidence. The mere appears to have originated in Devensian time, together with the other meres of Holderness (see next chapter). In Late-Devensian time the mere was an open-water lake into which clay and silt were freely transported, probably aided by solifluction, forming the deposits between 1.65 and 1.55m. This phase came to an end about 9880±60 b.p. Open water conditions continued, but the deposit became more organic, probably reflecting the growth of algae in the lake. **Typha** was present around the margins of the lake. Trees growing around the lake contributed increasing amounts of wood to the sediments. By about 7000 b.p. or a little later, the lake was sufficiently infilled to allow the spread of fen and fen carr across the sampling site. The fen species included **Cladium mariscus** and the fen carr may have been dominated by **Alnus**. After about 5000 b.p. the fen carr was exploited by man for timber. The openings thus created were colonised by **Cladium mariscus** and other sedges. The record ceased when soil erosion from the surrounding deforested land covered the site with silty colluvium, at a date to be discussed below.

History of the regional vegetation

It is difficult to draw conclusions from a single diagram with only two dates, but a few suggestions may be made here, to be amplified in the next chapter. In the Late Devensian, the vegetation appears to have included **Betula**, Gramineae and Cyperaceae, but little more can be said about it. In the later stages of the Late Devensian, before 9880±60 b.p., a **Betula** woodland appears to have covered the landscape and this was soon accompanied by **Corylus**. The latter may have dominated the vegetation until about 7000 b.p., but **Pinus** and **Salix** were also present. About 7000 b.p., mixed forest of **Quercus**, **Alnus**, **Ulmus** and **Tilia** immigrated and rapidly came to dominate the forests. The **Alnus** could have been growing in the fen carr around the lake. **Fraxinus** appeared later and in lesser quantity. At about 5000 b.p. (estimated: see next chapter) the first forest clearance took place. The weed **Plantago** appeared and Gramineae increased, suggesting pastoral usage (Godwin 1968), but cereals were also grown. The chief trees felled were **Ulmus**, **Alnus** and **Tilia**. **Alnus** could have been removed from the fen carr. Some trees, notably **Fraxinus** and **Betula**, appear to have gained a short-term advantage from the clearance, perhaps by growing on abandoned land. Some form of shifting agriculture <u>might</u> have been practised.

The forest recovered completely from this phase, but clearance then began again, and this time disturbance was continuous until the end of the record. The date of this is unknown, but the record ceases because the site was covered with silty colluvium. If, as is suspected, this is the product of soil erosion from the surrounding land, resulting from agricultural activities, then the date of 4500+50 b.p. at 0-0.2m is probably too old. Soil erosion is known to introduce old carbon in quantity sufficient to cause large errors in ^{14}C dates from depositional sites. The disturbance in this second clearance phase is again consistent with mixed farming. Cereal pollen is present throughout, but so is **Plantago** which is usually taken to suggest the presence of pasture.

FLANDRIAN PLANT MACROFOSSILS FROM SKIPSEA WITHOW MERE

by Allan R. Hall

Plant macrofossils were taken from the Flandrian organic muds and carr peats of section 7 (Figure 3.1 and 3.7) in March 1979. Three samples have been studied:

- sample 7/M/2 from carr peats (Unit 8d) at a depth of 20cms on Figure 7.2;
- sample 7/M/6 from woody peat with sand partings at a depth of 50cms (Figure 7.1)
- sample 7/M/15 from organic muds (Unit 6) at a depth of 140cms on Figure 7.1.

The results are given in Table 5.2.

In sample 7/M/15 (silty woody detritus) near the base of the Flandrian, a number of elements of the Late-Devensian assemblage (described in chapter 5) were still present, notably **Schoenoplectus**, **Populus** and **Betula**. A single fruit of **Alnus** indicates the start of local alder woodland (cf. Figure 7.1).

There was still a component of aquatic taxa (**Nymphaea** and **Potamogeton** spp.) together with tall herbs of water-side and marsh/fen habitats (**Alisma**, **Eupatorium**, **Filipendula**, **Potentilla palustris** and **Solanum dulcamara**).

Sample 7/M/6 (sandy coarse woody detritus) was very rich in remains of alder (fruits, female cone axes, wood, buds and anthers all being recorded), with evidence of other woody taxa from the local forest: hazel (**Corylus**), bird-cherry (**Prunus padus**) and **Prunus** sp., oak (**Quercus**) and the now much less frequent birch. Both **Antitrichia curtipendula** and **Neckera complanata** and perhaps also **Hypnum cupressiforme** were probably corticolous (living on bark) in the woodland. Indeed, the sediment gives the impression of having formed from drifted woody debris, probably not transported very far.

There were few non-woody taxa in this sample, perhaps reflecting shade by overhanging trees. The stinging nettle (**Urtica dioica**) is a plant typical of the fen woodland or alder carr that no doubt fringed the mere at this time.

The uppermost sample analysed (7/M/2, a coarse woody detritus) continues this pattern, with alder again the most frequent taxon recorded. The tentatively identified immature fruit of lime (**Tilia** sp.) and cupule fragments of yew (**Taxus baccata**) add to the list of woody taxa for the site, whilst the modest count of **Alisma** fruits perhaps represents an increase in areas of open water or a reduction of shading at the water's edge.

TIMBER ORIENTATION STUDIES

by DDG.

The abundance and apparent preferred orientation of tree trunks and large branches in Flandrian Units 7 and 8 are the two most distinctive aspects of these lake margin deposits.

The orientation and dip of tree trunks in Unit 7 - shallow water/lake margin deposits - are shown in Figure 7.4 (sections 5-7) and Figure 7.3 (sections 6-4). It is clear from these diagrams that the trunks and branches have not simply pitched down slope into the lake: rather they are preferentially orientated towards the north-northeast. Modern analogues (Plate 1.2) suggests windthrow is an important toppling agent in alder/oak carr in Holderness. If this was the agent responsible for the preferred alignment and dip at Skipsea Withow mere, then the dominant wind of the time would have come from the south-southwest: this is a more southerly source than predominates today. The reliability of this analysis is uncertain.

TOWARDS A VEGETATIONAL HISTORY OF THE MERES OF HOLDERNESS

by J.R. Flenley

The discussion in Chapters 1 and 2 demonstrated that Skipsea Withow is not by any means the only fresh water deposit in Holderness. The uneven topography of the Devensian till formerly bore numerous meres of which the only survivor is Hornsea Mere. The former existence of many other meres (Figure 7.5) is clear from historical records, place names, topography, vegetation and sedimentology, as reviewed in Chapter 2 and in T. Sheppard (1912) and J. Sheppard (1956). The fascinating history of the drainage of all but Hornsea Mere has been assembled by J. Sheppard (1956, 1957).

The Holderness meres appear to have been of two types. Larger meres, typically elongate and at least 1km long by 200m wide, include Hornsea Mere, Hornsea Old Mere, Lambwath Mere, Skipsea Bail Mere and Skipsea Low Mere (Figures 1.6 and 7.5). These occupy major depressions in the till surface, and the fact that three of them run in a west-east direction suggests that they might mark the sites of former valleys in the underlying chalk (Valentin 1957), which would presumably have drained to the east.

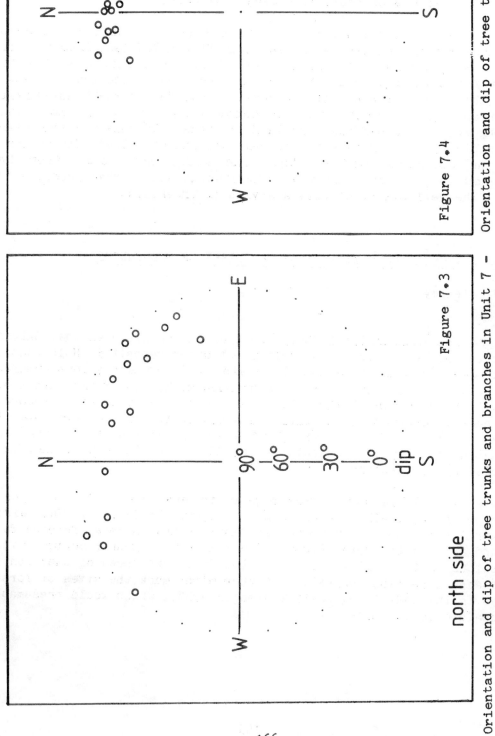

Figure 7.3

north side

Figure 7.4

south side

Orientation and dip of tree trunks and branches in Unit 7 - sections 6-4 - north side of the exposures of Skipsea Withow mere (Figure 3.1).

Orientation and dip of tree trunks and branches in Unit 7 - sections 5-7 - south side of the exposures of Skipsea Withow mere (Figure 3.1).

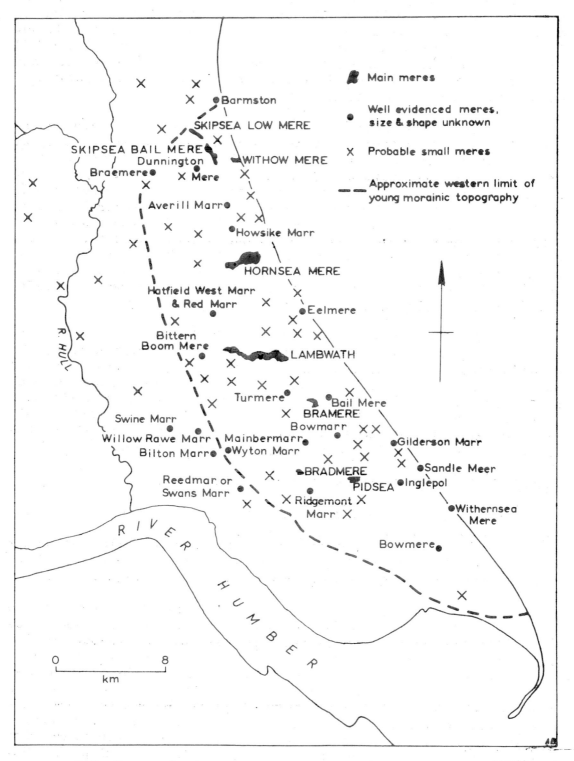

Figure 7.5 The ancient meres of Holderness (after Sheppard 1956)

The smaller meres, typically about 100m or less across and often circular or oval in shape, are probably features of till deposition. Some deep ones are possibly kettle holes (i.e. formed by melting out of a large ice block after deposition), e.g. The Bog at Roos. Others, generally shallower, may result simply from uneven deposition of till e.g. Gilderson Marr near Tunstall. Skipsea Withow is probably of this last type, although topography inland (Plate 2.1) suggests a considerable enlargement of the site in that direction, and we cannot know its former extent seaward; thus it may be a remnant of one of the larger meres (see Chapter 2).

The meres seem to have been of some archaeological significance. Mesolithic fish spears have been found not only at Skipsea Withow but also at Hornsea Old Mere, before the coastal exposure there was covered by a sea wall (Armstrong 1923b). A Neolithic dwelling platform was excavated in Skipsea Low Mere (Smith 1911). Bronze Age platforms have been excavated at several sites: e.g. Skipsea Low Mere and the passage between Skipsea Low Mere and Skipsea Bail Mere (Smith 1911). In Norman times, Skipsea Bail Mere provided a natural moat for the keep of Skipsea Brough, the castle of Drogo, Lord of Holderness (English 1979). There is documentation of the importance of fisheries in at least the larger meres in monastic times (Sheppard 1956, 1957).

The two Skipsea meres are remarkable in another way: they are the only locations for in situ records of **Trapa natans**, the Water Chestnut, in the British Flandrian (Flenley, Maloney, Ford and Hallam 1975, Flenley and Maloney 1976). This species now grows no nearer than central France, and its occurrence could indicate mid-post glacial temperatures higher than those of the present day. Alternatively, or additionally, man may have been involved, as the fruits are widely used by man in Europe and elsewhere (Hegi 1909-31).

POLLEN DIAGRAMS FROM HOLDERNESS MERES: THE DATA

The main detailed pollen diagrams published from Holderness meres are those from The Bog at Roos, and from Hornsea Old Mere (Beckett 1981). These establish a system of regional pollen assemblage biozones to which other diagrams may be related. A summary of the diagram from The Bog is included here for comparison (Figure 7.6).

Other diagrams available include those for Skipsea Withow (see Chapter 5) and several unpublished diagrams. The drained meres have afforded suitable material for palynology classes at the Department of Geography of the University of Hull for many years, and a number of useful outline diagrams have resulted. The ones included here are those from as near as possible to Skipsea Withow, i.e. from Skipsea Bail Mere (1982 class, Figure 7.7) and Skipsea Low Mere (1974 class, Figure 7.8). It is worthy of record that stratigraphy suggesting the presence of a full Late-Glacial and Flandrian has also been recorded at Bittern Boom Mere (+11m), Inglepol or Inglepool (+5m) and Gilderson Marr (+2m), and pollen diagrams from the two last sites confirmed this.

DISCUSSION

Stratigraphy

All the meres (if they have been bored sufficiently deeply) show similar stratigraphy at the base, the Late-Glacial being largely represented by inorganic deposits. Usually these are grey or pink silts, presumably the result of solifluction. In the deepest - and perhaps formerly largest - mere investigated, the Old Mere at Hornsea, a coarse chalky gravel was found as well as clay (Beckett 1981).

The Late-Glacial clay is interrupted by a darker, more organic clay-mud, c. 20 to 50cms in thickness, which appears to represent the Windermere Interstadial of Pennington (1977). In at least three sites, however (The Bog, Skipsea Bail Mere and the Inglepol), there is also a lower band of darker, more organic clay-mud, usually c. 2-5cms in thickness. At Roos this gave a ^{14}C date of 13,0435+270 b.p. (Birm-317). Although there is a possibility of such early dates being contaminated by older carbon derived from the till, this seems a reasonable minimum age for the deglaciation of Holderness. Taken with the date of 18,240+250 b.p. (Birm-108) for the Dimlington Moss Silts (Catt and Penny 1966), it brackets the deposition of the Skipsea and Withernsea tills.

The Flandrian begins everywhere with deposition of an organic lake mud (gyttja). In the larger meres, this continues until near the surface, but the smaller meres soon turned over to peat formation as their basins were more rapidly filled to near the water surface. Trees probably grew on the peat in some sites, as they do not (aided by drainage) at The Bog. In all sites except The Bog, the uppermost part of the sediment shows a return to mineral deposition. This is probably the result of soil erosion on the surrounding slopes, following deforestation. It is not impossible that mineral material was actually dumped on some sites to aid reclamation. Drainage of the meres was sometimes carried out by means of new surface ditches (e.g. at the Inglepol), or perhaps by canalisation of existing streams (? Skipsea Bail Mere and Skipsea Low Mere). Alternatively, underground pipes were put in, e.g. at The Bog, Roos and at Bittern Boom Mere, leading to one of the major drainage channels.

Pollen assemblages

Each diagram has been zoned according to its own pollen assemblages, and these zones are shown on the individual diagrams. In addition, an attempt has been made to correlate the diagrams with each other and with the regional pollen assemblage zones of Beckett (1981); the results of this exercise are shown in Table 7.1. Beckett did not feel that he had sufficient information to establish regional pollen assemblage zones for the Late-Glacial and this has been attempted for the first time here. The extent to which this correlation is successful will now be considered, and the regional vegetational history reviewed.

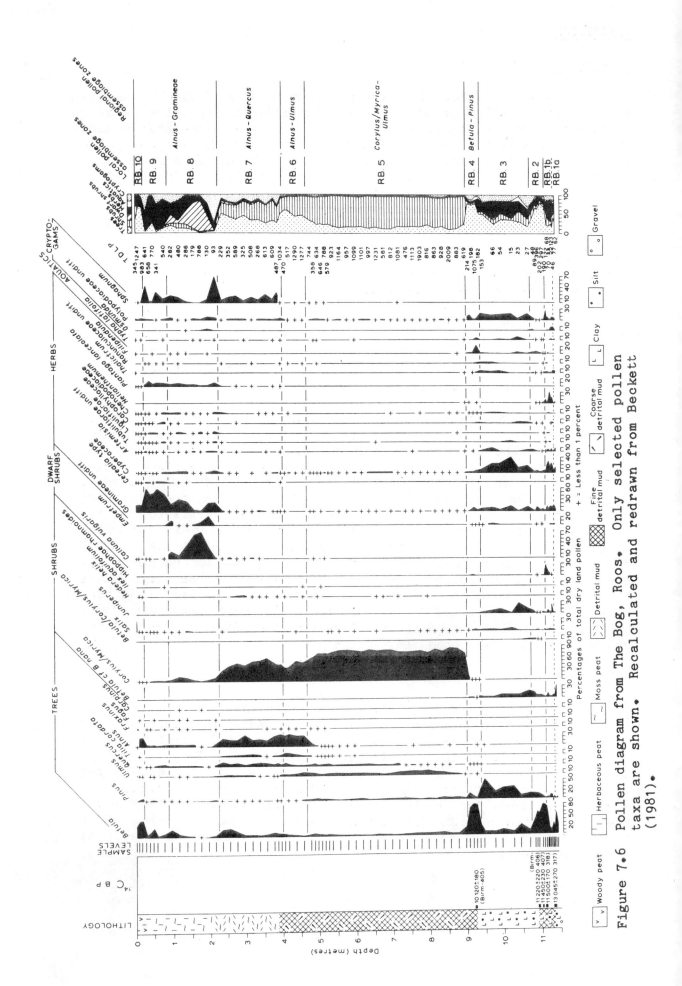

Figure 7.6 Pollen diagram from The Bog, Roos. Only selected pollen taxa are shown. Recalculated and redrawn from Beckett (1981).

C-14 Date B.P. if known	Regional Pollen Assemblage Zone	The Bog, Roos	Old Mere, Hornsea	Skipsea Withow Mere	Skipsea Bail Mere	Skipsea Low Mere
	Alnus-Gramineae	RB 10				
		RB 9	HO 5	WM 6	SB 7	SL 5
		RB 8				
	Alnus-Quercus	RB 7	HO 4	WM 5	SB 6	SL 4
	Alnus-Ulmus	RB 6	HO 3	WM 4	SB 5	SL 3
9880 ± 60 (SRR-1944)	Corylus/Myrica-Ulmus	RB 5	HO 2	WM 3	SB 4	SL 2
10,120 ± 180 (Birm-405)	Betula-Pinus	RB 4	HO 1	WM 2	SB 3	SL 1
	Cyperaceae - herbs	RB 3		-	SB 2	
11,200 ± 220 (Birm-406) 11,500 ± 170 (Birm-318)	Betula-herbs	RB 2		WM 1	SB 1	
13,045 ± 270 (Birm-317)	Helianthemum - herbs	RB 1b				
		RB 1a				

Table 7.1.   A Correlation of Pollen Diagrams from Holderness.

The earliest zone recorded (from c. 13,000 b.p.) is present only at The Bog, Roos, and Skipsea Withow and is designated the **Helianthemum** - herbs Regional Pollen Assemblage Biozone (RPAZ). At Roos and Skipsea Withow this is subdivided, but further evidence would be needed to substantiate a division at the regional level. The landscape was open, with few trees (Beckett 1981, Chapter 5, this volume). Shrubs (**Salix, Juniperus, Hippophäe rhamnoides** and **Betula nana**) were present but did not exclude numerous herbs. The regular presence of **Helianthemum**, which is now typical of chalk grassland, testifies to the unleached, calcareous nature of the soil newly developed on the till.

The **Betula**-herbs RPAZ covers the period c. 12,000 b.p. to c. 11,000 b.p. (Beckett 1981), and is represented at three sites: The Bog at Roos, Skipsea Withow Mere and Skipsea Bail Mere (2 samples). Pollen of tree birches is abundant (>50% of total dry land pollen and spores) at the small meres but less so (c. 20%) at Skipsea Bail Mere and less still at Skipsea Withow. It seems clear, however, that birch woodland was present, although this may have been patchy. Other tree pollen is probably derived or wind blown. Climate may well have been similar to that of the present day.

The Cyperaceae - herbs RPAZ, roughly 11,000 b.p. to c. 10,200 b.p., seems to represent a distinctly colder phase. Tree birches were not eliminated altogether at Roos or Skipsea Withow, although they are absent in the single sample from Skipsea Bail Mere. **Pinus** pollen, present at Roos and Skipsea Withow, is probably wind blown from much further south. The vegetation may have been a sparse tundra, with occasional birch in favourable microhabitats.

Birch woodland reappeared in Holderness before 10,120±180 b.p. (Birm-405) (**Betula-Pinus** RPAZ). This zone is represented at all five sites. **Pinus** is now present in quantity sufficient to suggest it grew locally although other tree and **Corylus** pollen was probably carried in on the wind. Climate could have been as warm as at present, the low tree diversity being due simply to slow migration from southern refugia.

The next RPAZ is designated **Corylus/Myrica-Ulmus**. Pollen of **Corylus** and **Myrica** are not readily distinguishable, but in Holderness it is likely that the pollen is nearly all derived from **Corylus**. **Ulmus** and **Quercus** arrive early in this zone at Roos and Hornsea but later at Skipsea Withow. At the other sites the diagrams are too sketchy to permit close correlation at this time. It is not unlikely, however, that immigration would proceed in an irregular manner if it was not closely controlled by climatic change. A single grain of **Trapa** at this level in Skipsea Bail Mere is probably the result of contamination in sampling.

The maximum development of forest in Holderness coincided with the ensuing **Alnus-Ulmus** RPAZ. Non-tree pollen is usually at a minimum, and forest tree diversity increases with the use of **Alnus** and **Tilia**, both previously present but in smaller quantities in most areas. Again it is unnecessary to invoke climatic change; delayed immigration may be the explanation.

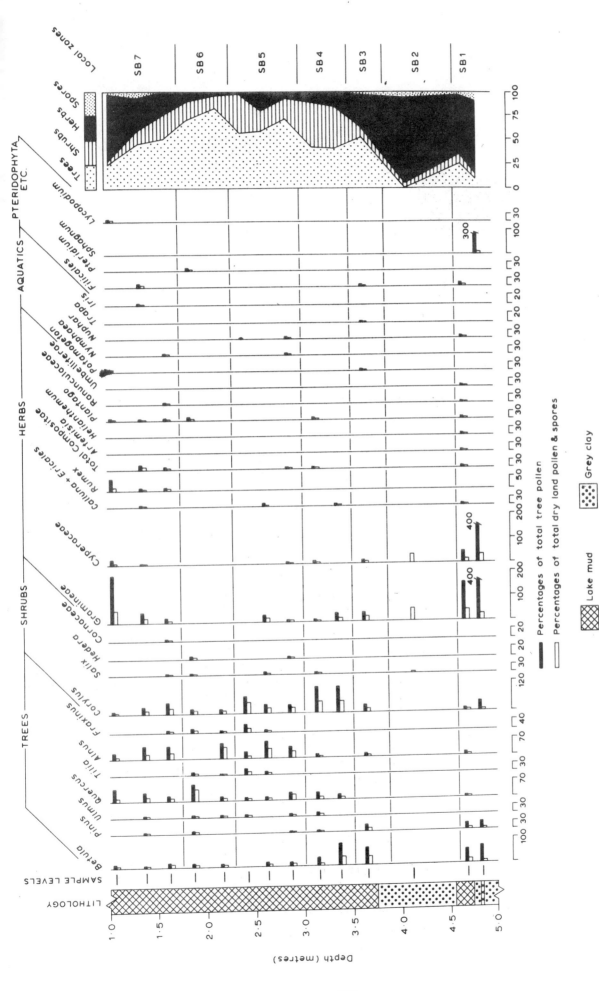

Figure 7.7 Outline pollen diagram from Skipsea Bail Mere. Analysis by University of Hull 2nd year Palynology Class, 1982.

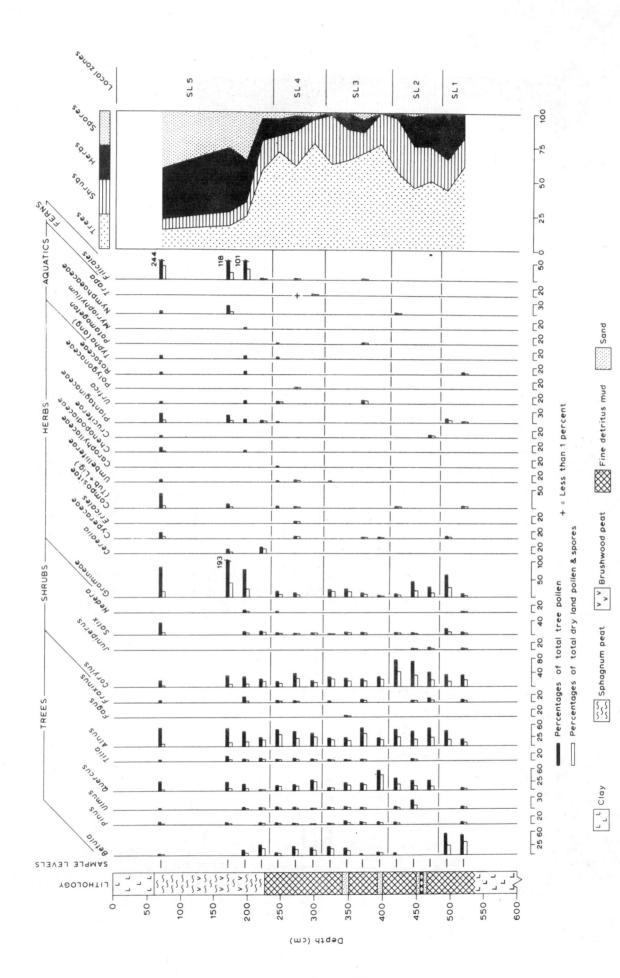

Figure 7.8 Outline pollen diagram from Skipsea Low Mere. Analysis by University of Hull 2nd year Palynology Class, 1974.

174

The well-known elm decline (usually dated to about 5000 b.p.) ushers in the succeeding **Alnus-Quercus** RPAZ. The first clear evidence of man's influence on the vegetation is present in the form of pollen of cereals and weeds. Tree pollen is spectacularly reduced at Skipsea Withow. Pollen of **Trapa natans** is present at Skipsea Low Mere (Figure 7.9). It was also found in this zone at Skipsea Bail Mere (Flenley, Maloney, Ford and Hallam 1975), although it is not recorded in Figure 7.7). Its presence in Skipsea Bail Mere over a long period within this zone was however confirmed by Elaine Smith (unpubished dissertation, University of Hull, Department of Geography), who not only found pollen, but also fruit spines. The presence of **Trapa** has usually been taken to indicate summers warmer than at present in Britain (Godwin 1956), but it is also possible that the occurrence is related to man, and one cannot but note with interest the presence of Bronze Age dwelling platforms in both meres where **Trapa** has been found (Flenley and Maloney 1976).

The uppermost parts of the diagrams differ widely, and all have been lumped in a rather unsatisfactory **Alnus**-Gramineae RPAZ. Forest clearance, doubtless occurring in different ways and at different times, is evidenced in all the diagrams. Tree pollen is reduced spectacularly at Roos, then shows a recovery, a further clearance and a later recovery (perhaps due to tree growth on The Bog itself after drainage). At Hornsea and Skipsea Bail Mere, clearance seems to have been progressive, although the evidence from the latter site is scanty, and both are incomplete at the top. At Skipsea Withow the record is again incomplete and dating is confused: it is possible the zone is not represented at all, although there is evidence of forest reduction at 40cms. At Skipsea Low Mere the record is exiguous but suggests a rather complete clearance early in the time represented by the zone. In the best record, at Roos, the herbs present suggest the initial clearance was for mixed farming. For instance the presence of **Plantago lanceolata** suggests pastoral land, but that of Chenopodiaceae suggests arable. Cereal pollen is regularly present later in the zone, and **Plantago lanceolata** is reduced in amount, which accords with the present day importance of arable farming.

CONCLUSIONS

It is clear that the meres of Holderness provide a series of records through the last 13,000 years which display considerable variations on a basic theme. The pattern of Late-Glacial oscillation, Flandrian forestation and later deforestation is everywhere present, but the details are different. This is particularly so during the last 5000 years, in which the forests have been removed. It seems that the abundance of sites will eventually make possible a remarkably detailed reconstruction of the impact of man on the vegetation of Holderness.

CHAPTER 8

ARCHAEOLOGICAL REMAINS FROM SKIPSEA WITHOW MERE AND THEIR WIDER SIGNIFICANCE

INTRODUCTION

It is abundantly clear from Chapters 1 and 2 that there has been a comparative abundance of archaeological finds from the meres and wetlands of Holderness. This is the case for the Mesolithic blade, scrapers and harpoons which pre-occupied Armstrong and Sheppard and have been found frequently since that time (Davis-King 1980) and for carved and worked timbers dated to the Bronze Age and Iron Age. For example, Smith (1911) records numerous sites in the Skipsea meres -Bail Mere, Low Mere and the Barmston drain where stakes, piles and ?platform structures occur. Worked or carved wood remains have been recovered at no less than fourteen sites in Holderness in the recent review of prehistoric woodworking by Coles, Heal and Orme (1978). Prehistoric wooden boats from Humberside are described by Wright and Churchill (1965). The utilisation of wood during the Mesolithic is of course well known from the Star Carr site further north in Yorkshire. Nevertheless, despite the frequency with which 'finds' have been noted, reliable information on their dating, correlation and environmental and palaeoecological significance is very restricted in scope and quantity. In particular, the significance of these finds, especially the later prehistoric wood remains, for our understanding of the nature and utilisation of the prehistoric landscape, largely remains to be explored.

In this study, the finds of Mesolithic and early Neolithic age which have been discovered from the Withow mere exposures are discussed.

PALAEOLITHIC AND MESOLITHIC FINDS FROM THE SKIPSEA WITHOW MERE DEPOSITS

by Paul Mellars

There are three main finds recovered from the Skipsea Withow Mere deposits to be discussed here:

1. the flint blade discovered during the recent investigations;

2. the barbed bone point discovered by B. Morfitt in 1903, and discussed in many subsequent papers (Armstrong 1922, 1923a, 1923b, Sheppard 1923, Read, Woodward and Kendall 1923, Godwin and Godwin 1933, Clark and Godwin 1956 etc.); and

3. the small series of flints excavated by Armstrong in 1923, mainly from deposits of 'blue-grey silt' exposed on the foreshore.

<u>The Skipsea Withow blade</u> (Figure 8.1)

As discussed earlier, this was discovered in October 1978 by K. Dash, in the course of taking samples from the lower silt deposits exposed in the basal part of the Skipsea Withow Mere series. The environmental associations of the blade point clearly to a period of cold climate, which is stratigraphically earlier than a ^{14}C determination of 9980±100 b.p. On stratigraphic and palaeontological grounds (Chapters 3, 5 and 6) the blade is referred to pollen zone I of the Godwin (1975) scheme.

The blade is illustrated in Figure 8.1. As will be seen, the piece exhibits a rather impressive level of blade technology, with regular, parallel edges and a marked degree of convexity when viewed in long section. The blade shows a very small striking platform and pronounced bulb of percussion, and apparently some deliberate 'trimming back' of the striking platform before detachment from the core. The lower end of the blade is broken, apparently as the result of a blow delivered (deliberately or accidentally) from the dorsal surface. There are no signs of secondary retouching, and there are no indications of any damage to the edges of the blade that can be attributed with certainty to utilisation - as opposed, for example, to accidental damage either prior to or during excavation. In general, the piece shows a remarkably fresh state of preservation, with no indication of patination or abrasion prior to incorporation into the lake sediments. The raw material is a good quality translucent flint, of a medium to orange-brown in colour, and shows a small patch of cortex on the lower right-hand corner of the blade.

On technological grounds, parallels for blades of this kind could be found in industries of either Late-Devensian or early Flandrian age in Britain. Certainly, similar pieces could be found in the assemblages from Star Carr and Flixton site 1, dated to pollen zone IV of Godwin (1975), or in many of the assemblages from British cave sites collectively referred to the 'Creswellian' tradition, and probably spanning the period from late pollen zone I to early pollen zone III (cf. Clark 1954, Moore 1950, Campbell 1977, Jacobi 1980). Blade technology of this kind would be much more difficult to parallel in any later industries from Britain - for example, those of the later Mesolithic or subsequent Neolithic/Bronze Age date. The character of the piece is therefore generally consistent with the dating inferred from the stratigraphic and palaeoecological data.

<u>The Skipsea Withow 'harpoon'</u> (Figure 8.2)

The discovery of this piece by B. Morfitt in 1903 precipitated a major controversy, and led to a spate of later publications (Armstrong 1922, 1923a, 1923b, Sheppard 1923, Read Woodward and Kendall 1923, Godwin and Godwin 1933, etc.). The most coherent account of the discovery remains that provided by Armstrong (1922, 1923b - based on the notebooks kept by Morfitt at the time of the original discovery) who states that the barbed point was discovered by Morfitt below a depth of approximately 1.5 metres of peat, embedded in an underlying deposit of 'silt'. The point was said to have been found 'immediately' below the complete skeleton of a giant elk

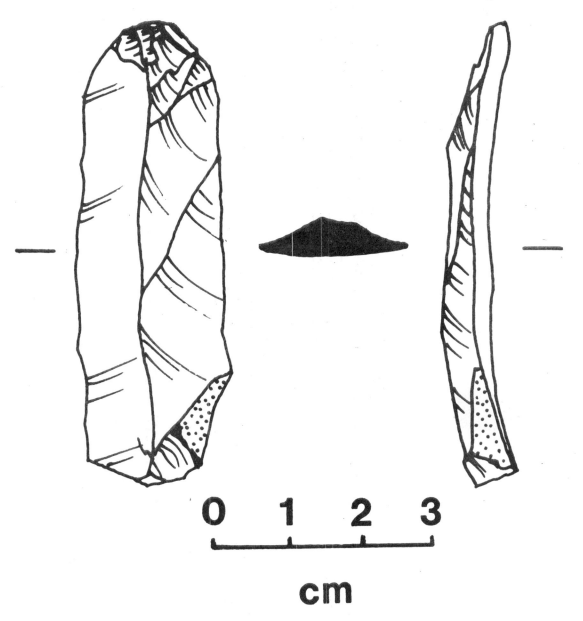

0 1 2 3

cm

Figure 8.1 Flint blade found during recent investigations at Skipsea
Withow.

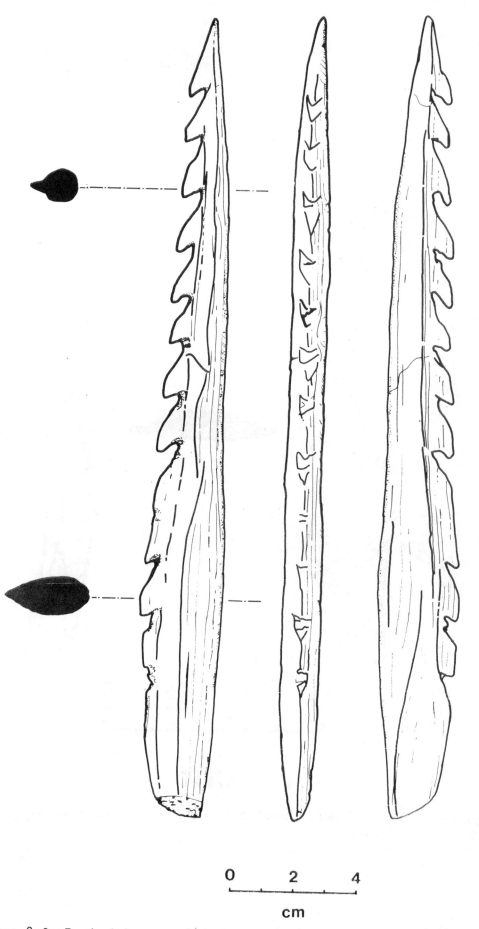

Figure 8.2 Barbed bone point from Skipsea Withow, excavated by B.
Morfitt, 1903. After Clark and Godwin 1956, Fig. 4.

(**Megaceros giganteus**), which was reputedly embedded within the base of the overlying peat deposits (cf. Armstrong 1922:131, 1923b:60, and Chapters 1, 2, 3 here).

The problems of assessing the true chronological position of the barbed point remain very difficult, and have been discussed in an earlier section. Pollen analyses undertaken by H. and M.E. Godwin in 1932 indicated that the point could be no later than pollen zone IV (i.e. later Boreal) in age, but left the possibility of an earlier date open (Godwin and Godwin 1933:38-42). As discussed earlier, the recent work points in favour of a much earlier Late-Glacial date, probably within the range of 10,000-10,450 b.p. A dating within this range would clearly accord well with Armstrong's assertion (unfortunately not accompanied by any detailed records) that remains of reindeer were recovered 'at the same level as the harpoon' (Armstrong 1922:131). The sedimentological and stratigraphic evidence presented in Chapter 3 suggests the present Unit 5 (Figure 3.3) may have been the source of these finds.

The character and technology of manufacture of the barbed point have been discussed in some detail in an earlier paper by Clark and Godwin (1956). As Clark pointed out, all of the essential details of the piece - the fine, close spacing of the barbs, the 'criss-cross' pattern of shaping the barbs, and the use of bone as opposed to antler as the raw material - can be paralleled in several other discoveries of barbed points from the Holderness region of east Yorkshire, notably those from Brandesburton, 10km southeast of Skipsea, and from a poorly-documented site at Hornsea, some 7km to the south on the same coast. Unfortunately, neither of these sites is dated. The main point emphasised by Clark was the contrast between these pieces and those from Star Carr (dated to pollen zone IV) in which both the technique of manufacture and the raw material (i.e. red-deer antler as opposed to bone) differed from those of the Skipsea Withow, Brandesburton and Hornsea specimens (Clark and Godwin 1956:11).

In a recent study, Wymer, Jacobi and Rose (1975) have suggested that barbed points of the type represented by the Skipsea Withow and related Holderness finds may represent a generally earlier phase of technology than that of the Star Carr finds. A closely similar specimen from Sproughton, Suffolk, for example, is clearly earlier than a ^{14}C determination of 9880±120 b.p., and is most probably of either pollen zone III or very early zone IV age (Wymer et al. 1975, Wymer 1976, Rose 1976). In other words, the age inferred for the Sproughton specimen is similar to that proposed on the basis of the recent work for the Skipsea Withow find. On the basis of the combined evidence from Sproughton and Skipsea Withow, therefore, barbed points of this type may well be particularly characteristic of the pollen zone III/early zone IV time range in eastern England. Interestingly, the two barbed points of bone found in association with an elk skeleton (**Alces alces**) at High Furlong, Lancashire, and dated to pollen zone II, differ in certain respects from the Skipsea/Sproughton form, and show closer analogies with the later specimens from Star Carr (Hallam, Edwards, Barnes and Stuart 1973).

Artefacts excavated by Armstrong (1923) (Figure 8.3)

Limited excavations were carried out by A.L. Armstrong at Skipsea Withow in May, 1923, following the exposure of large areas of silt deposits in the foreshore area as a result of heavy tides. Only brief details of these excavations were published, of which the most complete are provided in the paper published in **Man** in September 1923 (Armstrong 1923a). Here, Armstrong states that almost all of the deposits on the foreshore consisted of 'blue' or 'blue-grey' silt, although he notes that thin patches of peat could be seen overlying the silt deposits in a few places.

During the course of Armstrong's excavations a total of only seven supposed artefacts were recovered in situ, of which five were clearly embedded within the silt, while the other two were found either within the peat, or at the junction between the peat and silt. Armstrong noted that the flints recovered from the silt were 'stained from black to greenish grey' in colour, while those from the peat were 'stained yellow to brown'.

Potentially the main interest attaches to the series recovered from within the 'blue-silt' deposit since, on the basis of evidence discussed in earlier sections, these must almost certainly be of Late-Devensian age - i.e. broadly within the range from late pollen zone I to zone III. Unfortunately, Armstrong's own illustrations of these pieces are by no means entirely clear cf. Figure 8.3 and the character of the flints is difficult to assess. In fact, of the three pieces illustrated by Armstrong, only one (a small flake recovered at a depth of approximately 60cms within the silt - No. A2 of Armstrong's report) is reasonably convincing as an artefact (Figure 8.3, No. 2). The other two pieces (Nos. A1 and A3 of Armstrong's report - Figure 8.3 Nos. 1 and 3) are much less convincing, and could well represent flints with purely natural damage or flaking, perhaps derived by reworking from the underlying boulder-clay deposits. Two other pieces recovered from the silt are not illustrated by Armstrong and are therefore even more difficult to assess; one is described as 'a quartzite hammer stone, or pounder, abraded and battered at one end by use' while the other is described simply as 'a thin quartzite flake showing signs of use as a scraper' (Armstrong 1923a:137).

The two flints found by Armstrong either within the overlying peat deposits or at the junction between the peat and silt are much more convincing as artefacts, but are typologically not very distinctive. The small end scraper recovered from the junction between the peat and silt in the exposed face of the cliff (Armstrong 1923a:Figure A5, Figure 8.3 No. 5) is a carefully worked implement, but could be paralleled equally well in either late glacial or early postglacial (i.e. early Mesolithic) industries. Potentially more interesting are two additional artefacts, discovered long before the time of Armstrong's excavation, but assumed by Armstrong (mainly on the basis of colour and patination) to have been derived from the peat deposits at Skipsea rather than the underlying silts. One of these is a classic obliquely-blunted point of characteristic early Mesolithic type, while the other is a small, transversely-sharpened flint axe of probably similar age (respectively Figure A7 and Figure B of Armstrong's report; c.f. Figure 8.3 No. 6 and Figure 8.4). The

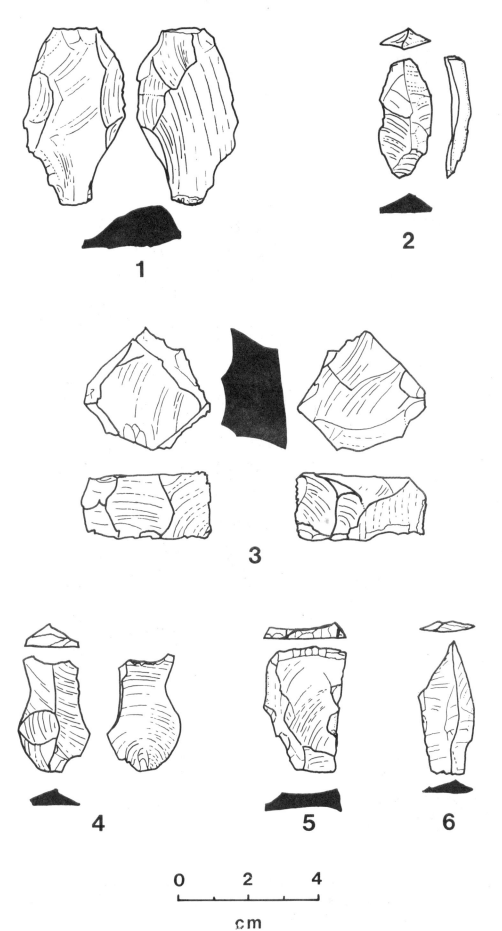

Figure 8.3 Flints from Skipsea Withow discovered by Armstrong and
others. Nos. 1-3 excavated by Armstrong from 'blue-grey
silt' deposits; Nos. 4-5 excavated by Armstrong from within
peat deposits (No. 4) or at junction of peat and silt (No.
5); No. 6 found on beach but assumed (from patina) to
derive from peat deposits. After Armstrong 1923a, Figure A
(page 135).

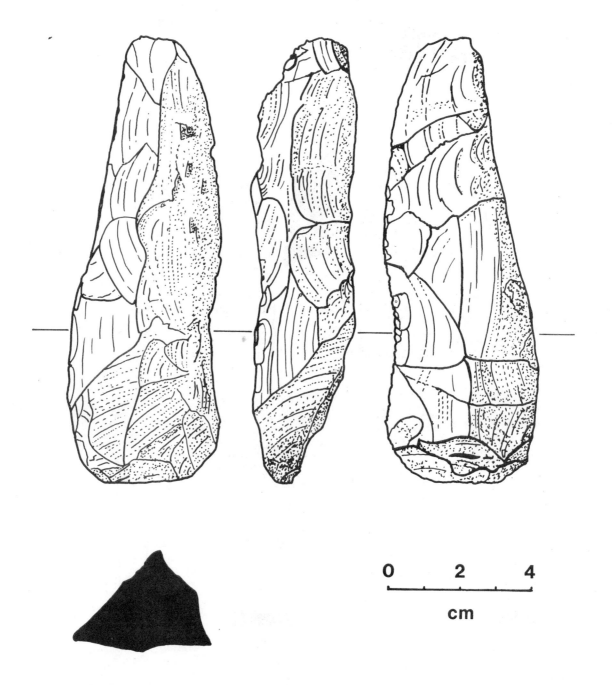

Figure 8.4   Transversely-sharpened flint axe, presumed to derive from
peat deposits at Skipsea Withow.   After Armstrong 1923a,
figure B (page 136).

presence of these pieces clearly hints at the existence of at least some traces of early Mesolithic activity within the early Flandrian deposits at Skipsea, but in the absence of any clear indication of their exact stratigraphic position within the deposits, any closer assessment of their age is impossible.

CONCLUSIONS

The main importance of the finds discussed above is the evidence they provide for some form of occupation within the vicinity of the Skipsea Withow Mere deposits during Late-Devensian times. The Skipsea Withow blade dates to an early stage of the development of the lake in pollen zone I (i.e. broadly from 14,000-c. 12,000 b.p.). Other finds date broadly to the pollen zone III-IV transition. Further finds of well documented Late-Devensian age are still very scarce in eastern England. The concentration of horse bones excavated by John Moore from Flixton site 2 appears to be well dated to either pollen zone II or early pollen zone III (Moore 1954:192-4, Walker and Godwin 1954:49-51) but the archaeological associations of this consist of only two rather undiagnostic flint artefacts. The single end-scraper recovered by Buckland from Messingham, Lincolnshire, is stratigraphically earlier than a ^{14}C date of 10,550+250 b.p. (BIRM 707) and is claimed to date from a period of rigorous climate during Late-Devensian pollen zone III (c.f. Jacobi 1980:65). Other discoveries of typologically late-glacial material are known essentially from surface exposures (e.g. Jacobi 1980:65-6) and could potentially cover a wide range of time.

The Skipsea Withow finds therefore serve to reinforce the potential importance of Late-Devensian occupation in northeastern England, and should encourage a more determined search for further traces of this occupation - particularly in the Holderness region and the Vale of Pickering, where the prospects of recovering traces of this occupation in datable contexts are relatively high. Evidence is urgently needed not only on the detailed character of this occupation (in terms of both the typology of the industries and the associated economic and settlement patterns) but also on the precise age and duration of this occupation within the Late-Devensian sequence as a whole.

P.M.

NEOLITHIC WOODWORKING AND WOODLAND MANAGEMENT

Between 1978 and 1984 a series of 'worked' wooden remains have been recovered from site SS1 on section 4, in the middle of Unit 8 (Figure 3.1 and inset). They were obtained from one horizon which continued under a collapsed pill box floor. The source deposits were detrital and in situ marsh and carr peats which are strongly laminated with many densely packed, horizontally bedded timbers, mainly alder, with oak and ash. Sandy partings are common, suggesting soil erosion on the nearby slopes. The deposit indicates a reworked carr peat; probably within or close to growing trees - as suggested in the modern lake margin carr woodland from Hornsea mere illustrated in Plates 1.1 and 1.2.

AN EARLY NEOLITHIC ROD

The worked rod shown in Plate 8.1 was found interbedded with horzontally bedded, detrital peats and brushwood 0.4m below the centre of the collapsing pill box base (Figure 3.1, site of SS1 inset). Consequently it must either have been discarded or reworked.

The wood is alder (**Alnus** sp.), and the rod was taken from a stem approximately 40 years old (Hillam, pers. comm). Its upper end was an apparently natural, rectangular fracture, which might have occurred before or after final burial. The other end had been carved to a crudely rounded point with a series of rough facets produced by an axe or knife (Plate 8.1). There is minimal abrasion of the sharper facet edges suggesting very limited reworking or exposure before final burial. There are many parallels for this rod in the Somerset Levels trackways (Somerset Levels Papers, 1975-1980). Probably the most likely use of this timber was as a stake or pile driven into the water-logged peat-soil of the alder carr woodland, and intended to support another structure such as a platform or trackway, etc.

This worked rod was dated by radiocarbon assay to 4770±70 radiocarbon years b.p. (HAR 3378). There are no reasons to doubt the reliability of this date. The wood did not appear to be contaminated. The age difference between the timber, and the peat dated at the top of Unit 5 to 4500±50 b.p. (SRR 1942) suggests a plausible sedimentation rate of 0.5 to 1.5m of detrital peats and timbers in a period of approximately three hundred years.

The interest of this Neolithic rod lies in its great age, placed by the radiocarbon date firmly in the early Neolithic, and amongst the earliest Neolithic trackways or platforms so far found in the British Isles (see Coles et al. 1978). For example, the Skipsea radiocarbon date lies well within the range of the radiocarbon dates for the very old Sweet Track in the Somerset Levels given by Morgan (1979) and Coles (1979).

IN SITU ROD AND PEG

A further rod and peg were found 5m north of the first at exactly the same stratigraphic horizon within the carr-peat. However, these were noted in situ, still pushed vertically into the peat, their upper parts exposed by erosion and slumping. The rod illustrated in Plate 8.2 is also made from Alder (**Alnus**), again about 40 years of age (Hillam pers. comm). Its lower end forms an 'elbow'; this form is obtained by breaking and/or cutting the stem from the side of a basal coppiced stool (Coles, Heal and Orme 1978) in a process described by these authors. The fractured elbow has been further trimmed by axe or knife to leave facets before the elbow was inserted into the peat soil; its expanded, hooked end providing good anchorage in this difficult substrate. It therefore indicates deliberate management of woodland.

Plate 8.1 Carved rod of Alder (**Alnus**) showing carved facets: reworked and found interbedded with detrital peats: radiocarbon dated to 4770+70 yrs b.p. (HAR 3378).

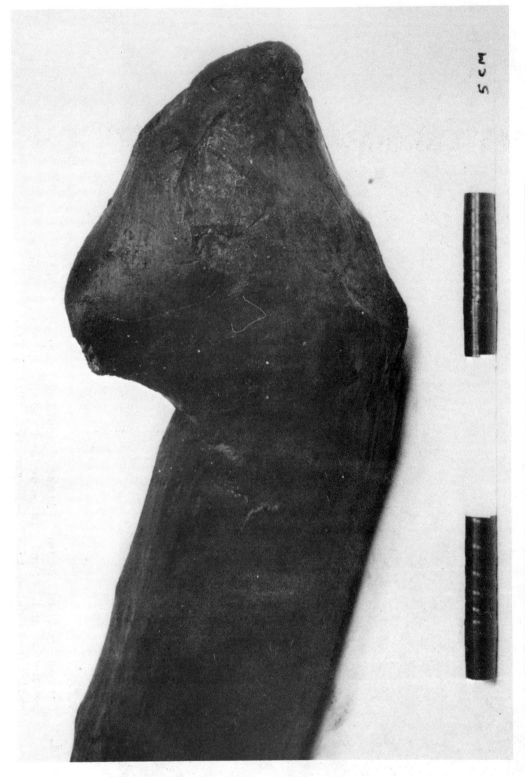

5 cm

Plate 8.2 Alder rod displaying an 'elbow' due to coppicing: find spot
is site SS 1 in Figure 3.1 inset.

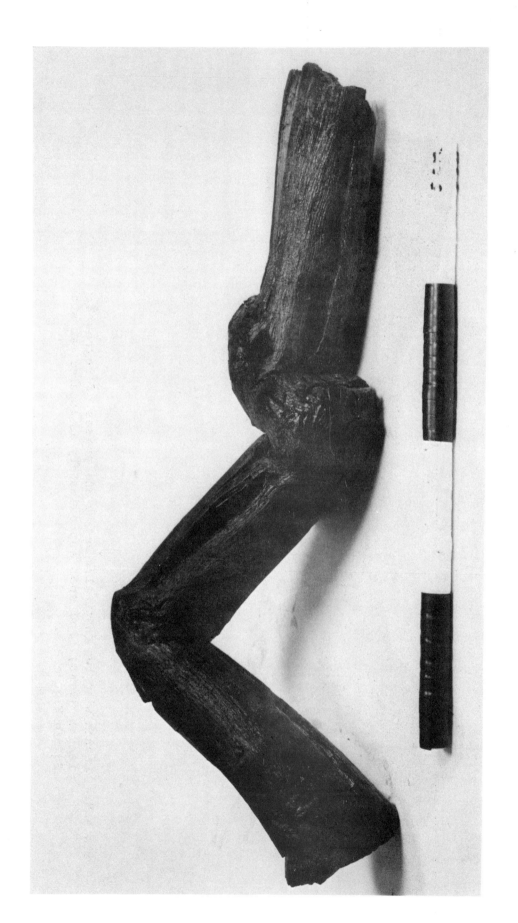

Plate 8.3 Zig-zag peg caused by pushing/hammering the peg into the peat surface: the find spot is site SS1 in Figure 3.1.

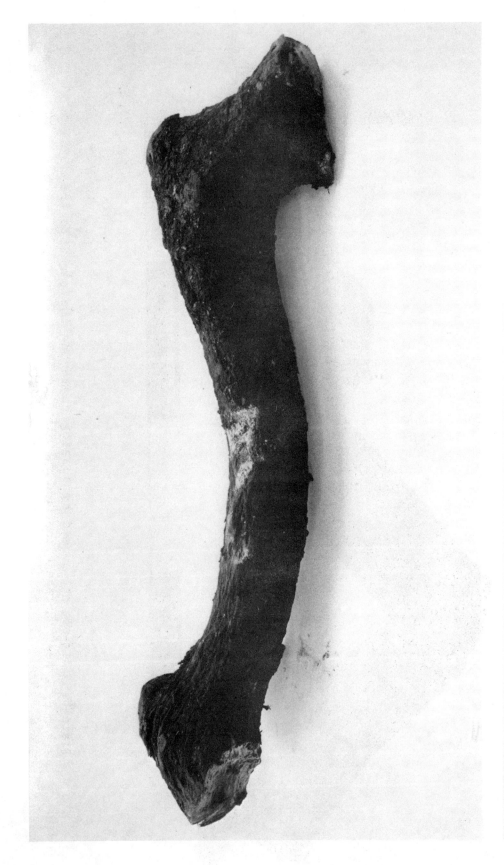

Plate 8.4 Branch with two (natural?) breaks and phases of regrowth:
length 30cms; find spot approximately as located at site
SS1 in Figure 3.1.

PLATE 8.5.

The zig-zag peg is illustrated in Plate 8.3. It was found 1m further north from the second rod, and is of Hazel (**Corylus**). The tip was not found. The bending and buckling is not a natural growth shape of wood, either above or below ground. It was probably caused by continued hammering when the peg met buried Alder wood at depth. Again the feature is similar to finds in the Somerset Levels trackways, from which Coles et al. (1978) show how a zig-zag peg timber was used to stake planks to a peat surface. These authors also point out the peg must have been used 'green'; seasoned wood would have fractured and split, rather than bent and buckled in this manner.

UNPROVENANCED TIMBERS

In 1984 cliff falls of peat from Unit 8 at section 4 yielded further timbers of interest, from approximately the same horizon as those described above.

The first is shown in Plate 8.4. The two marked breaks do appear to be original and preserved within the peat. It is unclear whether or not these original breaks indicate natural or human activity.

The second timber is ash (Plate 8.5). It has a clear stake-like form. However, no axe marks are preserved on its point, and it is not inconceivable that the point-shape represents the effect of natural rotting within the peaty soil.

These latter timbers have not been dated. There is, however, no reason to suspect they are significantly different in age to the dated rod, although they may slightly pre-date or post-date it. They are all overlain by the same further series of laminated detrital and carr-peats. Consequently the dated rod, and adjacent rod and peg, indicate early Neolithic exploitation of the margins of Skipsea Withow Mere and utilisation of the alder carr timber. By analogy with evidence from Somerset, the timbers suggest active woodland management by coppicing. The worked timbers from the Withow lake margin appear to be notably older than many other stakes and piles recorded from Holderness (Smith 1911) and generally attributed to the Bronze Age. The significance of this observation remains to be determined.

CHAPTER 9

SYNTHESIS AND CONCLUSIONS

INTRODUCTION.

The discussion section of each of the preceding chapters has indicated the important information, ideas and explanations that have been derived from each type of investigation. Several general points merit further emphasis and elaboration. This may be achieved by reference to the chart below which facilitates comparison between the various lithological units recognised in the field, sample provenance and the local assemblage zones recognised in the molluscan and palaeobotanical studies of the complex late Devensian sequence at the Withow mere:

Unit No.	Sample No.	Local molluscan assemblage zones	Local pollen and plant macrofossil assemblage zones
10	1		
9	2		
3e	138b	D	————
3e	135		
3e	136		SKJ
4vii	137		————
	138a		
4iv	5		SKH
4iv	6	————	————
4d	7		
4d	8		
4d	9	C_2	
4d	11		
4d	12	————	
4d	13		SKG
4d	14		
4d	15		
4ii	16	C_1	
4ii	23		
4ii	17		
4ii	24	————	————
4ii	25		
4ii	18	B_2	SKF
4c	19		
4c	20?	————	————
4c	21		
4c	30		
4b	22	B_1	SKE
4b	32		
3b	33	————	
3b	34		
4a	35	A_4	————
4a	36		
4a	37		SKD
3a3	38	————	————

$3a_3$	39			SKC
$3a_2$	40	A_3		
$3a_2$	41	——		
$3a_2$	42			SKB
$3a_1$	43	A_2		
$3a_1$	44			
$3a_1$	45	A_1		——
3/1/1	LS4			SKA
and	LS5			
2/3	LS6			
	LS7			

THE ECOLOGICAL HISTORY OF THE WITHOW MERE AND ITS CATCHMENT.

The Late Devensian: Deglaciation

The contained rock types and pre-Quaternary palynomorphs in the Skipsea till demonstrate that the parent ice sheet had flowed in a generally southerly direction to the area along the general line of the Northumberland-Durham-Yorkshire coast. Unpublished till fabric studies from Skipsea suggest it had adopted a slightly south-westward direction into Holderness after passing the barrier of Flamborough Head. The radiocarbon date of 13,045±270 b.p. (BIRM 317) on "pioneer" mosses above the till at The Roos (Beckett, 1981) still provides the best estimate of the date by which the deglaciation of Holderness had occurred. The present data are not capable of further resolving the discussion on the character of the glacial episode (multiple re-advances as opposed to a multiple-layer ice sheet in the Devensian) which affected the region. Both plant micro- and macrofossil studies have demonstrated that "warm stage" biological indicators have been re-worked from the Skipsea till into the Withow mere site.

The initial deglacial history of the till is known in more detail than is commonly the case. Initially weathering features and tension cracks developed; presumably reflecting a partial drying out of the till surface. Gleying suggests the immature, skeletal soils were subject to periodic waterlogging. Mudflows and slumps occurred, followed by shallow faulting of the surface materials. A wet, unstable ground surface on sloping ground is suggested. The origin of the depression which was to form the later Withow mere, similarly remains obscure. The present data suggest that in its earliest deglacial phases, the Withow lake was either not present, or more probably, it was developing in the lower parts of the hollow to the east of the current exposures.

The episode of dessiccation, weathering and mass-movement was followed by the deposition of this hillwash deposit and then by the inundation of the existing sequence by the waters of a lake which reached 8+m above the present beach; almost to the highest point reached by the present cliff face. Elutriation by waves, or shallow currents, appears to have removed the fine grade sediment fraction from these newly submerged lake margin deposits. This left a pebble-rich lag deposit (Unit 2b).

In general Units 2a and 2b imply rapid melting and thawing, although there is no other evidence from the site to suggest that the climate in this deglacial phase was notably warm or even mild.

Ameliorating conditions

The next phase of deposition is recorded only at the highest margins of the former lake. The presence of texturally varved sediments (Units 3/1/1-4) indicate the repeated freezing of the lake. The deposition of very fine grained clays within this unit occurred at times of ice cover.

"Pioneer" plant and animal species are shown to have colonised both the lake and the surrounding catchment at this time. **Chara** -stoneworts - and pondweeds grew in the deeper water; the lake margins were colonised by **Hippuris** and **Eleocharis** (SKA). The adjacent hillslope soils were immature, contained little organic matter, and were covered in a mosaic of mosses, light demanding herbs and shrubs, and eroding, open ground. The lake was rapidly colonised by freshwater molluscs, especially bivalves (A$_1$). Water conditions were improving. The input of organic detritus was continuing, causing the oxidisable organic carbon content of the lacustrine sediments to rise from the very low initial levels. Water hardness was increasing from very low levels to moderately high levels as carbonates were washed from the chalk-rich till-soils into the lake. The frequency with which the lake froze was declining. The sediments accumulating at the lake margin reflected this change. The "textural" varves were replaced by layers of carbonate precipitates suggesting notably hard water. On several occasions the lake margin was sufficiently stable for fringing reedswamp to spread onto the lake margin sediments, eventually to form thin layers of peaty silt. The rate of erosion of the catchment soils was declining causing fewer re-cycled palynomorphs to be deposited in the lake. The vegetation of the catchment was still open in aspect, but was now starting to reflect milder, stable conditions. Thickets or a parkland of birch and poplar-aspen developed within a widespread ground cover of light-demanding and, increasingly, warmth-demanding herbs. Dwarf birch was present, as was the meadowsweet, **Filipendula**, which has a present northern limit coinciding with the 14°C July isotherm in northwestern Europe (Seddon 1962).

The accumulating lake margin deposits were subject to disruption by local, small scale faulting. Lake levels also fluctuated, causing the erosion of the lake margin and the truncation of the lake margin sediments. The causes of these events are not clear. It is likely they reflect the general climatic improvement, thawing and dewatering of the slope and marginal deposits.

The "Skipsea blade" found in these deposits indicates human activity in this early "deglacial" landscape. The present evidence suggests the need to revise impressions of the geography of the Holderness landscape at this time. Several points merit emphasis. First, there is no reason to suspect that the generally <u>high</u> lake levels evidenced were caused by factors other than climatic in origin. If climate was the forcing factor, then the Withow situation of high lake levels is likely to have occurred throughout Holderness. Second, general ideas on the past geography of the region tend to reflect the impression derived from the reconstruction of the medieval landscape - i.e. low, undulating topography interspersed with meres and marsh. However, if the evidence from the Withow site was replicated from other lake margin sites, then a considerable shift of emphasis in interpretation is required. This area of Holderness would then be seen as an area of lakes, streams and marsh interspersed with islands and sinuous ridges. Such a landscape in an ameliorating climate is likely to have been relatively benign and relatively rich in biological resources.

Fluctuations in an improving environment

The next major event was a substantial drop in lake level to below the height of the present beach. This lowering resulted in further erosion of the abandoned lake margin deposits. The cause of the drop in level is not clear. One, or several of many factors, might have been important. Higher temperatures might have increased evaporation and/or precipitation input might have declined. The spreading tree/shrub cover "pumping" water from the ground through evapotranspiration may have reduced surface and soil water throughput to the lake. Alternatively, the final melting of large, incorporated ice-blocks nearby in the till may have promoted temporary breaching or draining of the lake. These questions may be resolved by replicate studies of nearby meres.

The period following this lowering (LMAZ A_{2-3i}; SKB/C; Unit $3a_1-3a_3$) records the re-establishment of the ameliorating trend noted earlier. The lake level returned to within 2-3m of its former level. Water conditions were good. The dominant deposit was the "sticky-plastic" blue, grey silt noted by earlier authors. The lake and its margin now supported a relatively rich flora of vascular plants, as well as desmids, Zygnemataceae, **Pediastrum**, and dinoflagellates. The rich and abundant molluscan fauna included several taxa requiring summer warmth. Erosion of the surrounding hillslope soils was decreasing even further in intensity, yielding fewer derived microfossils. There was a relatively complete ground cover with grasses, herbs, dwarf shrubs. Finds of the pollen of tree birch suggests it had joined the **B. nana - Populus** thickets by zone SKB. Slightly later in SKC, macrofossils of tree birch and juniper occur, demonstrating the increasing diversity of the ground cover, and suggesting the presence of a birch-poplar/aspen-juniper parkland. At several points in the central areas of the exposure, these strata ($3a_{2-3}$) are overlain unconformably by peats. It is possible that some of the artifacts and vertebrate remains recorded by Armstrong (1923a, b) derive from this deposit. However, no evidence of the "punt-holes" inferred by Armstrong was detected. The favourability and resource potential of the lake and its catchment must have been high at this time.

Deterioration: Unit 4a -LMAZ A4- SKD

Until this point in time the general picture is of an improving environment punctuated by local changes in the geography. However, at this level, both the molluscan and palaeobotanical studies record an environmental deterioration. The re-cycled pollen increase, suggesting accelerated soil erosion in the catchment. Juniper and tree birch become much less frequent; whereas the more cold tolerant taxa -**B. nana** - continue. The deterioration was not sufficiently strong to induce any notable reduction in the open-ground or ground-cover species present. The molluscan fauna declines rapidly in both diversity and numerical abundance. The nutrient status of the lake appears to decline. This combination of responses suggests a minor climatic deterioration may have occurred.

Stability and instability

At, or shortly after this deterioration, the history of the mere becomes more complex. The most notable event is the start of the input into the lake of very coarse clastic sediments at the south west margins of the present exposure from pockets of coarse glacial sands and gravels interbedded in the till at this location. The stratigraphy of the site indicates the extremely localised nature of the mass movement process involved. These gravels do not occur on the northern face of the modern exposure and thin rapidly to the south.

The graded bedding and inter-digitating grey-blue silts which indicate an aquatic depositioal environment are restricted to the lower half of the complex gravel member (SKB$_{1-2}$; LMAZ E-F), the absence of these properties in the upper components of these deposits suggests that they are sub-aerial in origin. The cause(s) of the mass-movement/instability are obscure. Several mechanisms, acting singly or in combination, may be involved. The climatic deterioration associated with Unit 4a may have served as a trigger. Major storms or the continuing process of lake bank erosion may have contributed.

This period of geomorphic instability was accompanied by limnological and biological stability. The molluscan data indicates a biologically mature lake fringed with well developed hydroseral successions. A mild summer climate is similarly indicated.

The palaeobotanical data suggest that only limited soil erosion was occurring elsewhere in the catchment. Once again, the ground vegetation appears to have been once again a birch-poplar/aspen parkland with juniper and a ground cover of grasses, herbs and shrubs, including some thermophiles. The climatic amelioration continued until the base of Unit 4iv - 6: when a sudden and marked deterioration is indicated. Although it cannot be rigorously demonstrated it appears likely that some of the more recent episodes of faulting and slides affecting these gravels were induced during and after this change.

A Major Climatic Deterioration

All lines of palaeontological evidence point to a sudden and distinct climatic decline. The palynological indications of soil erosion in the catchment increase markedly in comparison to the earlier periods. The lake fauna shows a very marked decline in species diversity and overall numerical abundance. The vegetation of the lake becomes extremely poor: its productivity must have been very low. Warmth-indicating molluscs disappear. The plant macrofossils indicate a decline in the abundance of tree species and loss of thermophiles. The landscape ceased to be a parkland with herbs and grasses. It became a sedge-grass tundra with exposed soil patches and a few tree birch surviving in favoured locations.

The Flandrian: Amelioration

The character of the finer-grained sediments deposited at the lake margin in the early Holocene (SKH) remained broadly the same as in the Late Devensian - grey/blue "plastic silts". The landscape was progressively recolonised by the more thermophilous and familiar tree taxa which were associated with a diverse shrub-herb flora. Tree birch replaced dwarf birch, only to subsequently decline in abundance due to competition. The most notable local events in the history of the lake were:

i. a very marked lowering of lake level which resulted in the exposure, erosion and on the northern exposures, weathering and soil development on the exposed Late Devensian lake silts. Lake levels fell below modern beach level. It is difficult to envisage other than climatic causes of this change. The "buff-silts" produced by soil development and weathering of the Lake Devensian lake margin deposits may have been the equivalent of those which were noted by Godwin and Godwin (1933). Mixed cold/warm plant-animal assemblages and archaeological remains might be anticipated at this level.

ii. the return of lake levels almost to their Late Devensian level: (c. 3-4m above modern beach level) and a marked change in sedimentary type to organic muds indicative of a nutrient-rich biologically active lake. This change occurred at or before 9,880±60 b.p. It is possible the "peat-stained" or immediately "sub-peat" artefacts of Armstrong derive from theses early Flandrian deposits.

At about 7,000 b.p. the catchment was dominated by a mixed forest assemblage of oak, alder, elm and lime. The lake was now sufficiently infilled for Alder carr to start to extend away from the lake margin across the sample site. The palaeontological data indicate open water conditions still prevailed nearby in the lake. Large vertebrates occasionally became trapped and died in the organic sediments. The climate of the time might have been slightly milder than at present; with the dominant wind direction being being from the S.S.W. rather than W or S.W.

Forest clearance and management

There is abundant evidence of forest clearance and early agriculture dating from the period 5000 years b.p. Elm, alder and lime were the main trees felled, with plantains and grasses being favoured in the grazed pastures. Cereal cultivation was also practised. The site is also interesting because of the clear evidence of deliberate woodland management - the coppicing of Alder carr - and the construction of structures requiring piles and pegs at the lake margin. Presumably these were intended to aid exploitation of other biological resources in and around the lake. Further episodes of clearance and agriculture are recorded before the site was buried in the hillwash resulting from soil erosion sometime after c. 4,500 b.p. The historical data indicate that the mere continued to be important into late Medieval times, when it was presumably breached by coastal erosion.

COMPARISONS FURTHER AFIELD

Several important points may be made. In spite of the immense complexity of the geomorphic history of the lake margin environment, and the major extent to which purely local features are dominant in the palaeontological record for the Lake Devensian, it has proved possible to correlate on biostratigraphic grounds both the palaeobotanical data and the molluscan remains. These correlations appear to be more than a correlation of biofacies. The patterns detected generally match those from elsewhere in Holderness and further afield in the British Isles. In particular there is a remarkable degree of similarity between the pattern of climatic change revealed at Skipsea Withow and other Late Devensian lake sites from Britain described in Pennington (1977), Coope (1977) Beckett (1981) and the emerging sequence at Creswell Crags (Jenkinson and Gilbertson, 1984). Nevertheless, there is every reason to suspect some degrees of diachroneity exists at and between zone boundaries.

A clear four-fold division of the Late Devensian is evidenced at Skipsea. An initial phase of rapid warming following upon deglaciation reaches a peak, with mild - or even warm - summer temperatures suggested. This corresponds fairly precisely to the pre-interstadial and Lake Windermere interstadial of Coope (1977). This was succeeded at Skipsea Withow by a short-lived climatic deterioration. Many sites elsewhere record this episode which is dated to c. 12,200 to c. 12,000 years b.p. (Coope 1977:329). A period of fairly stable mild, but not cold climate follows. This corresponds to the milder part of the Windermere interstadial which was previously often referred to as the Allerød interstadial. The severe, sudden climatic deterioration of the Loch Lomond stadial stands out clearly in the impoverished floras and faunas of the Withow mere and other British sites. Consequently the detailed palaeoclimatic and palaeontological information from the Withow site will provide an important link between the more "oceanic" sites of western Britain and those of the European mainland.

In many ways the Flandrian history of the area is more conventional; with the exceptions of the evidence of very early woodland management and the suggestions of water chestnuts being used (?grown/encouraged?) for food.

METHODOLOGICAL CONSIDERATIONS

It is interesting to compare the information derived from the investigations of the margins of this mere with that which would have been obtained by an investigation using more conventional coring techniques and/or of the more central areas of a lake.

It has proved possible to identify regional trends in the pollen evidence from the swamping effects of local environments and their fluctuations. Nevertheless, this was not always a confident activity and has been carried out only because of the wealth of information available from other investigations in Holderness and elsewhere.

The more "conventional" studies would (probably) have failed to identify the following features or concepts noted at Skipsea Withow.

1.   The great fluctuations in lake level which have occurred in the Late Devensian and early Flandrian would not have been elucidated in detail. Whilst we can only speculate on their cause, they have profound significance for palaeogeographical reconstruction and the assessment of plant resource availability. The prospect of a shift of interpretation from a Holderness formerly being a great till sheet interspersed with meres, to that of a very large area of interconnected lakes and streams interspersed with discontinuous islands and gravelly ridges is both tantalising and important.

2.   The abundance of macrofossils at this lake margin environment has clarified many issues. For example, it is now clear that tree birch did survive during the Loch Lomond stadial this far north on the eastern side of the Pennines. Similarly, the site has yielded fascinating evidence of Neolithic woodland management.

3.   The presence of normal faulting, lateral slides and extensive slumping and mudflows is interesting in its own right. When more fully understood, these superficial tectonic structures may yield information of further palaeoenvironmental significance. It is clear from the stratigraphy that these features have also disrupted the stratification and have brought the lake margin deposits together with field relationships which are familiar to the geologist, but less frequently encountered in archaeology or limnology. Cores or small trial pits are unlikely to have detected the crucial displacements.

4.   The distribution of the biological remains merits emphasis. In the Late Devensian deposits they are richest in the areas of sedimentation that reflect the idiosyncracies of lake margin mass-movements and erosion.

5.   Two types of investigations have yielded information which has proved very useful, albeit initially unexpected: (a) the studies of pre-Quaternary palynomorphs (Hunt 1984) have yielded valuable data on:

      i.   erosional rates and vegetation cover on the soils of the catchment;

      ii.   the background "noise" in the palaeontological record provided by derived, reworked biological remains;

      iii.   corroborated ideas on climatic fluctuations; and

      iv.   indicated the route traversed by the Late Devensian icesheet(s) to Skipsea.

and (b) the studies of the freshwater molluscan remains have provided not only the expected good guide to habitat conditions, but have also been shown to be most interesting indicators of palaeoclimate and useful for correlation.

6. The more obvious lithological properties of the sediments are especially interesting. The textural properties of the earliest lake silts reflect the changing climate of the period through the impact of lake freezing. The chemical properties of the sediments also reflect biological and environmental changes within and outside the lake. In general they match the sequence established at nearby Barmston by Varley (1968) and more generally through the British Isles (Mackereth 1965, 1966). However, the major fluctuations associated with the coarse gravel unit are demonstrated by the palaeontological studies to be associated with purely <u>local</u> geomorphic processes: a conclusion not easily reached by initial field examination of the site. Comparison with the published stratigraphies of other Holderness meres (e.g. Hornsea Old Mere, Sheppard 1906, 1912) indicates that major changes in the extent of carbonate-rich lake deposits have also occurred during the Flandrian in Holderness, but that the extent to which they reflect local, as opposed to regional forcing factors remains uncertain.

"In Memorium" for a lost mere

These studies of the lost meres of Holderness have provided just another small piece of information with which to understand the origins and development of our landscape. The misfortunes of the Withow site have nevertheless resulted in both the development of interesting ideas from a category of depositional environment which is frequently overlooked, and provided staunch support for Sheppard's (1909:500) advocacy of palaeoecological research in Holderness.

MOLLUSCAN TAXONOMY, ECOLOGY AND PALAEOECOLOGY

by N.M.Thew.

Note: LD - Late Devensian, MD - Middle Devensian, ED - Early Devensian
       Ip - Ipswichian, Wo - Wolstonian, Ho - Hoxnian: pollen zone
       I-VIIb refers to the Godwin (1975) scheme - see also Table 2.1.

A. LAND SPECIES

Succinea oblonga (Draparnaud)

Fairly specialist.   Shell: thin, requiring little calcium.
Ecological distribution: lives in damp, sparsely vegetated places;
e.g. marshes etc. Characteristically on dried out bare muddy surfaces
(Kerney and Cameron 1979).
Dispersal and colonisation: moderately rapid dispersal.
Breeding and growth: annual, with replacement.
Palaeoecology: uncertain as there has been some confusion with
Catinella arenaria. Holyoak (1982) claims this species is only
present in interglacials and interstadials.

Catinella arenaria (Bouchard-Chantereaux)

Fairly generalist.   Shell: thin, requiring little calcium.
Ecological distribution: lives in damp, sparsely vegetated hollows;
prefers bare mud in marshes.
Geographical distribution: Holarctic, to 70°N (Kerney and Cameron
1979).
Dispersal and colonisation: dispersal moderately rapid.
Breeding and growth: annual breeding, with replacement.
Palaeoecology: despite some confusion with **Succinea oblonga**, Holyoak
(1982) claims that this species is known from Devensian stadials.

Oxyloma pfeifferi (Rossmäsler)

A generalist species.   Shell: thin, requiring little calcium.
Ecological distribution: lives in marshes and permanently wet
terrestrial habitats; tolerant of acidity (with pH as low as 5 -
Bishop 1976).
Geographical distribution: Holarctic - beyond 70°N (Kerney and
Cameron 1979).
Dispersal and colonisation: rapid (Valovirta 1977).
Breeding and growth: annual, with replacement; growth and time of
breeding vary with climate and location.
Palaeoecology: similar habitats; known throughout Wolstonian and
Devensian cold stages.

Cochlicopa lubrica (Müller)

A generalist species.   Shell: thin, requires little calcium.
Ecological distribution: ubiquitous but requires moderately damp
conditions (Paul 1975); tolerant of acidity (pH of 5 or over - Bishop
1976, Walden 1981 - though Berry (1973) states that numbers drop
sharply under 5.6).
Geographical distribution: Holarctic - beyond 70°N in FennoScandia
(Kerney and Cameron 1979).
Dispersal and colonisation: fairly rapid (Valovirta 1977).
Breeding and growth: annual, with replacement; adults hibernate in
winter, juveniles remain active in U.K., eggs hatch in September (Paul
1975).
Palaeoecology: similar habitats; present in Early Devensian at
Cambridge (Lambert et al 1963) and Wretton (West et al 1974)
and Late Devensian from pollen zone Ib (Allison et al 1952, Evans
1967, Kerney 1963) - also the interstadial material at Fisherton (ED or
MD - Green et al 1983).

Vertigo lilljeborgii (Westerlund)

A specialist species.
Shell: fairly robust requiring moderate calcium.
Ecological distribution: lives on saturated, decaying vegetation in
marshes and alder fens at the margins of lakes and rivers, usually in
places subject to flooding; rarely associated with other species of
Vertigo (Kerney and Cameron 1979).
Dispersal and colonisation: not known.
Breeding and growth: annual breeding, with replacement.
Palaeoecology: poorly known. It is only known from one other
non-Flandrian site - Sturton, N. Lincolnshire which is late Devensian
and a lowland site (Preece, in press). All the Flandrian records (3
fossil and a handful of modern) are from highland locations (R. Preece,
pers. comm.).

Vertigo geyeri (Lindholm)

Specialist (Norris and Pickerell 1972, Coles and Coleville 1979).
Shell: fairly robust requiring moderate calcium.
Ecological distribution: this species lives only in neutral or fairly
calcareous (pH 6.5) wet fenland with a good growth of narrow leafed
plants (sedges, grasses and rushes), and a stable water level.
Geographical distribution: northern limit of c. 68° in
FennoScandia.
Dispersal and colonisation: moderately fast where suitable habitats.
Breeding and growth: annual.
Palaeoecology: in Late Devensian only appears at very end of pollen
zone Ic (Kerney 1963).

Vertigo genesii (Gredler)

Fairly specialist (Kerney and Cameron 1979).
As above but lives in marshy upland locations associated with water
seepage; again, requires neutral or calcareous locations; similar
northern limit but also absent in U.K.
Palaeoecology: appears from pollen zone Ia onwards (Allison et al
1952, Kerney 1963).

Pupilla muscorum (L.)

Fairly specialist.
Shell: fairly robust requiring moderate calcium.
Ecological distribution: widely held to be a xerophile found in only
very dry locations where few competing species can survive (Kerney and
Cameron 1979): but also rarely found in wet locations (Boycott 1934)
but with a slightly different morphology corresponding closely to a
damp-loving species found in the Alps (Kerney et al 1964).
Geographical distribution: found N. of 70°N in FennoScandia.
Dispersal and colonisation: rapid (Valovirta 1977).
Breeding and growth: annual.
Palaeoecology: found throughout Wolstonian and Devensian cold periods;
found fairly commonly in damp locations in association with marsh and
freshwater species, but only Kerney et al (1964) notes that the
morphology was of the damp variant, in such a case.

Vallonia pulchella (Müller)

A generalist species.
Shell: fairly robust requiring moderate calcium.
Ecological distribution: lives in fairly wet to marshy locations in
open fairly calcareous habitats (Kerney and Cameron 1979).
Geographical distribution: found to 71°N in Norway.
Dispersal and colonisation: rapid (Valovirta 1977).
Breeding and growth: annual.
Palaeoecology: known from ED sites, the late Devensian from pollen
zone Ia onwards, and also from the Upton Warren interstadial deposits
(MD) at Isleworth (Kerney et al 1982) and Fisherton (ED or MD? -
Green et al 1983); always from damp habitats.

Punctum pygmaeum (Draparnaud)

A generalist species.
Shell: fairly robust but very small requiring little calcium.
Ecological distribution: lives in moderately most to marshy locations;
resistant to acidity (Bishop 1976); prefers shade (Evans and Jones
1973) and vegetation (Kerney and Cameron 1979).
Geographical distribution: beyond 70°N in FennoScandia (Kerney and
Cameron 1979).
Dispersal and colonisation: being so small it is very easily dispersed
and colonises well (Valovirta 1977, Paul 1979).
Breeding and growth: annual.
Palaeoecology: always in damp locations; known from ED sites, the late
Devensian from pollen zone Ia, and from interstadial deposits at
Isleworth (MD - ibid) and Fisherton (ED or MD? - ibid): like **V.
pulchella**, however, not from very cold climate deposits.

Vitrina pellucida (Müller)

A generalist species.   Shell: thin requiring little calcium.
Ecological distribution: lives in moderately damp to fairly wet
locations; very acid tolerant (Bishop 1976, 1977); prefers shade (Evans
and Jones 1973) and vegetation (Paul 1975).
Geographical location: found beyond 70°N in FennoScandia (Kerney and

Cameron 1979).
Dispersal and colonisation: fairly rapid (Valovirta 1977).
Food, breeding and growth: sometimes carnivorous (Evans and Jones 1973); adults are most active in winter in U.K.; annual breeding with replacement, eggs being laid in spring, the adults then dying (Paul 1975).
Palaeoecology: not known from ED or MD but found locally from pollen zone Ib onwards in LD (Kerney 1963).

Deroceras agrestre (L.)

A generalist species.   Shell: a slug species.
Ecological distribution: found in meadows and wet upland pastures, in relatively wild or undisturbed locations (Kerney and Cameron 1979); acid tolerant (over 5.0 pH - Walden 1981).
Geographical distribution: extends beyond 70°N in FennoScandia (Kerney and Cameron 1979).
Dispersal and colonisation: rapid (Valovirta 1977).
Palaeoecology: ubiquitous.

Euconulus fulvus (Müller)

A generalist species.   Shell: variable thickness.
Ecological distribution: ubiquitous catholic species but requires fairly damp conditions, tolerant of acidity (Bishop 1976, Kerney and Cameron 1979).
Geographical distribution: Holarctic; beyond 70°N in FennoScandia (Kerney and Cameron 1979).
Dispersal and colonisation: rapid (Valovirta 1977).
Breeding and growth: annual breeding, with replacement.
Palaeoecology: known from the ED, MD, LD. Holyoak (1982) says this species is known from Late Devensian interstadials.

Cecilioides acicula (Müller)

A fairly specialist species.
Shell: fairly thin requiring little calcium.
Ecological distribution: this burrowing species is commonly found at depths of 1.5 to 2m (Evans and Jones 1973, Kerney and Cameron 1979) usually in rock crevices or among plant roots, and on calcareous soils (Kerney and Cameron 1979).
Geographical distribution: restricted to 58°N (Kerney and Cameron 1979).
Dispersal and colonisation: no data.
Breeding and growth: annual.
Palaeoecology: absent from cold periods.

Lymnaea truncutula (Müller)

A generalist species.
Shell: can be thin or thicker, depending on habitat.
Ecological distribution: technically an aquatic species; Boycott (1936) and then Kerney (e.g. 1971) have preferred to group it with the land snails. This is really a hygrophilous land species capable of living in damp terrestrial, or commonly wet lakeside or riverside marsh locations, rarely in truly aquatic habitats (Macan 1950, Okeland 1969,

Paul 1975); fairly tolerant of acidic conditions (Bishop 1977, Okeland 1969) and fairly tolerant of poor vegetation (Okeland 1969) - responds fairly well to improvements in both.
Geographical distribution: beyond 70°N in Norway (Okeland 1969).
Dispersal and colonisation: fairly rapid.
Food: restricted diet of plant detritus, but efficient digestion as some sand is present in the gut (Reavell 1980).
Breeding and growth: 70 to 150 eggs: 2 or 3 broods per summer with replacement (Calow 1978).
Palaeoecology: found throughout Wolstonian and Devensian so obviously extremely hardy; always in marsh rather than aquatic habitats.

B. FRESHWATER GASTROPODS

Prosobranchs:

Valvata cristata (Müller)

Fairly specialist.   Shell: robust, requires a lot of calcium.
Ecological distribution: requires rich vegetation (commonly reed beds) in fairly eutrophic, shallow water, with a soft substrate (Fretter and Graham 1978, Okeland 1969); intolerant of either exposed, fast water locations (because of lack of vegetation) or soft/acidic water (Okelund 1969); common at lake margins, and in eutrophic ditches and ponds; burrows into substrate in winter.
Geographical distribution: found to 65°N in Sweden and Finland (Sparks 1957), absent beyond S. of Norway (Okeland 1969), but found in Siberia E. to the river Amur (Fretter and Graham 1978).
Dispersal and colonisation: fairly rapid where suitable habitats.
Food: as **V. piscinalis.**
Breeding and growth: lays eggs on weeds and stones, growth halts over winter; one brood per summer with replacement.
Palaeoecology: known from ED interstadials at Sedgwick, Cambridge (Lambert et al 1963), and Wretton (West et al 1974), but not from MD interstadials like the Upton Warren at Isleworth. Known from pollen zone II in the LD at the White Bog, Co. Down (Stelfox et al 1972). Typically dominant in Ho and Ip II sites where suitable large pond deposits (e.g. Sparks 1976, West and Sparks 1960) but rare or secondary with river terrace-type deposits.

Valvata piscinalis (Müller)

A fairly generalist species.
Shell: robust, requiring considerable calcium.
Ecological distribution: requires eutrophic water; can tolerate poor vegetation but needs moderate calcium carbonate (Macan 1950, Okeland 1969), and a soft substrate (Fretter and Graham 1978); common in lakes and slow moving rivers, absent in littoral zone and fast currents but can live to depths of 10m (Macan 1950, Fretter and Graham 1978).
Geographical distribution: found to beyond 70°N in Norway (Okeland 1969).
Dispersal and colonisation: fairly rapid.
Food: feeds by crawling over substrate, possibly by filtering (Fretter and Graham 1978); restricted diet of plant detritus (Reavell 1980).

Breeding and growth: annual, one brood with replacement (Calow 1978).
Lives on vegetation and substrate in summer, burrows to hibernate in
winter (M. Young 1975); breeds in spring to summer with 50 to 400 eggs
laid on vegetation or stones.
Palaeoecology: present in ED, MD and LD where suitable habitats, i.e.
absent from rapidly accumulating braided river gravels. Typical of
warm stage terrace deposits with **Bithynia tentaculata, Pisidium
amnicum, P. henslowanum, P. nitidum** and **P. subtruncatum.**

Bithynia tentaculata (L.)

A fairly specialist species.
Shell: thick and robust requiring considerable calcium.
Ecological distribution: requires fairly abundant vegetation (Powell
and South 1978, Fretter and Graham 1978), with calcareous water, for
breeding to take place (J. Young 1975, Dussart 1976): also need
eutrophic but not fast-flowing water. Common in lakes and slow-flowing
rivers with a soft-substrate.
Geographical distribution: reaches 66°-67°N in FennoScandia but also
found in Soviet Arctic (Green et al 1983).
Dispersal and colonisation: rapid (Boeters 1979, 1982).
Food: feeds by both filtering suspended matter, and also by grazing
over the substrate (Fretter and Graham 1978) hence its fairly varied
diet with plant detritus, plus secondary algae etc; sand grains in the
gut increase digestive efficiency.
Breeding and growth: this biennial species breeds in spring to summer
without replacement. This is also a viviparous species with separate
males and females. One hundred and twenty eggs are laid which climb
vegetation after hatching. Hibernates buried in soft substrate (Calow
1978, Fretter and Graham 1978).
Palaeoecology: present during interstadials in the ED (Sedgwick and
Wretton) MD (Isleworth and Fisherton) and LD (pollen zone II at
Nazeing): (Lambert et al 1963, West et al 1974, Green et al
1983, Kerney et al 1982, Allison et al 1952). During warm
stages it is dominant in slow-moving river assemblages, and very
prominent in lake and large pool faunas.

Bithynia leachii (Sheppard)

Frequently found with **B. tentaculata** though more restricted to
vegetation and only found in hard water.
Distribution is more restricted to the N. in FennoScandia (64°N?).
Lives for one or sometimes two years. Viviparous. Less common than
B. tentaculata; less tolerant of moving water, though needs to be
eutrophic.
Palaeoecology: this species is unknown from the MD or LD but is
present in ED interstadials (e.g. Wretton - West et al 1974). It
is found with **B. tentaculata** in warm period deposits.

<u>Pulmonates:</u>

Lymnaea stagnalis (L.)

Shell: fairly robust, requires moderate calcium carbonate.
Ecological distribution: it is only found in hard water (Macan 1950,
1969, Okeland 1969); prefers good vegetation, but intolerant of much
water movement (Okeland 1969, Boycott 1936, Ellis 1969); found in
sheltered lake margins and large ponds.
Geographical distribution: found N. of Arctic Circle in FennoScandia
(Okeland 1969).
Dispersal and colonisation: slow (Ellis 1969, Okeland 1969).
Food: very varied diet with very high sand intake allowing efficient
digestion (Reavell 1980).
Breeding and growth: this biennial species produces one brood per year
without replacement; 1000 to 1500 eggs.
Palaeoecology: this species is known from interstadial deposits within
the ED (Sedgwick and Wretton), MD (Isleworth) and LD; at Nazeing it is
also known from late pollen zone III, a stadial of the LD; it is always
in small numbers (Lambert <u>et al</u> 1961, West <u>et al</u> 1974, Kerney
<u>et al</u> 1982, Allison <u>et al</u> 1951). It is common, but in small
numbers during warm period deposits but rare in river terrace
sequences.

Lymnaea peregra (Müller)

A very generalised species.
Shell: varies greatly; thin in acidic water.
Ecological distribution: this is probably the most ubiquitous species
being extraordinarily genetically flexible (Calow 1981); it can live in
acidic, poorly vegetated, fast flowing, littoral, or deep water
locations (Macan 1950, Okeland 1969, 1979, Dussart 1976, J. Young
1975). It is less abundant, however, in situations of intense
competition (Calow 1981).
Geographical distribution: ubiquitous, beyond 70°N (Okeland 1969,
1979).
Dispersal and colonisation: very rapid (Boeters 1979, 1982).
Food: very varied, and very efficient with a very high sand content in
the gut (Reavell 1980).
Breeding and growth: annual but one or two broods per season with
replacement; avoids muddy substrates (M. Young 1975) and prefers stony
bottoms. Unlike most pulmonates can live at depth by breathing
dissolved oxygen so can tolerate colder regional temperatures (Macan
1950); in U.K. remains active through the winter (Boycott 1936); 300 to
1100 eggs laid.
Palaeoecology: ubiquitous in all deposits with aquatic environments
available. Often dominant in terrace type assemblages laid down during
rigorous climates.

Myxas glutinosa (Müller)

A specialist species.
Shell: fairly robust, requiring moderate calcium.
Ecological distribution: requires stony rather than mud substrate,
tolerant of fairly poor vegetation; common at shallow lake margins, in
drainage ditches, and slow rivers; requires hard water (Boycott 1936).

Geographical distribution: northern limit of 63ºN in Finland (Sparks 1957) and S.E. Sweden (Okeland 1969).

Dispersal and colonisation: dispersal rapid but colonisation poor causing localised distributions with rapidly changing numbers (Ellis 1969).

Palaeoecology: absent from cold phases except for an appearance during pollen zone II at Nazeing; present in warm periods in small numbers, typically with the **V. cristata - B. tentaculata** and **V. piscinalis - A. crista - Anisus vorticulus** etc. Facies characteristic of pollen zone II-III, large shallow ponds.

Physa fontinalis (L.)

A fairly specialist species.

Shell: thin and fragile - requires little calcium.

Ecological distribution: requires abundant vegetation (Macan 1950, Okeland 1969, Powell and South 1978), plus eutrophic, moderately calcareous water (Macan 1969, Okeland 1969, J. Young 1975, Dussart 1976). Common in lake margins and in slow-flowing rivers.

Geographical distribution: restricted to southern Norway (Okeland 1969).

Dispersal and colonisation: fairly rapid.

Food: fairly varied diet with efficient digestion as some sand is present within the gut.

Breeding and growth: one or two broods per season, sometimes with the first brood living on after egg laying; 50 to 200 eggs (Calow 1978). Remain on vegetation throughout the year, with an aversion to substrate mud (M. Young 1975).

Palaeoecology: absent from cold period; present in small quantities in large pond and slow-river assemblages from pollen zone II-III of the Ho and Ip.

Planorbis planorbis (L.)

A fairly specialist species. Shell: demands moderate calcium.

Ecological distribution: requires both vegetation and fairly hard, shallow water (Boycott 1936, Macan 1950, Ellis 1969, Dussart 1976, Powell and Smith 1978). Commonly in small water bodies with little water movement.

Geographical distribution: limited to S.E. Norway, and to c. 66ºN in Sweden.

Dispersal and colonisation: moderate.

Palaeoecology: known from ED, and LD interstadials; also known from zone III stadial at Nazeing. Commonly present in small numbers in Ho and Ip large pond deposits with the **Valvata cristata -Bithynia tentaculata** dominated facies.

Gyraulus laevis (Alder)

A fairly specialist species.

Shell: size and thickness varies with location.

Ecological distribution: the modern ecology is poorly known. Boycott (1936) states: "a wild species, mostly north-western, and living characteristically in sllow, low-lying mountain lakes, generally near the sea, either among the weeds or on bare stones". In Ireland it is confined to lakes with clear water, free from much vegetation and with clean stony shores and bottoms (Stelfox et al 1972); Kerney et al (1982) describes these habitats as 'raw', with poor natural vegetation (cf. Norris et al 1971 - 'undisturbed' habitats). This species is tolerant of slightly brackish water, being found in typically western, 'maritime' coasts (e.g. Norway - Okeland 1969). In Caithness it is quite common in lochs and old quarries (Meiklejohn 1975). Boycott (1936) also notes that in aquaria fairly hard water is needed.

Geographical distribution: found to 65°N in FennoScandia (Green et al 1983), and also in the Siberian arctic.

Palaeoecology: within the cold phases this species is well-documented from both terrace deposits (e.g. Brandon and Beckford from MD faunas within the Avon number 2 terrace - Shotton 1968, Briggs et al 1975), and interstadial deposits - e.g. Sedgwick, Wretton and Fisherton (ED), Upton Warren and Isleworth (MD) and Nazeing (LD) (Lambert et al 1961, West et al 1974, Green et al 1983). It is also commonly found in zone I deposits from warm interglacial periods (best seen at Hoxne - West 1956) and also from zone late III, and IV, e.g. Stutton - Ip, Sparks and West 1964). This suggests that the species is both 'catholic' in the sense of being able to colonise rapidly, and tolerate fairly 'raw' conditions, and a 'slum' species in being unable to withstand competition, and hence specialising in colonising relatively ill-developed (biologically) habitats. The presence of this species in a spring fed stream at Burton Salmon in pollen zone VIIa Flandrian deposits is therefore interesting (Norris et al 1971).

Armiger crista (L.)

A fairly specialist species. Shell: thin, requiring little calcium.

Ecological distribution: contrary to Boycott's (1936) placement of this species as tolerant of soft water, studies by Macan (1950) and Okeland (1969) show this to require both calcareous water and a fairly well-developed vegetation. Much more common in large ponds than lakes, and seems to prefer quiet water.

Geographical distribution: in Norway found fairly far N., but onlyu to 65°N. in Sweden and Finland(Sparks 1957).

Dispersal and colonisation: rapid (Boycott 1936).

Food: fairly restricted diet - mostly plant detritus, as well as algae and a few bacteria (Reavell 1980).

Breeding and growth: annual, with replacement, c. 30 eggs (Boycott 1936).

Palaeoecology: absent from stadials of cold phases but commonly present in ED, MD and LD interstadials, but absent from terrace type deposits except the Taele gravels (W-interstadial). Also common with G. laevis as an early coloniser of large ponds during warm phases - e.g. Hoxne and Hatfield (Ho) and Wortwell (Ip) (Sparks and West 1964, 1968) - but continues significant into zone II (e.g. Swanton Morley, Bobbitshole and Selsey - Sparks 1957, 1976, West and Sparks 1960) where suitable habitats; important also in Ip zone IV deposits e.g. Stutton (Sparks and West 1964).

Anisus leucostoma (Millet)

A specialised 'slum' species.

Shell: little calcium required.

Ecological distribution: specialises in semi-terrestrial type habitats like marshes, and ponds prone to periodic drying out. Tolerant of

water acidity (Macan 1950, Meiklejohn 1973) intolerant of fast flow (Okeland 1969). Most commonly in ponds and ditches, and sometimes in lake margin and slow river marshes, but never in best locations as cannot withstand competition.
Geographical distribution: beyond 65°N in FennoScandia (Sparks and West 1963).
Dispersal and colonisation: very rapid (Boycott 1936).
Palaeoecology: common in terrace deposits from cold periods, as well as pond deposits from interstadials, often with **G. laevis** where it represents an early coloniser. Also present in early and late warm period ponds, as well as in 'slum' marsh locations throughout.

Bathyomphalus contortus (L.)

Fairly generalised.   Shell: thin, requiring little calcium.
Ecological distribution: most common in submerged vegetation (Macan 1950) but can tolerate poor vegetation as well as soft water (Okeland 1969). Requires fairly eutrophic water conditions, and is most common in slow rivers, lake margins and large ponds.
Geographical distribution: beyond the Arctic Circle in Norway (Okeland 1969).
Dispersal and colonisation: fairly rapid.
Food: fairly varied, mostly plant detritus (Reavell 1980).
Breeding and growth: one or two broods per season with replacement (Calow 1978); c. 30 to 40 eggs.
Palaeoecology: present in ED, and LD interstadial deposits, plus pollen zone III at Nazeing (Allison et al 1951). During warm phases it is rarely common, being significant only at Hatfield (Ho II) with abundant **A. crista** (Sparks and West 1970).

Hippeutis complanatus (L.)

Specialised.
Shell: fragile and thin, requiring little calcium.
Ecological distribution: requires both abundant vegetation and hard, eutrophic water, so found only in large ponds, lake margins (Okeland 1969, J. Young 1975) and occasionally in sheltered stretches in rivers.
Geographical distribution: to 63°N in Finland (Sparks 1957).
Dispersal and colonisation: efficient dispersal (Macan 1950).
Food: fairly restricted diet of plant detritus, plus some algae with a few sand grains to aid digestion (Reavell 1980).
Breeding and growth: annual, with replacement.
Palaeoecology: known from ED interstadials at Wretton and Sedgwick (West et al 1974, Lambert et al 1961). During the warmer phases this species is seen only in small numbers in the early and late phases, and in terrace deposits, but represents a significant element within the **Valvata cristata - Bithynia tentaculata** facies characteristic of zone II-III eutrophic well-vegetated pond deposits - e.g. Bobbitshole, Wretton and Swanton Morley (Sparks 1957, 1976, West 1970).

Acroloxus lacustris (L.)

Specialised.
Shell: fairly robust - requires moderate calcium.
Ecological distribution: requires abundant vegetation, and shallow, eutrophic, hard water (Okeland 1969 plus Boycott 1936, Macan 1950,

Ellis 1969, Young 1975); requires stones or vegetation to cling to.
Most common in ponds and in sheltered lake sites plus sheltered river
locations.
Geographical distribution: found only in S. Norway and S. Sweden in
FennoScandia (Sparks 1957, Okeland 1969).
Breeding and growth: annual with replacement, 80 to 100 eggs (Calow
1978).
Palaeoecology: very similar to **H. complanatus**.

C. FRESHWATER BIVALVES

Anodonta cygnaea (L.)

Specialised.
Shell: very large - requires abundant calcium.
Ecological distribution: requires both hard water, and a firm, muddy
bottom in which to live permanently embedded. Common in rivers,
canals, lakes etc. where these conditions fulfilled; intolerant of
rapid currents (Boycott 1936, Ellis 1962). Need fish for the parasitic
juvenile phase, so a fairly advanced biological community is required.
Geographical distribution: northern limit is the summer isotherm of
+14°C, so limited to c. Arctic Circle in FennoScandia, but extends
into Siberia (Ellis 1962).
Dispersal and colonisation: dispersed by fish.
Breeding and growth: thousands of eggs released (Boycott 1936).
Palaeoecology: no data.

Sphaerium corneum (L.)

Fairly generalised.
Shell: large, requiring abundant calcium.
Ecological distribution: most common where hard water with rich
organic substrate, and eutrophic, moving water is found, but can
tolerate some acidity, and is known from high energy littoral, stony
locations (Dussart 1976, 1979, Paul 1976). Boycott (1936) claims this
to be an indicator of 'good' molluscan conditions.
Geographical distribution: found beyond 70°N in Norway (Okeland
1979).
Dispersal and colonisation: efficient.
Breeding and growth: like all Pisidia and **Sphaerium** spp. this is
ovoviviparous, producing juvenile individuals from brood pouches.
Produces 2 or 3 broods within a season without replacement, individuals
living c. 1 year with a few surviving to 2 years. Up to 11 spat per
individual. Spat and adults overwinter with little growth (Dussart
1979).
Palaeoecology: present within interstadials of the ED, MD and LD,
where most significant within river assemblages; also present during
stadials (Holyoak 1982). During the warmer periods the species is
fairly significant with the fluvial facies dominated by **Bithynia
tentaculata - Valvata piscinalis - Pisidium nitidum - P.
henslowanum**, with significant **P. subtruncatum - P. amnicum -
P. casertanum** (e.g. Swanscombe [Ho] - Kerney 1971a), and
Grantchester and Wretten (Ip) (Sparks 1964a, Sparks and West 1970).
Also present in large pond facies dominated by **Valvata cristata -
Bithynia tentaculata**, plus significant **P. milium, P. nitidum**
and **P. subtruncatum** (e.g. Hatfield - Ho - Sparks and West 1970).

Sphaerium lacustre (Müller)

Fairly generalised.   Shell: requires moderate calcium.
Ecological distribution: tolerant of some acidity, and drying out;
more commonly found in ponds and ditches than in running water (Boycott
1936, Macan 1950, Ellis 1962).
Geographical distribution: reaches Arctic Circle in FennoScandia
(Ellis 1962).
Palaeoecology: only known from ED interstadials. Always with S.
corneum. Present in both fluvial and pond facies. Most common
seemingly at the end of warm periods e.g. Stutton (Ip IV - Sparks and
West 1964), indicative perhaps of a vulnerability to competition.

Pisidium amnicum (Müller)

Fairly specialised.
Shell: robust - requires considerable calcium.
Ecological distribution: requires hard, eutrophic, moving water with a
sandy substrate (Bass 1979); commonly found in rivers, streams and lake
shores.
Geographical distribution: scarce in N. FennoScandia, possibly because
of a lack of suitable habitats (Gibbard et al 1982) but extends E.
into Siberia (Ellis 1962).
Food: filter feeder.
Breeding and growth: two or three broods released in Spring to Autumn,
with c. 13 spat. A few live to 2 years.
Palaeoecology: present during Devensian stadials and interstadials
(Holyoak 1982); characteristically within fluvial sediments. Within
warm periods it is commonly within a fluvial facies, with small numbers
found within large eutrophic ponds (e.g. Bobbitshole - Sparks 1957).

Pisidium casertanum (Poli)

A very generalised species. Shell: thickness varies with conditions.
Ecological distribution: extremely tolerant of acidity and poor
vegetation; plus fairly tolerant of water currents, and drying out
(Boycott 1936, Ellis 1962, Macan 1950, Bishop 1977). In high Alpine
lakes found with **P. hibernicum, P. personatum,** while in lowland
Alpine lakes often found with **P. lilljeborgii** (Jayet 1973). In
Canadian lakes commonly found with **P. nitidum** and especially **P.
lilljeborgii** being found in small eutrophic lake basins with fine
organic substrate (Green 1971). In U.K. commonly found with **P.
nitidum** and **P. subtruncatum** (Bishop and Hewitt 1976). In deep
water found with **P. conventus** and **P. personatum** (Macan 1950).
Geographical distribution: widespread, found beyond 70°N in
FennoScandia (Okeland 1979, Ellis 1962).
Dispersal and colonisation: rapid (Boycott 1936).
Food: feed by grazing with their feet cilia (Dussart 1979)
Breeding and growth: annual, small number of spat (fry).
Palaeoecology: like **Lymnaea peregra** this species is widely found
within stadial and interstadial deposits (Holyoak 1982) within the
Devensian and Wolstonian. Within the warmer periods it is more common
in fluvial assemblages, but is also significant within large pond
deposits. Also significant in the White Bog Zone II LD lake deposit
with **P. nitidum** and **P. hibernicum** (Stelfox et al 1972).

P. casertanum var. ponderosa

Ellis (1962) says this variety is only found 'in specially favourable
habitats such as large riveres'.
Palaeoecology: ED: Sedgewick)   fluvial
                     Wretton)
           Ho I: Hatfield - large pond
          Ip III: Wretton)
                            fluvial
                Grantchester
(Lambert et al 1961, West et al 1974, Sparks and West 1970a, b,
Sparks 1964a).
Always with P. casertanum; seems to be present in fluvial locations
and large ponds, especially during early and late successional stages
within warm periods.

Pisidium personatum (Malm)

Specialised.
Shell: small and fairly thin - requires little calcium.
Ecological distribution: this is a specialist 'slum' species found
only inmarginal locations like damp and drying out habitats (Boycott
1936, Meiklejohn 1973, Paul 1975), in exposed littoral locations (Paul
1976), and at depth in lakes like Windermere (Macan 1950); also in high
mountain lakes with P. casertanum and P. hibernicum (Jayet
1973).
Geographical distribution: not N. of Arctic Circle (Ellis 1962).
Dispersal and colonisation: rapid (Boycott 1936).
Feeding: like most Pisidia this is a filter feeder.
Palaeoecology: in Devensian only known from pollen zone I in LD at
Nazeing (Allison et al 1951). Known from Wretton and Stutton (West
et al 1974, Sparks and West 1964) where marginal to a fluvial
fauna.

Pisidium obtusale (Lamarck) and P. obtusale var. lapponicum

Fairly specialist.
Shell: small but fairly robust - moderate calcium.
Ecological distribution: Kuiper (in Stelfox et al 1972) claims a
definite gradational change between these two species varieties.
Boycott (1936) claims this to be a specialist 'slum' dweller, but it is
not nearly as extreme as P. personatum, and is rarely found with
it. Often found in shallow water and marshy locations at lake margins,
slow-river margins and marshy ponds; tolerant of acidic water (Macan
1950, Ellis 1962). In N. European plains and in U.K. normally found
with P. hibernicum, P. nitidum, P. milium, P.
casertanum and P. lilljeborgii (Jayet 1973, Ellis 1962). In N.
Sweden found with P. hibernicum, P. lilljeborgii and P.
conventus (Kuiper in Stelfox et al 1972).
Geographical distribution: though Dance (in Coope et al 1961)
claims lapponicum is the northern variety, Kuiper (1972) claims that
both varieties extend into N. FennoScandia.
Palaeoecology: known from Devensian and Wolstonian stadial (?) and
interstadial deposits (Holyoak 1982). In these and warm stages, found
with slow-moving river and pond assemblages, especially the latter;

e.g. Bobbitshole (Ip IIb - Sparks 1957) with **P. nitidum** - **P. subtruncatum** - **P. milium** and **P. amnicum.** In LD known from pollen zones I to III at Nazeing and zone II at the White Bog (Stelfox et al 1972).

Pisidum milium (Held)

Fairly specialist.   Shell: moderate calcium.
Ecological distribution: common in ponds, lakes and rivers where eutrophic water and well-vegetated water found; lives on vegetation not on the substrate (Boycott 1936, Ellis 1962, Meiklejohn 1973). Often with **P. nitidum** but less common in rovers as prefers quieter moving water (Kerney et al 1982). In Pyrrenean shallow lakes found with **P. lilljeborgii** - **P. hibernicum** - **P. nitidum.**
Geographical distribution: not found beyond Arctic Circle.
Palaeoecology: present in Devensian interstadials but not stadials (Holyoak 1982). In interstadials and interglacials commonly in slow rivers and ponds with **P. nitidum** - **P. subtruncatum** and also **S. corneum** - **P. casertanum** and often with **P. henslowanum** - **P. amnicum.**

Pisidium subtruncatum (Malm)

Fairly general.   Shell: moderate calcium.
Ecological distribution: found where moving eutrophic water occurs; common in slow rivers, lakes, etc; tolerant of soft water but not so common. In moving water commonly found with **P. nitidum** (Ellis 1962).
Geographical distribution: found beyond Arctic Circle in FennoScandia (Ellis 1962).
Palaeoecology: known from stadial deposits (Holyoak 1982); more common from interstadials and interglacials where most common in slow-moving river assemblages - e.g. Grantchester (Ip), Swanscombe (Ho) and Isleworth (MD); also fairly significant in large eutrophic ponds like Bobbitshole (Ip) (Sparks 1957, 1964a, Kerney 1971a, Kerney et al 1982).

Pisidium lilljeborgii (Clessin)

Fairly specialist.   Shell: moderate calcium.
Ecological distribution: Boycott (1936), Macan (1950), Ellis (1962) and Meiklejohn (1973) all mention this species as being common with a sandy substrate; this may be a myth perpetuated or it may suggest a genuine conflict with Meier-brook's (1969) experimental and empirical data and Green's (1971) observations, who note that **P. lilljeborgii** prefers a fine, organic-rich substrate often being found with **P. casertanum** in the zone deeper than **P. nitidum** - **P. hibernicum.** Common in smaller, eutrophic lakes with **P. hibernicum, P. casertanum** and **P. nitidum** (Green 1971, Jayet 1973) and often with **P. milium** also in lowland lakes. Further N. in FennoScandia known also to inhabit marshy areas of shallow lakes (Kuiper in Stelfox et al 1972). Commonly in lakes, and also found in large eutrophic ponds, often with soft water.

Geographical distribution: extends into N. of FennoScandia (Kuiper in Stelfox et al 1972).
Palaeoecology: rarely recorded. Only from the White Bog, Co. Down, N.E. Ireland (see notes with **P. conventus**) - pollen zone II; plus from LD deposits from the Lea Valley at Nazeing (Allison et al 1952).

Pisidium henslowanum (Westerlund)

Fairly specialist.   Shell: requires a lot of calcium.
Ecological distribution: requires both moving water, a fairly coarse sandy or stony substrate, and hard water (Boycott 1936, Ellis 1962). Commonly in streams, rivers, and larger lakes with some water movement.
Geographical distribution: found to 65°N in FennoScandia (Kerney et al 1982) where it is commonly inappendiculate at the Northern edge of its range (Gibbard et al 1982); but also extends into Siberia (Green et al 1983). Like **P. amnicum** restriction of range could be due to lack of a suitable habitat.
Palaeoecology: known from stadial terrace deposits (Holyoak 1982). Common in river assemblages from interstadials and interglacials where invariably paired with **P. nitidum** with lesser amounts of S. **corneum** - **P. casertanum** and **P. subtruncatum**. In large ponds also have **P. milium** (e.g. Bobbitshole - Sparks 1957).

Pisidium hibernicum (Westerlund)

Fairly specialist.   Shell: moderate calcium required.
Ecological distribution: Meier-brook (1969) with experimental and empirical observation established that this species was much more mobile than other **Pisidia**, spending much of its time crawling over the surface. Hence it requires a reasonably coarse substrate, and is commonly found in the detrital zone of lake shores or slow-moving rivers; requires eutrophic moving water and is rare in closed ponds.
In rivers found with **P. subtruncatum** - **P. nitidum** - **P. milium** - **P. lilljeborgii**; in highland lakes with **P. casertanum** and **P. conventus** (Jayet 1973, Kuiper 1972).
Geographical distribution: found in N. FennoScandia (Kuiper in Stelfox et al 1972).
Palaeoecology: known from:
  (i)   Wretton: Ip II-III, +ED interstadial river assemblage;
  (ii) Swanscombe: Ho IIb-III - river assemblage;
  (iii) Nazeing: pollen zone III in LD - river assemblage.
all in fairly small numbers (Sparks and West 1970, Kerney 1971a, Allison et al 1951). Plus - dominant with **P. nitidum** in a pollen zone II lake deposit at the White Bog, NE Ireland (Stelfox et al 1972 - see note under **P. conventus**).

Pisidium nitidum (Jenyns)

Generalist.   Shell: thin - moderate calcium.
Ecological distribution: Meier-brook (1969) found **P. nitidum** paired with **P. hibernicum** in the coarser detritus and vegetation zone; burrows into sediment; decreases markedly below 4m depth, which explains why it is less common in deep mountain lakes. Prefers

well-oxygenated, eutrophic water, but can tolerate low calcium, so common in small closed lake basins (Green 1971); also Green says species prefers medium-grained, organic-rich substrate where it is found with **P. lilljeborgii** and **P. casertanum.** Common in slow-moving rivers, at lake margins and in large eutrophic ponds. Geographgical distribution: into N. of FennoScandian (Ellis 1962, Kuiper in Stelfox et al 1972).

Palaeoecology: almost ubiquitous where there is clean, moving water; found in stadial terrace sequences in small numbers (e.g. Hanborough Terrace - ?W (Briggs and Gilbertson 1973), and Beckford terrace - MD (Briggs et al 1975); most common in interstadial and interglacial river assemblages (see **P. henslowanum**), but also significant in large ponds (e.g. Bobbitshole - Sparks 1957) and lakes (e.g. White Bog, N.E. Ireland (Stellfox et al 1972) - also see **P. hibernicum**).

LATE DEVENSIAN VERTEBRATE REMAINS

by R.D.S. Jenkinson

The vertebrate remains found in the present study were:

23 Unit 4

Rana sp. 1 x distal calcaneum/astragalus - fractured
1 x complete phalange
1 x urostyle, proximal
1 x astragalus/calcaneum, complete
1 x shaft fragment (mid)
1 x distal epiphysis of tibia
3 x shaft bone flakes

P8LG 1 Unit 4

Rana sp. 1 x mandible pair (i.e. 2 both sides) complete
1 x astragalus/calcaneum, proximal only
1 x Lt. illium fragment
1 x limb shaft

Soricidae sp.
1 x femur shaft

P8LG 3a4: Unit 4

Soricidae sp.
1 x femur proximal
1 x Rt. distal tibia
1 x illium fragment

Rana sp. 2 x shaft fragment
1 x sphenoid
1 x vertebrae fragment

P8LG 2: Unit 4

Rana sp. 1 x distal radiocubitos
1 x Lt. scapula
1 x Lt. Fronto parietal
2 x calcaneum/astragalus flake
1 x phalange
1 x acetabulam fragment
1 x neural spine fragment

Unit 4 11

Vole sp. dentine plate from lower molar

Unit 4 12

Microtus sp.
lower incisor root. Seed?

Unit 1/2 LS.7

Microtus sp.
molar (dm) fragment - <u>very</u> abraded crown and roots
completely worn away.

Unit 4 12

Indet sp.
2 very abraded bone lumps - one may be a cranium fragment of
Lacerta sp. (lizard).

Unit 4 13

Lacerta sp.
vertebrae

Unit 4 14

Vole sp. m fragment lateral side broken inhibiting identification.

Unit 4 18

Vole sp. dentine plate from (molar)?

Unit 4 19

Vole sp. two dentine plates from lower molar.

It is difficult to estimate the numbers of animals represented -
however an estimate for frogs and shrews is set out below.

23 **Rana** sp.   1
P8LG 1 **Rana** sp.   2
Soricidae sp.   1
P8LG3 + 4 Soricidae sp.   1
Rana sp.   1
P8LG 2 **Rana** sp.   1

Habitat

Interpretation is necessarily restricted. **Rana** are extremely common in most environments with the exclusion of permanently frozen areas. They indicate the present of water in the vicinity. This need not be nearby or exist all year round.

Soricidae sp. - the present of shrew is interesting. On the bones preserved it is not possible to differentiate between Water Shrew, **Neomys fodiens**, or Common Shrew, **Sorex araneus**. They are definitely not pygmy shrew. Water shrew is almost wholly aquatic and associated with clear water streams. Both species prefer areas of dense cover (rocks, leaf litter or vegetation). Their life territory is small and they are therefore a more reliable indicator of conditions around the sample site.

The various species of vole are tolerant of a wide range of conditions. Lizards prefer warm conditions and usually sandy soil areas with open spaces.

Much further research is needed to establish the provenance and significance of the faunal remains noted in earlier surveys.

FLANDRIAN VERTEBRATES

A single vertebral process of pike (**Esox lucius** L.) was identified from sample 7/M/15 - near the base of the Flandrian - by A.K.G. Jones. A fine skeleton of red deer was recovered from the peat at Skipsea Withow by Thomas Sheppard (1923); exhibited at the Hull Museum.

Much further stratigraphic work is necessary before the vertebrate remains described from the site by Phillips (1829) and Armstrong (1923a, b) can be studied in an appropriate chronological, stratigraphic and environmental context.

INSECTS.

by H.K. Kenward

The macrofossil studies in Chapters 5 and 6 also detected the remains of various invertebrate groups apart from the Mollusca. Earthworm egg cases, caddis larval cases and **Daphnia** ephippia are most common. Their stratigraphic distribution is given in Table 5.3.

Two finds of insects merit note. A small, poorly preserved insect assemblage was recorded from Late-Devensian sample 7/M/16. It contained the typical Late-Devensian beetle **Arpedium brachypterum** (Grav.), together with species consistent with, though not directly indicative of, cold climatic conditions.

In Mid-Flandrian deposit 7/M/3 a single pronotum of **Platystethus nodifrons** (Mannrh.) was detected. This waterside species is confined nowadays to southern England: a feature of possible palaeobiological and palaeoclimatic significance. In general, the upper alder carr detritus peat (Unit 8: Figure 3.1) yielded species which are characteristic of swamps and fen woodland (including <u>Oxytelus</u> <u>fulvipes</u> Er.,reported by Kenward 1980). The insect material in these upper layers is still under study. Its poor state of preservation and the presence of a number of terrestrial species suggests inwashing of the fauna into the peat from the surrounding land by former streams, floods or overland flow.

APPENDIX 2

ROUTINE SAMPLE PREPARATIONS AND ANALYSIS

MACROFOSSILS

A vertical sampling thickness of 15mm was employed in the field. The plant macrofossils and insect remains were obtained by washing through a bank of sieves with the finest mesh of 300 microns, following the procedures outlined in Kenward, Hall and Jones (1980). The molluscs were extracted after immersion in a weak solution of detergent, or in a very weak solution of hydrogen peroxide, and washing through a 0.5mm mesh sieve. All specimens were identified with the aid of low-powered stereo microscopes.

POLLEN, SPORES AND DINOFLAGELLATES

Two procedures have been followed. Samples from sections 1, 2 and 7 were prepared using the standard techniques outlined in West (1977). These involved acetolysis and treatment in hydrofluoric acid. The samples from section 8 were prepared using the swirling method described in Hunt (1984). This technique does not involve noxious acids and has the additional advantage of permitting the recovery of siliceous and organic-walled microfossils in addition to pollen and spores. Specimens were identified with the aid of high powered binocular microscopes equipped with phase contrast optical systems.

SEDIMENTOLOGY

The particle size distributions of the coarse fraction was determined using a sieve shaker and nest of sieves at 1/2 phi intervals. The fine fraction was investigated using the modified Bouyucos (Kaddah 1974) hydrometer method. 'Carbonate equivalent' was measured with a modified Collins calcimeter (Avery and Bascomb 1974) and organic carbon by the low temperature loss-on-ignition procedure of Ball (1964).

PALAEOMAGNETISM

Field sampling followed the method proposed by Tarling (1983:79) for subaerially exposed soft sediments. This comprised driving short lengths of plastic tubing into a cleaned, horizontal sediment surface. The upper surface of the tube/sediment surface was sealed with wax and magnetic north marked on the wax and tube. The lower surface was sealed in a similar manner. Replicate samples were obtained for each level. We are grateful to Miss Katherine Groves for obtaining these samples in the field.

The laboratory procedures are described in Chapter 4.

BIBLIOGRAPHY

Allison, J., Godwin, H. and Warren, S.H. (1952) Late-Glacial deposits at Nazeing in the Lea Valley, North London. **Philosophical Transactions of the Royal Society of London B236**, 169-240.

Allison, K.J. (1976) **The East Riding of Yorkshire Landscape.** London: Hodder and Stoughton.

Andrews, E.B. (1968) An anatomical and histological study of the nervous system of **Bithynia tentaculata** (Prosobranchia) with special reference to possible neurosecretory activity. **Proceedings of the Malacological Society 38**, 213-232.

Armstrong, A.L. (1922) Two East Yorkshire bone harpoons. **Man 75**, 130-131.

Armstrong, A.L. (1923a) Further evidence of Maglemose culture in East Yorkshire. **Man 83**, 135-138.

Armstrong, A.L. (1923b) The Maglemose remains of Holderness and their Baltic counterparts. **Proceedings of the Prehistoric Society of East Anglia 4**, 57-70.

Armstrong, A.L. (1923c) On two bone points from Hornsea, East Yorkshire. **Man 31**, 49-50.

Avery, B.W. and Bascomb, E.L. (eds.) (1974) **Soil Survey Laboratory Methods.** Soil Survey Technical Monograph No. 6. Harpenden, U.K. Soil Survey of England and Wales.

Ball, D.F. (1964) Loss-on-ignition as an estimate of organic matter and organic carbon in non-calcareous soils. **Journal of Soil Science 15**, 84-92.

Bartley, D.D. (1962) The stratigraphy and pollen analysis of lake deposits near Tadcaster, Yorkshire. **New Phytologist 61**, 277-287.

Bartley, D.D. (1966) Pollen analysis of some lake deposits near Bamburgh, Northumberland. **New Phytologist 65**, 141-157.

Bartley, D.D., Chambers, C. and Hart-Jones, B. (1976) The vegetational history of parts of south and east Durham. **New Phytologist 77**, 437-468.

Bartlett, J.E. (1969) Further finds of Maglemosian barbed bone points from Brandesburton, East Yorkshire. **Kingston-upon-Hull Museums Bulletin 2**, 4-6.

Bass, J.A.B. (1979) Growth and fecundity of **Pisidium amnicum** (Muller, Bivalvia Sphaeridae) in the Tadnoll Brook, Dorset, England. **Journal of Conchology (London) 30**, 129-134.

Beckett, S.C. (1977) Hornsea mere. In **Yorkshire and Lincolnshire** ed. J.A. Catt. Birmingham, INQUA, 37-38.

Beckett, S.A. (1981) Pollen diagrams from Holderness, North Humberside. **Journal of Biogeography 8**, 177-198.

Beedham, G.E. (1972) **The Identification of the British Mollusca.** London: Hulton.

Bell, F.G. (1969) The occurrence of southern, steppe, and halophyte elements in the Weichselian (Last Glacial) floras from southern Britain. **New Phytologist 68**, 913-922.

Bell, F.G. (1970) Late Pleistocene floras from Earith, Huntingdonshire. **Philosophical Transactions of the Royal Society of London B258**, 347-378.

Bellamy, D.J., Bradshaw, M.E., Millington, G.R. and Simmons, I.G. (1966) Two Quaternary deposits in the Lower Tees basin. **New Phytologist 65**, 425-442.

Berry, F.G. (1973) Patterns of snail distribution at Ham Street Woods Nature Reserve, East Kent. **Journal of Conchology (London) 28**, 23-35.

Best, S.E.J. (1930) **East Yorkshire: A Study in Agricultural Geography.** London: Longmans, Green and Co.

Bisat, W.S. (1932) Glacial and Post-Glacial Sections on the Humber shore at North Ferriby. **Transactions of the Hull Geological Society 7(3)**, (1930-1931), 83-95.

Bisat, W.S. (1939a) Older and Newer Drift in East Yorkshire. **Proceedings of the Yorkshire Geological Society 24**, 137-151.

Bisat, W.S. (1939b - 1940) The relationship of the "Basement Clays" of Dimlington, Bridlington and Filey Bays. **The Naturalist,** 133-135 and 161-168.

Bisat, W.S. (1954) In Summer Field Meeting in East Yorkshire. V. Wilson et al. **Proceedings of the Geologists' Association 65(4)**, 313-327.

Bisat, W.S. and Dell (1941) The occurrence of a bed containing moss in the boulder clays of Dimlington. **Proceedings of the Yorkshire Geological Society 24**, 219-222.

Bishop, M.J. (1976) The Mollusca of some poor fens in County Cork, Ireland. **Journal of Conchology (London) 29**, 57-60.

Bishop, M.J. (1977) The habitats of Mollusca in the Central Highlands of Scotland. **Journal of Conchology (London) 29**, 189-197.

Boetters, H.D. (1979) Species concept of Prosobranch Freshwater Molluscs in Western Europe I. **Malacologia 18**, 57-60.

Boetters, H.D. (1982) Species concept of Prosobranch Freshwater Molluscs in Western Europe II. **Malacologia 22**, 499-504.

Boulton, G.S., James, A.S., Clayton, K.M. and Kenning, (1977) A British Ice sheet model and patterns of glacial erosion and deposition in Britain. In **British Quaternary Studies** F.W. Shotton (ed.) Oxford: Clarendon Press.

Boycott, A.E. (1934) The habitats of Land Mollusca in Britain. **Journal of Ecology 22**, 1-38.

Boycott, A.E. (1936) The habitats of Freshwater Mollusca in Britain. **Journal of Animal Ecology 5**, 116-186.

Boylan, P.J. (1966) New records of Holocene Mollusca from East Yorkshire. **The Naturalist 899**, 113-118.

Boylan, P.J. (1967) The Pleistocene Mammalia of the Sewerby-Hessle buried cliff, East Yorkshire. **Proceedings of the Yorkshire Geological Society 36**, 115-125.

Breuil, H. (1922) Observations on the Pre-Neolithic industries of Scotland. **Proceedings of the Society of Antiquaries of Scotland 56**, 261-281.

Briggs, D.J. (1977a) **Sources and Methods in Geography: Sediments.** London: Butterworths.

Briggs, D.J. (1977a) **Sources and Methods in Geography: Soils.** London: Butterworths.

Briggs, D.J. and Gilbertson, D.D. (1973) The age of the Hanborough Terrace of the River Evenlode, Oxfordshire. **Proceedings of the Geologists' Association 84(2)**, 155-173.

Briggs, D.J. and Gilbertson, D.D. (1980) Quaternary processes and environments in the Upper Thames Basin. **Transactions of the Institute of British Geographers NS5**, 53-65.

Briggs, D.J., Coope, G.R. and Gilbertson, D.D. (1975) Late Pleistocene Terrace Gravels at Beckford, Worcestershire. **Geological Journal 10(1)**, 1-16.

Briggs, D.J., Coope, G.R. and Gilbertson, D.D. (1984) **The Chronology and Environmental Framework of Early Man in the Upper Thames: A New Model.** Oxford, British Archaeological Reports.

Brown, A. (1977) Late Devensian and Flandrian vegetational history of Bodmin Moor, Cornwall. **Philosophical Transactions of the Royal Society of London B276**, 251-320.

Cain, A.J. (1981) Variation in the shell shape and size of Helicid snail in relation to other Pulmonates in faunas of the Palaearctic region. **Malacologia 21**, 149-176.

Calow, P. (1978) The evolution of life-cycle strategies in Freshwater Gastropods. **Malacologia 17**, 351-364.

Calow, P. (1981) Adaptational aspects of growth and reproduction in **Lymnaea peregra** (Gastropoda: Pulmonata) from exposed and sheltered aquatic habitats. **Malacologia 21**, 5-13.

Campbell, J.M. (1977) **The Upper Palaeolithic of Britain.** Oxford: Clarendon Press.

Catt, J.A. (1977) (ed) **Yorkshire and Lincolnshire Guidebook to Excursion C7.** Birmingham: INQUA.

Catt, J.A. and Madgett, P.A. (1981) The work of W.S. Bisat, F.R.S. on the Yorkshire Coast. In **The Quaternary in Britain.** J. Neale and J. Flenley (eds.). Oxford: Pergamon. 119-136.

Catt, J.A. and Penney, L.F. (1966) The Pleistocene deposits of Holderness, East Yorkshire. **Proceedings of the Yorkshire Geological Society 35**, 375-420.

Catt, J.A., Weir, A.H. and Madgett, P.A. (1974) The loess of Eastern Yorkshire and Lincolnshire. **Proceedings of the Yorkshire Geological Society 40**, 23-39.

Clark, J.G.D. (1954) **Excavations at Star Carr.** London: Cambridge University Press.

Clark, J.G.D. and Godwin, H. (1956) A Maglemosian site at Brandesburton, Holderness, Yorkshire. **Proceedings of the Prehistoric Society 22**, 6-22.

Coles, B. and Colville, B. (1979) **Catinella arenaria** (Bouchard-Chantereux) and **Vertigo geyeri** Lindholm, from a base-rich fen in North West England. **Journal of Conchology (London) 30**, 99-100.

Coles, J.M. (1979) Radiocarbon dates: Third list. **Somerset Levels Papers 5**, 101.

Coles, J.M., Heal, S.V.E. and Orme, B.J. (1978) The use and character of wood in Prehistoric Britain and Ireland. **Proceedings of the Prehistoric Society 44**, 1-45.

Cookson, I.C. (1953) Records of the occurrence of **Botryococcus brannii, Pediastrum** and the **Hystrichosphaerideae** in the Cainozoic deposits of Australia. **Memoirs of the National Museum, Melbourne 18**, 107-121.

Coope, G.R. (1977) Fossil coleoptera assemblages as sensitive indicators of climatic change during the Devensian (Last) cold stage. **Philosophical Transactions of the Royal Society of London B280**, 313-340.

Coope, G.R. and Pennington, W. (1977) The Windermere interstadial of the Late Devensian. **Philosophical Transactions of the Royal Society of London B280**, 337-339.

Coope, G.R., Shotton, F.W. and Strachan, I. (1961) A Late Pleistocene fauna and flora from Upton Warren, Worcestershire. **Philosophical Transactions of the Royal Society of London B244**, 279-421.

Creer, K.M., Gross, D.L. and Lineback, J.A. (1976) Origin of regional geomagnetic variations recorded by Wisconsinian and Holocene sediments from Lake Michigan, U.S.A., and Lake Windermere, England. **Bulletin of the Geological Society of America 87**, 531-540.

Creer, K.M., Mackereth, F.H., Molyneux, L. and Thompson, R. (1972) Geomagnetic secular variation recorded in the stable magnetic remanence of recent sediments. **Earth and Planetary Science Letters 14**, 115-127.

Dance, S.P. (1961) On the genus **Pisidium** at Upton Warren. **Philosophical Transactions of the Royal Society of London B244**, 418-421.

Davis-King, S. (1980) A note on new barbed points from Brandesburton, North Humberside. **Archaeological Journal 137**, 22-26.

de Boer, G. (1964) Spurn Head: its history and evolution. **Transactions of the Institute of British Geographers 34**, 71-89.

de Boer, G. (1981) Spurn Point: Erosion and protection after 1849. In **The Quaternary in Britain.** J. Neale and J. Flenley (eds). Oxford: Pergamon. 206-215.

Dickson, J.H. (1973) **Bryophytes of the Pleistocene.** Cambridge: Cambridge University Press.

Drake, H.C. and Sheppard, T. (1910) Classified list of organic remains from the rocks of the East Riding of Yorkshire. **Proceedings of the Yorkshire Geological Society 17(1)**, 4-71.

Dunlop, D.J. and Stirling, J.M. (1977) 'Hard' viscous remanent magnetization (VRM) in fine-grained hematite. **Geophysical Research Letters 4**, 163-166.

Dussart, G.B.J. (1976) The ecology of Freshwater Molluscs in northwest England in relation to water chemistry. **Journal of Molluscan Studies 42**, 181-198.

Dussart, G.B.J. (1979) **Sphaerium corneum** and **Pisidium** spp. - the ecology of freshwater bivalve molluscs in relation to water chemistry. **Journal of Molluscan Studies 45**, 19-34.

Edwards, C.A. (1981) The tills of Filey Bay. In **The Quaternary in Britain.** (eds) J. Neale and J. Flenley. Oxford: Pergamon. 108-118.

Ellis, A.E. (1951) Census of the distribution of British non-marine Mollusca. 7th ed. **Journal of Conchology London 23**, 6-7.

Ellis, A.E. (1962) **British Freshwater Bivalves.** Synopses of the British Fauna, No. 13. Linnean Society of London.

Ellis, A.E. (1969) **British Snails.** Oxford: Clarendon Press.

Ellis, A.E. (1978) **British Freshwater Bivalve Mollusa.** London: Academic Press.

Ellis, A.E. (1979) **British Snails.** Oxford: Clarendon Press. 3rd edn.

English, B. (1979) **The Lords of Holderness 1086-1260: a study in feudal society.** Oxford: Oxford University Press.

Evans, J.G. (1966) Late-glacial and Post-glacial sub-aerial deposits at Pitstone, Buckinghamshire. **Proceedings of the Geologists' Association 77**, 347-364.

Evans, J.G. (1967) **The Stratification of Mollusca in Chalk Soils and their Relevance to Archaeology.** Unpublished Ph.D. Thesis, University of London.

Evans, J.G. (1972) **Land Snails in Archaeology: With Special Reference to the British Isles.** London: Seminar Press.

Evans, J.G. and Jones, H. (1973) Subfossil and modern land snail faunas from rock-rubble habitats. **Journal of Conchology 28**, 103-130.

Erdtman, G., Berglund, B. and Praglowski, J. (1961) **An Introduction to a Scandinavian Pollen Flora.** Stockholm: Almquist and Wicksell.

Erdtman, G., Praglowski, J. and Nilsson, S. (1963) **An Introduction to a Scandinavian Pollen Flora** Vol. 2. Stockholm: Almquist and Wicksell.

Etheridge, B. (with J. Phillips) (1875) **Illustrations of the Geology of Yorkshire.** Brown, Hall. 3rd ed.

Faegri, K. and Iversen, J. (1975) **A Textbook of Pollen Analysis.** Copenhagen: Munksgaard.

Flenley, J.R., Bridger, J.F.D., Madgett, P.A. and Beckett, S. (eds) (1972) **East Yorkshire and North Lincolnshire.** Hull: Q.R.A.

Flenley, J.R. and Neale, J. (eds) (1981) **The Quaternary in Britain** Oxford: Pergamon.

Flenley, J.R., Maloney, B.K., Ford, D. and Hallam, G. (1975) **Trapa natans** in the British Flandrian. **Nature, London 257**, 39-41.

Flenley, J.R. and Maloney, B.K. (1976) Reply to a comment by P.A. Tallentire. **Nature, London 261**, 347.

Fitter, R.L. (1978) **Atlas of Wild Flowers of Britain and Northern Europe.** London: Collins.

Franks, J.W., Sutcliffe, A.J., Kerney, M.P. and Coope, G.R. (1958) Haunt of elephant and rhinoceros: the Trafalgar Square of 100,000 years ago - new discoveries. **Illustrated London News** 1011-1013.

Fretter, V. and Graham, A. (1978) The Prosobranch Molluscs of Britain and Denmark. Part 3 - Neritacea; Vivaparacea, Valvatacea, Terrestrial and Freshwater; Littorinacea and Rissoacea. Supplement No. 5. **Journal of Molluscan Studies.**

Gale, S.J., Hunt, C.O. and Southgate, G.A. (1984) Kirkhead Cave: biostratigraphy and magnetostratigraphy. **Archaeometry 26**, in press.

Gaunt, G.D. and Tooley, M.J. (1974) Evidence for Flandrian sea level changes in the Humber estuary and adjacent areas. **Bulletin of the Geological Survey of Great Britain 48**, 25-41.

Gibbard, P.L., Coope, G.R., Hall, A.R., Preece, R.C. and Robinson, J.E. (1982) Middle Devensian deposits beneath the 'Upper Floodplain' terrace of the River Thames at Kempton Park, Sunbury, England. **Proceedings of the Geologists' Association 93**, 275-289.

Gilbertson, D.D. (1980) The Palaeoecology of Middle Pleistocene Mollusca from Sugworth, Oxfordshire. **Philosophical Transactions of the Royal Society of London B289**, 107-118.

Gilbertson, D.D. (1984) Early Neolithic utilisation and management of Alder Carr at Skipsea Withow mere, Holderness. **Yorkshire Archaeological Journal 56**, 17-22.

Gilbertson, D.D. and Hawkins, A.B. (1978) **The Pleistocene Succession at Kenn, Somerset.** Bulletin of the Geological Survey of Great Britain, No. 66. London: H.M.S.O.

Godwin, H. (1943) Coastal peat beds of the British Isles and North Sea. **Journal of Ecology 31**, 199-247.

Godwin, H. (1945) Coastal peat beds of the North Sea region as indices of land and sea level changes. **New Phytologist 44**, 26-69.

Godwin, H. (1956) **The History of the British Flora.** London: Cambridge University Press.

Godwin, H. (1968) Studies of the Post-glacial history of British vegetation: Organic deposits at Old Buckenham Mere, Norfolk. **New Phytologist 67**, 95-107.

Godwin, H. (1975) **The History of the British Flora**. 2nd ed. London: Cambridge University Press.

Godwin, H. and Godwin, H.E. (1933) British Maglemose harpoon sites. **Antiquity 7**, 36-48.

Green, C.P., Keen, D.H., McGregor, D.F.M., Robinson, J.E. and Williams, R.B. (1983) Stratigraphy and environmental significance of Pleistocene deposits at Fisherton near Salisbury, Wilshire. **Proceedings of the Geologists' Association 94**, 17-22.

Green, R.H. (1971) A multivariate statistical approach to the Hutchinsonian niche: Bivalve molluscs of Central Canada. **Ecology 52**, 543-556.

Grichuk, G.P. Vegetation. In **The Palaeogeography of Europe during the Late Pleistocene, Reconstruction and Models**. Moscow. (in Russian - quoted in Starkel, 1977, **op cit**).

Hallam, J.S., Edwards, B.J.N., Barnes, B. and Stuart, A.J. (1973) The remains of a Late-Glacial elk associated with barbed points from High Furlong, near Blackpool, Lancashire. **Proceedings of the Prehistoric Society 39**, 100-128.

Hammen, T. van der, Maarleveld, G.C., Vogel, J.C. and Zagwijn, W.H. (1967) Stratigraphy, climatic succession and radiocarbon dating of the Last Glacial in the Netherlands. **Geologie en Mijnbouw 46**, 79-95.

Irving, E. (1957) The origin of palaeomagnetism of the Torridonian Sandstones of north-west Scotland. **Philosophical Transactions of the Royal Society, London A250**, 110.

Jacobi, R.M. (1978) Northern England in the eighth millennium b.c.: an essay. In **The Early Postglacial Settlement of Europe**. P.A.M. Mellars (ed). 295-332. London: Duckworth.

Jacobi, R.M. (1980) The Upper Palaeolithic of Britain, with special reference to Wales. In **Culture and Environment in Prehistoric Wales**. J.A. Taylor (ed.) Oxford: British Archaeological Reports **76**, 15-100.

Janus, H. (1965) **The Young Specialist Looks at Molluscs**. London: Burke.

Jayet, A. (1973) Sur Quelques **Pisidium** Haut-Alpines. **Malacologia 14**, 415-418.

Jenkinson, R.D.S. and Gilbertson, D.D. 1984. **In the Shadow of Extinction: The Archaeology and Palaeoecology of the Lake, Fissures and Smaller Caves at Creswell Crags S.S.S.I.**. Sheffield, University of Sheffield Monographs in Prehistory and Archaeology.

Jones, R.L. (1976a) The activities of Mesolithic Man: further palaeobotanical evidence from North East Yorkshire. In **Geoarchaeology: Earth Science and the Past.** D.A. Davidson and M.L. Shackley (eds.) London: Duckworth.

Jones, R.L. (1976b) Late Quaternary vegetational history of the North York Moors: IV. Seamer Carrs. **Journal of Biogeography 3,** 397-406.

Jones, R.L. (1977) Late Quaternary vegetational history of the North York Moors: V. The Cleveland Dales. **Journal of Biogeography 4,** 353-362.

Jones, R.L. and Cundill, P. (1978) **Introduction to Pollen Analysis.** Norwich. British Geomorphological Research Group Technical Bulletin No. 22.

Kaddah, M.T. (1974) The hydrometer method for detailed particle-size analysis. 1. Graphical interpretation of hydrometer readings and test of method. **Soil Science 118,** 102-108.

Keen, D.H., Jones, R.L. and Robinson, J.E. (1984) A Late Devensian and early Flandrian fauna and flora from Kildale, north-east Yorkshire. **Proceedings of the Yorkshire Geological Society 44**(4), 385-397.

Kendall, P.F. and Wroot, H.E. (1924) **Geology of Yorkshire.** (Reprint 1972). Menston, Yorks: Scolar Press.

Kennard, A.S. and Musham, J.F. (1937) On the Mollusca from a Holocene tufaceous deposit at Broughton-Brigg, Lincolnshire. **Proceedings of the Malacological Society 22,** 374-379.

Kenward, H.K. (1980) **Oxytelus fulvipes** Er. (Col., Staphylinidae) abundant at Askham Bogs. **Entomologists' Monthly Magazine 115,** 180.

Kenward, H.K., Hall, A.R. and Jones, A.K.G. (1980) A tested set of techniques for the extraction of plant and animal macrofossils from waterlogged archaeological deposits. **Science and Archaeology 22,** 3-15.

Kerney, M.P. (1959) An interglacial tufa near Hitchin, Hertfordshire. **Proceedings of the Geologists' Association 70,** 322-337.

Kerney, M.P. (1963) Late-glacial deposits on the chalk of south east England. **Philosophical Transactions of the Royal Society of London B246,** 203-254.

Kerney, M.P. (1971a) Interglacial deposits at Barnfield Pit, Swanscombe and their molluscan fauna. **Journal of the Geological Society 127,** 69-93.

Kerney, M.P. (1971b) A middle Weichselian deposit at Halling, Kent. **Proceedings of the Geologists' Association 82,** 1-12.

Kerney, M.P. (1976a) A list of the fresh and brackish-water Mollusca of the British Isles. **Journal of Conchology London 29,** 26-28.

Kerney, M.P. (1976b) **Atlas of the Non-Marine Mollusca of the British Isles.** European Invertebrate Survey. Cambridge: N.E.R.C.

Kerney, M.P. (1976c) Mollusca from an interglacial tufa in East Anglia. **Journal of Conchology, London 29,** 47-50.

Kerney, M.P. (1977a) British Quaternary non-marine Mollusca: a brief review. In **British Quaternary Studies: Recent Advances.** F.W. Shotton (ed.). 31-42. Oxford: Clarendon Press.

Kerney, M.P. (1977b) A proposed zonation scheme for Late Glacial and Post Glacial deposits using land Mollusca. **Journal of Archaeological Science 4,** 387-390.

Kerney, M.P., Brown, E.H. and Chandler, T.J. (1964) The Late-glacial and Post-glacial history of the Chalk escarpment near Brook, Kent. **Philosophical Transactions of the Royal Society of London B248,** 135-204.

Kerney, M.P. and Cameron, R.A.D. (1979) **A Field Guide to the Land Snails of Britain and North-west Europe.** London: Collins.

Kerney, M.P., Preece, R.C. and Turner, C. (1980) Molluscan and plant biostratigraphy of some Late Devensian and Flandrian deposits in Kent. **Philosophical Transactions of the Royal Society of London B291,** 1-43.

Kerney, M.P., Gibbard, P.L., Hall, A.R. and Robinson, J.E. (1982) Middle Devensian river deposits beneath the 'Upper Floodplain' terrace of the River Thames at Isleworth, W. London. **Proceedings of the Geologists' Association 93,** 385-393.

Lambert, C.A., Pearson, R.G. and Sparks, B.W. (1963) A flora and fauna from Late Pleistocene deposits at Sidgwick Avenue, Cambridge. **Proceedings of the Linnean Society 174,** 13-29.

Large, N.F. and Sparks, B.W. (1965) The non-marine Mollusca of the Cainscross Terrace near Stroud, Glos. **Geological Magazine 98,** 423-426.

Lowe, S. (1980) Radiocarbon dating and stratigraphic resolution in Welsh late-glacial chronology. **Nature, London 293,** 210-212.

Macan, T.T. (1950) Ecology of Freshwater Mollusca in the English Lake District. **Journal of Animal Ecology 19,** 124-146.

Macan, T.T. (1969) **A Key to the British Fresh- and Brackish-Water Gastropods.** 3rd. Edn. Windermere Freshwater Biological Association.

Mackereth, F.J.H. (1965) Chemical investigation of Lake Sediments and their interpretation. **Proceedings of the Royal Society of London B161**, 295-309.

Mackereth, F.J.H. (1966) Some chemical observations on Post-Glacial Lake Sediments. **Philosophical Transations of the Royal Society of London B250**, 165-213.

Mackereth, F.J.H. (1971) On the variation in direction of the horizontal component of remanent magnetization in lake sediments. **Earth and Planetary Science Letters 12**, 332-338.

Madgett, P.A. and Catt, J.A. (1978) Petrography, stratigraphy and weathering of Late Pleistocene tills in East Yorkshire, Lincolnshire and north Norfolk. **Proceedings of the Yorkshire Geological Society 42**, 55-108.

Marcussen, I. (1967) The freshwater molluscs in the Late-glacial and early Post-glacial deposits in the Bay of Barmosen, southern Sjaelland, Denmark. **Medd. Fra. Dansk Geol. For. 17**, 256-287.

Megaw, J.V. and Simpson, D.D.A. (1979) **British Prehistory: An Introduction**. Leicester: Leicester University Press.

Meier-Brook, C. (1969) Substrate relations in some **Pisidium** species (Sphaeriidae). **Malacologia 9**, 121-125.

Meiklejohn, R.G. (1973) A list of Caithness land and Freshwater Mollusca. **Journal of Conchology (London) 28**, 95-101.

Mitchell, G.F., Penny, L.F., Shotton, F.W. and West, R.G. (1973) **A Correlation of Quaternary Deposits in the British Isles.** Geological Society of London, Special Publication No. 4, 99 pp.

Mitchell, G.F. and West, R.G. (1977) A discussion on the changing environmental conditions in Great Britain and Ireland during the Devensian (Last) cold stage. **Philosophical Transactions of the Royal Society of London B280**, 103-374.

Molyneux, L. (1971) A complete result magnetometer for measuring the remanent magnetization of rocks. **Geophysical Journal of the Royal Astronomical Society 24**, 429-433.

Moore, J.W. (1950) Mesolithic sites in the neighbourhood of Flixton, north-east Yorkshire. **Proceedings of the Prehistoric Society 16**, 101-108.

Moore, J.W. (1954) Excavations at Flixton, site 2. In **Excavations at Star Carr.** J.G.D. Clark (ed.). 192-194. Cambridge: University Press.

Moore, P.D. and Webb, J.A. (1978) **An Illustrated Guide to Pollen Analysis.** London: Hodder and Stoughton.

Morgan, R. (1979) Tree-ring studies in the Somerset Levels: Floating Oak Tree-ring chronologies from the Trackways and their radiocarbon dating. **Somerset Levels Papers 5**, 98-100.

Norris, A. Bartley, D.D. and Gaunt, G.D. (1971) An account of the deposit of shell marl at Burton Salmon, West Yorkshire. **Naturalist 917**, 57-63.

Norris, A. and Colville, B. (1974) Notes on the occurrence of **Vertigo augustior** Jeffreys in Great Britain. **Journal of Conchology London 28**, 141-154.

Norris, G. and McAndrews, J.H. (1970) Dinoflagellate cysts from Post-Glacial lake muds. **Review of Palaeobotany and Palynology 10**, 131-156.

Okeland, J. (1964) The eutrophic lake Borrevan (Norway) - an ecological study on shore and bottom fauna with special reference to gastropods, including a hydrographic survey. **Folia Limnologica Scandinavia 13**, 1-337.

Okeland, J. (1969) Distribution and ecology of the Freshwater Snails (Gastropods) of Norway. **Malacologia 9**, 143-151.

Okeland, J. (1979a) Distribution of environmental factors and Freshwater Snails (Gastropods) in Norway: Use of European Invertebrate Survey principles. **Malacologia 18**, 211-222.

Okeland, J. (1979b) **Sphaeriidae** of Norway: A project for studying the ecological requirements and geographical distribution. **Malacologia 18**, 223-226.

Ordnance Survey (1977) **Kingston-upon-Hull**, Sheet 107. 1:50,000.

Pals, J.B., Van Geel, B. and Delfos, R.P.P. (1980) Palaeoecological studies in the Klokkweel Bog near Hoogkarspel (Province of Noord Holland). **Review of Palaeobotany and Palynology 30**, 371-418.

Paul, C.R. (1975) The ecology of Mollusca in ancient woodland I: The fauna of Hayley Wood, Cambridgeshire. **Journal of Conchology London 28**, 301-327.

Paul, C.R. (1976) The Non-marine Mollusca of Colonsay and Oronsay. **Journal of Conchology London 29**, 107-110.

Paul, C.R. (1978a) The ecology of Mollusca in Ancient Woodland II: Analyses of distribution and experiments in Hayley Wood, Cambridgeshire. **Journal of Conchology London 29**, 281-294.

Paul, C.R. (1978b) The ecology of Mollusca in Ancient Woodland III: Frequency of occurrence in West Cambridgeshire Woods. **Journal of Conchology London 29**, 295-300.

Pennington, W. (1977) The Late Devensian Flora and vegetation of Britain. **Philosophical Transactions of the Royal Society of London B280**, 247-272.

Pennington, W. (1980) Modern pollen samples from West Greenland and the interpretation of pollen data from the British Late Glacial (Late Devensian). **New Phytologist 84**, 171-201.

Penny, L.F. (1963) Vertebrate remains from Kelsey Hill, Burstwick and Keyingham. **Hull Museum Publication 214**, 871-873.

Penny, L.F. (1974) Quaternary. In **The Geology and Mineral Resources of Yorkshire.** D.H. Rayer and J.E. Hemingway (eds.). pp. 245-264. York: Yorkshire Geological Society.

Penny, L.F. and Catt, J.A. (1967) Stone orientation and other structural features of tills in East Yorkshire. **Geological Magazine 104**, 344-360.

Penny, L.F., Coope, G.R. and Catt, J.A. (1969) Age and insect fauna of the Dimlington silts, East Yorkshire. **Nature 224**, 65-67.

Penny, L.F. and Rawson, P.F. (1969) Field meeting in East Yorkshire and North Lincolnshire. **Proceedings of the Geologists' Association 80**, 193-216.

Petch, T. (1904) The published records of Land and Freshwater Mollusca of the East Riding with additions. **Transactions of the Hull Scientific and Field Naturalists' Club** 3(2), 121-72.

Phillips, J. (1829) **Illustrations of the Geology of Yorkshire.** 1st edition. York. xvi + 192pp.

Phillips, J. (1835) **Illustrations of the Geology of Yorkshire: or a Description of the Strata and Other Organic Remains.** Part 1. **The Yorkshire Coast.** 2nd ed. London. vi + 184pp.

Phillips, J. with Etheridge, B. (1885) **Illustrations of the Geology of Yorkshire ....** 3rd ed. London.

Powell, A. and South, A. (1978) Studies on the faunas of gravel-pit lakes in South east England. **Journal of Molluscan Studies 44**, 327-339.

Preece, R.C. (1981) The value of shell microsculpture as a guide to the identification of land Mollusca from Quaternary deposits. **Journal of Conchology London** 30(5), 331-337.

Preece, R.C. and Robinson, J.E. (1982) Mollusc, Ostracod and plant remains from early Postglacial deposits near Staines. **The London Naturalist 61**, 6-15.

Preece, R.C. and Robinson, J.E, (1984) Late Devensian and Flandrian environmental history of the Ancholme Valley, Lincolnshire: Molluscan and Ostracod evidence. **Journal of Biogeography 11**, 319 - 352.

Prestwich, J. (1861) On the occurrence of **Cyrene fluminalis**, together
          with marine shells of recent species, in beds of sand and
          gravel over boulder clay near Hull. **Quarterly Journal of
          the Geological Society of London 17**, 446-456.

Read, C.H., Woodward, A.S. and Kendall, P.F. (1923) On two bone
          harpoons from Hornsea, East Yorkshire. **Man 31**, 49-50.

Reavell, P.E. (1980) A study of the diets of some British freshwater
          Gastropods. **Journal of Conchology London 30**, 253-271.

Reid, C. (1885) **The Geology of Holderness** Memoir of the Geological
          Survey of Great Britain. H.M.S.O. 177pp.

Robinson, J.E. (1972) Quaternary Ostracoda from East Yorkshire and
          North Lincolnshire. **Quaternary Research Association
          Newsletter 7**, 1-2.

Round, F.E. (1973) **The Biology of the Algae.** London: Edward Arnold.

Rose, J. (1976) The date of the buried channel deposits at Sproughton.
          East Anglian Archaeology 3, 11-15.

Seddon, B. (1962) Late-glacial deposits at Llyn Dwythwrch and Nant
          Francon, Caernarvonshire. **Philosophical Transactions of the
          Royal Society of London B244**, 459-481.

Sheppard, J.A. (1956) **The Draining of the Marshlands of East
          Yorkshire.** Unpublished Ph.D. thesis, University of Hull,
          429pp.

Sheppard, J.A. (1957) The medieval meres of Holderness. **Transactions
          of the Institute of British Geographers 23**, 75-86.

Sheppard, T. (1906) On a section in the Post-Glacial deposit at
          Hornsea. **Naturalist**, 420-424.

Sheppard, T. (1909) Change on the east coast of England within the
          historical period. **Geographical Journal 34**(5), 500-513.

Sheppard, T. (1912) **Lost Towns of the Yorkshire Coast.** Hull and
          London: Brown.

Sheppard, T. (1923a) Red deer skeleton from Holderness peat.
          Naturalist, 369-371.

Sheppard, T. (1923b) The Maglemose Harpoons. **Naturalist**, 169-179.

Sheppard, T. (1929) Unpublished correspondence: reproduced here as
          Figure 2.8.

Shotton, F.W. (1965) Normal faulting in British Pleistocene deposits.
          Quarterly Journal of the Geological Society of London 121,
          419-435.

Shotton, F.W. (1968) The Pleistocene succession around Brandon, Warwickshire. **Philosophical Transactions of the Royal Society of London B254**, 387-400.

Shotton, F.W. (1972) An example of hardwater error in radiocarbon dating of vegetable matter. **Nature, London 240**, 460-461.

Shotton, F.W. (1977) The Devensian stage: its development, limits and substages. **Philosophical Transactions of the Royal Society of London B280**, 107-118.

Shotton, F.W. (1981) Major contributions of North East England to the advancement of Quaternary Studies. In **The Quaternary in Britain**. J. Neale and J. Flenley (eds.). pp. 137-145. Oxford: Pergamon.

Smith, A.H. (1937) **The Place Names of the East Riding of Yorkshire and York**. English Place Names Society XIV. Cambridge: Cambridge University Press. 351pp.

Smith, D.B., Beaumont, P., Gaunt, G.D., Francis, E.A. and Penny, L.F. (1973) 5. North-east England. In **A Correlation of Quaternary Deposits in the British Isles**. Mitchell et al. Geological Society of London Special Report No. 4, 99pp.

Smith, R.A. (1911) Lake-dwellings in Holderness. **Archaeologia 62**, 593-610.

Somerset Levels Papers (1975-1980) University of Cambridge, Department of Archaeology and Anthropology/University of Exeter, Department of History and Archaeology.

Spalding, D.A.E. (1962) Hull Museum's Acquisition. **Naturalist**, 114.

Sparks, B.W. (1952) Notes on some Pleistocene sections at Barrington, Cambridgeshire. **Geological Magazine 89**, 163-174.

Sparks, B.W. (1953a) Fossil and recent English species of **Vallonia**. **Proceedings of the Malacological Society of London 30**, 110-121.

Sparks, B.W. (1953b) The former occurrence of both **Helicella striata** (Müller) and **H. geyeri** (Soos) in England. **Journal of Conchology London 23**, 372-378.

Sparks, B.W. (1957a) The non-marine Mollusca of the interglacial deposits at Bobbitshole, Ipswich. **Philosophical Transactions of the Royal Society of London B241**, 33-44.

Sparks, B.W. (1957b) The taele gravel near Thriplow, Cambridgeshire. **Geological Magazine 94**, 194-200.

Sparks, B.W. (1961) The ecological interpretation of Quaternary non-marine Mollusca. **Proceedings of the Linnean Society of London 172**, 71-80.

Sparks, B.W. (1964a) Non-marine Mollusca and Quaternary ecology. **Journal of Animal Ecology 33** (Supplement), 87-98.

Sparks, B.W. (1964b) The distribution of non-marine Mollusca in the Last Interglacial in south east England. **Proceedings of the Malacological Society of London 36**, 7-25.

Sparks, B.W. (1964c) A note on the Pleistocene deposit at Grantchester, Cambridgeshire. **Geological Magazine 101**, 334-339.

Sparks, B.W. (1970) Appendix. Non-marine Mollusca from the Marks Tey deposits. In The Middle Pleistocene deposits at Marks Tey, Essex. C. Turner. **Philosophical Transactions of the Royal Society of London B257**, 373-437.

Sparks, B.W. (1976) Appendix 4. The non-marine Mollusca from Swanton Morley sample D. In Pleistocene Vegetational History and Geology in Norfolk. L. Phillips. **Philosophical Transactions of the Royal Society of London B275**, 215-286.

Sparks, B.W. and Lambert, C.A. (1961) The Post-glacial deposits at Apethorpe, Northamptonshire. **Proceedings of the Malacological Society of London 34**, 302-315.

Sparks, B.W. and West, R.G. (1959) The palaecology of the interglacial deposits at Histon Road, Cambridge. **Eiszeitalter und Gegenwart 10**, 123-143.

Sparks, B.W. and West, R.G. (1964) The interglacial deposits at Stutton, Suffolk. **Proceedings of the Geologists' Association 74**, 419-432.

Sparks, B.W. and West, R.G. (1968) Interglacial deposits at Wortwell, Norfolk. **Geological Magazine 105**, 471-481.

Sparks, B.W. and West, R.G. (1970) Late Pleistocene deposits at Wretton, Norfolk. I. Ipswichian interglacial deposits. **Philosophical Transactions of the Royal Society of London B258**, 1-30.

Sparks, B.W., West, R.G., Williams, R.B.G. and Ransom, M. (1969) Hoxnian interglacial deposits near Hatfield, Hertfordshire. **Proceedings of the Geologists' Association 80**, 243-267.

Starkel, L. (1977) The palaeogeography of mid- and east-Europe during the last cold stage, with west European comparisons. **Philosophical Transactions of the Royal Society of London B280**, 351-372.

Stelfox, A.W., Kuiper, J.G.J., McMillan, N.F. and Mitchell, G.F. (1972) The Late Glacial and Post-Glacial Mollusca of the White Bog, Co. Down. **Proceedings of the Royal Irish Academy B72**, 185-207.

Straw, A. (1983) Pre-Devensian glaciation of Lincolnshire (Eastern England) and adjacent areas. **Quaternary Science Review 2**, 239-260.

Straw, A. and Clayton, K.M. (1979) **Eastern and Central England: The Geomorphology of the British Isles.** London: Methuen. 247pp.

Stuart, A.J. (1977) The vertebrates of the last cold stage in Britain and Ireland. **Philosophical Transactions of the Royal Society of London B280**, 295-312.

Suggate, R.P. and West, R.G. (1959) On the extent of the Last Glaciation in eastern England. **Proceedings of the Royal Society of London B150**, 263-283.

Tallentire, P. (1976) **Trapa natans** in the British Flandrian. **Nature 261**, 341.

Tarling, D.H. (1983) **Palaeomagnetism.** London: Chapman and Hall. 379pp.

Tew, J.F.B. and Cowie, J.D. (n.d.) **Agricultural Land Classification of England and Wales.** Report to accompanyt sheet 99. Min. Ag. Fish and Food. London.

Thew, N.M. (1983) Unpublished dissertation for the degree of Master of Arts by course work and dissertation. University of Sheffield.

Thompson, R. (1973) Palaeolimnology and palaeomagnetism. **Nature, Physical Science 242**, 182-184.

Thompson, R. (1977) Stratigraphic consequences of palaeomagnetic studies of Pleistocene and Recent sediments. **Journal of the Geological Society of London 133**, 51-59.

Tucker, P. (1980) A grain mobility model of post-depositional realignment. **Geophysical Journal of the Royal Astronomical Society 63**, 149-163.

Turner, J. and Hodgson, J. (1979) Studies in the vegetational history of the northern Pennines. I. Variations in the composition of early Flandrian forests. **Journal of Ecology 67**, 629-646.

Turner, J. and Kershaw, A.P. (1973) A late- and post-glacial pollen diagram from Cranberry Bog, near Beamish, County Durham. **New Phytologist 72**, 911-928.

Valentin, H. (1954) Der Landverlust in Holderness, Ostengland, von 1852 bis 1952. **Erde, Berlin 6**(3-4), 296-315.

Valentin, H. (1957) Glazialmorphologische Untersuchungen in Ostengland. **Abhandlungen Geographischen Institut. Universität Berlin**, 1-86.

Valentin, H. (1971) Land loss at Holderness. In **Applied Coastal Geomorphology.** J.A. Steers (ed.) pp. 116-137. London: Macmillan.

Valovirta, I. (1977) The Baltic Island survey. A malacological cooperation between Scotland and Finland 1974. **Malacologia** **16**, 271-277.

Van Geel, B. (1976) Fossil spores of Zygnemataceae in ditches of a prehistoric settlement in Hoogkarspel (The Netherlands). **Review of Palaeobotany and Palynology 22**, 337-344.

Van Geel, B. and Van der Hammen, T. (1978) Zygnemataceae in Quaternary Columbian sediments. **Review of Palaeobotany and Palynology 25**, 377-392.

Varley, W.T. (1968) Barmston and the Holderness crannogs. **East Riding Archaeologist 1**, 11-26.

Verosub, K.L. (1982) Geomagnetic excursions: a critical assessment of the evidence as recorded in sediments of the Brunhes Epoch. **Philosophical Transactions of the Royal Society of London A306**, 161-168.

Verosub, K.L. and Banerjee, S.K. (1977) Geomagnetic excusions and their paleomagnetic record. **Reviews of Geophysics and Space Physics 15**, 145-155.

Walden, H.W. (1976) A nomenclatural list of the Land Mollusca of the British Isles. **Journal of Conchology London 29**, 21-25.

Walden, H.W. (1981) Communities and diversity of Land Molluscs in Scandinavian woodlands. I: High diversity communities in taluses and boulder slopes in South West Sweden. **Journal of Conchology London 30**, 351-372.

Walker, D. and Godwin, H. (1954) Lake stratigraphy, pollen analysis and vegetational history. In **Excavations at Star Carr.** (ed.) J.G.D. Clark. pp. 25-69. London: Cambridge University Press.

West, R.G. (1956) The Quaternary deposits at Hoxne. **Philosophical Transactions of the Royal Society of London B239**, 265-356.

West, R.G. (1957) Interglacial deposits at Bobbitshole, Ipswich. **Philosophical Transactions of the Royal Society of London B241**, 1-31.

West, R.G. (1970) Pollen zones in the Pleistocene and their correlation. **New Phytologist 69**, 1179-1183.

West, R.G. (1977a) Early and Middle Devensian flora and vegetation. **Philosophical Transactions of the Royal Society of London B280**, 229-246.

West, R.G. (1977b) **Pleistocene Geology and Biology.** London: Longmans.

West, R.G., Dickson, C.A., Catt, J.A., Weir, A.H. and Sparks, B.W. (1974) Late Pleistocene deposits at Wretton. II. Devensian deposits. **Philosophical Transactions of the Royal Society of London B267**, 337-420.

West, R.G., Lambert, C.A. and Sparks, B.W. (1964) Interglacial deposits at Itford, Essex. **Philosophical Transactions of the Royal Society of London B247**, 185-212.

West, R.G. and Sparks, B.W. (1960) Coastal interglacial deposits of the English Channel. **Philosophical Transactions of the Royal Society of London B243**, 95-133.

Wilson, V. (1948) **British Regional Geology: East Yorkshire and Lincolnshire.** London: H.M.S.O.

Woodall, D. (1981) Unpublished dissertation for the degree of Master of Arts by course work and dissertation. University of Sheffield. 2 vols.

Wright, C.W. and Wright, E.V. (1933) Some notes on the Holocene deposits at North Ferriby. **Naturalist**, 210-212.

Wright, C.W. and Wright, E.V. (1947) Prehistoric boats from Ferriby, East Yorkshire. **Proceedings of the Prehistoric Society 13**, 114-138.

Wright, E.V. and Churchill, D.M. (1965) The boats from North Ferriby, Yorkshire, England with a review of the origins of the sewn boats of the Bronze Age. **Proceedings of the Prehistoric Society 31**, 1-24.

Wymer, J.J. (1976) A long blade industry from Sproughton, Suffolk. **East Anglian Archaeology 3**, 1-10.

Wymer, J.J., Jacobi, R.M. and Rose, J. (1975) Late Devensian and early Flandrian barbed points from Sproughton, Suffolk. **Proceedings of the Prehistoric Society 41**, 235-241.

Young, J.O. (1975) Preliminary field and laboratory studies on the survival and spawning of several species of Gastropodia in calcium-poor and calcium-rich waters. **Proceedings of the Malacological Society of London 41**, 429-437.

Young, M.R. (1975) The life-cycles of six species of freshwater molluscs in the Worcester-Birmingham Canal. **Proceedings of the Malacological Society of London 41**, 533-548.